PLUG-IN ELECTRIC VEHICLES

PLUG-IN ELECTRIC VEHICLES

WHAT ROLE FOR WASHINGTON?

David B. Sandalow
editor

BROOKINGS INSTITUTION PRESS
Washington, D.C.

Library of Congress Cataloging-in-Publication data

Plug-in electric vehicles : what role for Washington? / David B. Sandalow,
editor.
    p.   cm.
Includes bibliographical references and index.
Summary: "Explains the current landscape for plug-in electrics and implications for national security, the environment, and the economy. Discusses
what can and should be done by the U.S. government to advance the role of
plug-in electric vehicles"—Provided by publisher.
ISBN 978-0-8157-0305-1 (cloth : alk. paper)
1. Electric vehicle industry—United States.   2. Electric vehicles—
Government policy—United States.   3. Hybrid electric vehicles—
Government policy—United States.   I. Sandalow, David.
HD9710.U52P54 2009
388.3'2—dc22   2009000791

1 3 5 7 9 8 6 4 2

The paper used in this publication meets minimum requirements of the
American National Standard for Information Sciences—Permanence of Paper for
Printed Library Materials: ANSI Z39.48-1992.

Typeset in Sabon and Strayhorn

Composition by R. Lynn Rivenbark
Macon, Georgia

Printed by R. R. Donnelley
Harrisonburg, Virginia

Contents

PART TWO
Barriers

PART THREE
Policies

Foreword

STROBE TALBOTT

Throughout his historic campaign for the presidency, Barack Obama spoke of the challenge of oil dependence, describing it as central to "our economy, our security, and the very future of our planet." Senator John McCain often sounded similar themes. We at Brookings consider energy policy in its many dimensions to be a top priority, with all five of our research programs—Governance Studies, Economic Studies, Foreign Policy, Metropolitan Policy, and Global Economy and Development—addressing the subject in different ways. It is also an issue that has engaged our trustees, led by Pulitzer Prize–winning author Daniel Yergin, who, in addition to being part of the governance of the institution, has brought his own enormous expertise to bear on our projects and programs.

In his 1991 book, *The Prize*, Yergin wrote, "Today we are so dependent on oil, and oil is so embedded in our daily doings, that we hardly stop to comprehend its pervasive significance." That dependence is nowhere more complete than in our vehicle fleet. As Brookings senior fellow and energy policy expert David Sandalow emphasizes in his writings, more than 96 percent of the energy used to move our cars and trucks comes from this one fuel. Indeed, for more than a century, cars and trucks around the world have run almost exclusively on gasoline.

That may be changing, thanks to the arrival on the scene of the hybrid vehicle, which adds an electric motor to the familiar gasoline engine.

There are more than a million already on U.S. roads. Since Brookings is a notably green community, it's not surprising that our garage on Massachusetts Avenue in Washington is well populated with hybrids that get as much as 48 miles per gallon in city driving.

However, as Sandalow and others have argued, conventional hybrids have a fundamental limitation—they still depend on gasoline. Ways must be found to make sure that hybrids become a bridge to an even more revolutionary technology—the plug-in electric car. Plug-in electric vehicles can help end the near-total dominance of oil as a transportation fuel, with its far-reaching geopolitical, environmental, and economic consequences.

We must hasten the day when we can plug in our cars in our own garages at home—and better yet, recharge them from the sun during the day and from wind at night. Then we could drive around town without contributing to global warming.

That day may seem far off. The major barrier has been the cost of batteries, a key component of plug-in vehicles that accounts for a significant portion of their higher overall cost. Another obstacle is a deeply entrenched attachment to public policies that support continued reliance of our transportation system on oil. The chapters in this book—by a diverse and distinguished group of authors—aim squarely at those challenges, proposing thoughtful and wide-ranging policies to help bring plug-in vehicles to market soon.

We at Brookings believe that good policy recommendations stem from asking the right questions—questions that invite bold, imaginative, yet pragmatic answers. This book starts with these questions: What if our cars and trucks could draw power from the electric grid? What if cars could be recharged by solar panels during the day and by wind power at night? What would be the benefits? How about the costs and limitations? What could and should the U.S. federal government do to speed such a change? Should the federal government help put millions of plug-in electric vehicles on the road soon? If so, what would be the best ways to do so? What would the benefits and costs be? How quickly could favorable policies make a difference?

Among the difficulties in translating the right answers into the right policies is a combination of history and habit as well as a combination of politics and geopolitics. Oil's dominance as a transportation fuel has shaped U.S. foreign policy for more than fifty years. For decades, U.S. policymakers have given high priority to securing oil flows from the Persian Gulf to world markets, shaping U.S. policy in the region and throughout the broader Mideast. When U.S. policymakers address existential threats such as the potential proliferation of nuclear weapons in the region and the fight against al Qaeda, the need to secure oil flows is a constant concern and central constraint. Today, many policymakers can scarcely imagine a world in which that constraint has been lifted. Would that be possible if the world's vehicles ran on fuels other than oil?

Oil shapes geopolitical relationships more broadly. A growing body of academic literature explores the relationship between oil dependence and democracy, generally concluding that dependence on oil for export revenues inhibits the movement to democracy. For many of the world's poorest countries, the rising cost of oil imports in recent years has exceeded the benefits of any debt relief. If the world's vehicles ran on many fuels, instead of relying so heavily on just one, the impacts on political and economic development around the world could be far-reaching.

At the same time, automakers in the United States have struggled greatly in recent years. There are many causes, but according to a number of analysts, one of the most central is the failure to deliver innovative products that excite the buying public. Technological innovations in information technology, communications, and many other sectors have reshaped markets in recent years. Yet the automobile industry today relies almost entirely on a century-old technology—the internal combustion engine. The problem is especially acute for U.S. automakers, who have relied heavily on gas-guzzling products that lost favor with the public during the run-up in oil prices from 2002 through mid-2008.

However, as I write in early 2009, the old order is changing—in this arena as in so many others. All major U.S. automakers have now announced plans to sell plug-in electric vehicles in the next several years. Israel and Denmark have both launched aggressive plans to electrify their vehicle fleets. More broadly, billionaire oilman T. Boone Pickens has launched a high-profile campaign to promote natural gas vehicles. More than 90 percent of the cars made in Brazil last year could run on either gasoline or ethanol. Cracks in oil's near-total dominance of transportation fuel markets are beginning to emerge.

Will the global financial crisis slow progress on these fronts, along with so many others? Perhaps. Automakers struggling to survive are ill-equipped to invest in innovative technologies or new business models. Yet clean energy in all its facets can and must become one of the thriving industries of the next several decades, helping to transform the global economy and become a powerful engine of economic growth. In this "defining moment"—to quote President Obama—the essays in this volume help point the way.

Commentary

DAN REICHER

I am pleased to provide some opening thoughts on the game-changing opportunity presented by plug-in vehicles. I have been involved in the world of advanced vehicles for a number of years, in both the public and private sectors, moving from work on hybrids and natural gas vehicles to hydrogen and biofuel vehicles and more recently to plug-ins. This experience leaves me convinced that the United States is finally turning the corner on vehicles that can wean the country off oil and cut greenhouse gas emissions. Plug-in vehicles—both hybrids and all-electrics—are the most promising element of this long overdue transformation of the U.S. transportation system. President Barack Obama—a serious supporter of plug-ins in the Senate and on the campaign trail—is in a strong position to help the automobile industry take plug-ins to scale, with all the economic, environmental, and security benefits that that entails.

At Google we launched the RechargeIT initiative in 2007 to help accelerate the commercialization of plug-in vehicles. We converted hybrid Ford Escapes and Toyota Priuses to plug-ins and added them to our company fleet at Google's headquarters. The cars are charged under a parking structure covered by solar panels, part of one of the nation's largest corporate solar systems. In a 2007 experiment with Pacific Gas and Electric we demonstrated vehicle-to-grid (V2G) electricity flow. The utility sent the computer in one of our cars a signal over the Internet to stop charging and start sending electricity back to the grid from its battery. It worked. In order to advance the adoption and commercialization of plug-ins, we've also made several million dollars in equity investments in companies that develop innovative technologies as well as grants to support policy work.

The RechargeIT initiative recently conducted a driving experiment with plug-ins from our fleet to see how well they performed against standard cars. Using a variety of vehicles, professional drivers, and driving routes representing typical trips for U.S. drivers, we conducted a series of controlled tests over seven weeks. Our Toyota Prius plug-ins achieved as many as 93 miles per gallon on average for all trips and 115 miles per gallon for city trips. The plug-in Ford Escape achieved about 50 miles per gallon.

That kind of vehicle fuel economy, along with straightforward recharging infrastructure, has prompted auto companies large and small to commit to bringing plug-ins to market. General Motors, Toyota, Nissan, BMW, and other major car companies are expected to begin selling plug-ins in the 2009–2010 timeframe. Meanwhile, small companies like Tesla Motors and Hymotion have already brought plug-ins—both new and retrofitted vehicles—to market.

Public policy will play a crucial role in accelerating both innovation in plug-in technology and large-scale deployment of plug-in vehicles. In June 2008, Google.org co-hosted a conference with the Brookings Institution to showcase plug-ins and explore the role that government can play in accelerating their commercialization. Members of Congress, auto and utility executives, and technology experts discussed the promise of plug-ins and the need for government leadership to move them to market in large numbers.

We enjoyed excellent bipartisan attendance from Capitol Hill, including Senator Lamar Alexander (R-Tenn.), Representative John Dingell (D-Mich.), Senator Orrin Hatch (R-Utah), and Representative Jay Inslee (D-Wash.). Former CIA director Jim Woolsey passionately argued that U.S. dependence on oil is a national security emergency and pointed to countries like Japan and Brazil that have demonstrated the potential to overhaul an automotive fleet in a short period of time. Shai Agassi described Better Place Inc. and the company's plans to rapidly deploy electric vehicles in Israel and other countries. Tom Friedman of the *New York Times* moderated a panel discussion on federal policy in which panel members quickly turned to the importance of modernizing and greening the electricity grid to support plug-ins.

I hope that discussions at the conference—along with the diverse policy papers in this book—will lead to specific and actionable policy solutions. President Obama is well positioned to advance the public policies and R&D critical to accelerating the large-scale commercialization of these vehicles and at the same time have a positive effect on the troubled economy.

At a minimum, I believe that the following measures are needed:

—*Federal funding for research and development.* Federal R&D support is important to driving development of technologies related to plug-in vehicles. We must further develop power management devices, grid integration technologies, and, especially, better batteries to increase their durability and extend their range and reduce the cost of plug-in vehicles. Advanced biofuels, like cellulosic ethanol, also are likely to be attractive in plug-in hybrids. The federal government can play a critical role in helping to accelerate the necessary R&D on both fronts.

—*Investment in infrastructure.* Putting millions of plug-in cars and trucks on the road will require deployment of recharging stations and new power management hardware and software. The federal government should start investing in and offering industry incentives to develop the infrastructure necessary to support this transformation. Doing so will encourage the private sector to seize the opportunity to develop a U.S. grid smart enough to ultimately accommodate more than 100 million plug-in vehicles. It also will create jobs in the troubled U.S. economy.

—*Financial incentives to spur adoption.* Federal tax credits helped jump-start the mass market for hybrid technology pioneered by Honda, Toyota, and Ford. A comparable set of incentives to ensure the initial marketability of plug-in vehicles could similarly boost the momentum and mass market availability of plug-ins. The consumer plug-in incentives in the recently adopted $787 billion federal bailout bill are a good start. Manufacturing incentives also should be considered. In addition, we should look at incentives to get older, more polluting cars off the road and speed the turnover of the vehicle fleet. If designed properly, a "cash for clunkers" program could have an array of benefits.

—*Federal procurement.* The federal government should procure large numbers of plug-in vehicles for the federal fleet and develop charging infrastructure. Given the hundreds of thousands of vehicles in the federal fleet, that could accelerate the adoption of plug-ins. State and private fleet purchases would increase momentum even more.

—*Modernization of the regulatory system.* Reform of current utility rate design would permit real-time pricing of electric power, which would encourage consumers to recharge during off-peak periods. A modernized regulatory and pricing system would also encourage vehicle charging based on the availability of renewable electricity and the ability to provide critical services to the grid, such as frequency and voltage support. In addition, the federal government should foster national uniform data collection and publish protocols for electric vehicles and V2G, including standards for vehicle mileage, tailpipe emissions, and carbon reduction.

Google recently introduced an energy plan, Clean Energy 2030, that provides a blueprint for how, over the next two decades, the United States could significantly reduce fossil fuel use for electricity and transportation with positive net economics. Plug-in vehicles figure prominently in the plan, along with a national push for energy efficiency and a massive scale-up of renewable electricity. Over 100 million plug-ins powered largely by green electricity from a smart grid would be a major advance in our nation's efforts to confront climate change, advance energy security, and stimulate the economy. With a new president and Congress—and serious economic, security, and environmental imperatives—the moment could not be better to make a major national commitment to plug-ins. This book provides an important intellectual foundation for this critical effort.

PLUG-IN ELECTRIC VEHICLES

Plug-In Electric Vehicles:
What Role for Washington?

DAVID SANDALOW

Plug-in electric vehicles are coming. Major automakers plan to commercialize their first models soon. Israel and Denmark have ambitious plans to electrify large portions of their vehicle fleets. Hybrid vehicles—the precursor to plug-ins—are the most successful automotive innovation of the past decade, with more than 1 million now on U.S. roads and sales climbing sharply.

This private sector technology could have important public benefits. Last year, oil provided more than 96 percent of the fuel for U.S. cars and trucks. This near-total dependence empowers our enemies, imperils the planet, and strains family budgets whenever oil prices rise. No technology has more promise to break the grip of oil on the U.S. transport sector than the plug-in electric vehicle.

For decades, the U.S. government has played a central role in promoting the use of oil in cars and trucks. How does one measure the subsidy to a commodity, for example, from having the president of the United States and his vast entourage fly to Saudi Arabia to try to lower its price? Although the most recent effort in this regard (in summer 2008) was unsuccessful, presidents and secretaries of state from both parties have made securing the free flow of cheap oil a priority of U.S. foreign policy for generations. Oil has also benefited from conventional subsidies, such as tax preferences and favorable lease terms on public lands.

Against this backdrop, what role should the U.S. government play with respect to technologies that can help end oil dependence, such as plug-in electric vehicles? Should the federal government seek to promote their rapid deployment? If so, what would be the best tools? What benefits could be expected? What are the costs and risks? This volume offers answers to these questions.

FIRST, THE BASICS. A "plug-in electric vehicle" (PEV) is any car or truck that can be recharged from an external source of electricity, such as a wall socket. These vehicles can be "all-electric" (running on electricity only) or "plug-in hybrids" (running on both electricity and liquid fuels).

As noted above, conventional hybrid vehicles have been hugely successful in the past decade. More than 1 million of the most popular model—the Toyota Prius—have been sold worldwide, with more than half those sales in the United States. The Big Three U.S. automakers—GM, Ford, and Chrysler—plan to introduce hybrid engines in more than a dozen models over the next several years.

Conventional hybrids combine an internal combustion engine and electric motor. The internal combustion engine runs on gasoline, and the electric motor draws power from a battery. The battery is continually recharged with extra power from the engine (for example, when the car is going downhill) and energy captured from the brakes (in a process known as "regenerative braking"). When the battery is depleted, the vehicle runs on gas only. Conventional hybrids provide better fuel efficiency, torque, and other measures of engine performance than cars with only an internal combustion engine.

The next big step in automotive technology is the plug-in electric vehicle. Like conventional hybrids, PEVs combine an internal combustion engine and electric motor. However, as the name suggests, there is an important additional feature. Plug-in hybrids can be recharged from an external source of electricity. They can—quite literally—be plugged into a wall socket. The idea is simple, but the benefits to drivers are far-reaching:

—With plug-in electric vehicles, many drivers would need no petroleum products for their daily commute. Cars could be recharged at night, and many drivers could travel back and forth to work or around town using only the car's electric motor.

—Driving costs would drop dramatically. At national average electricity prices, PEVs would cost the equivalent of roughly 75 cents per gallon to drive when operating on their electric motors.

—As with many electric cars, torque and acceleration would be excellent.

Said one enthusiast who converted his vehicle to a plug-in: "Everyone wants to drive electric cars, they just don't know it yet."[1]

The biggest barrier to mass production is battery technology. Adding a plug-in feature to a conventional hybrid engine requires adjustments that increase the cost and weight of the batteries, while shortening their expected life. Extra costs, which now run roughly $8,000 to $11,000 per car, are expected to drop sharply with mass production and advances in battery technology. The amount of those price drops and the speed with which they occur could have far-reaching social consequences.

What benefits could widespread use of plug-in electric vehicles deliver? First, PEVs could transform geopolitics and improve U.S. national security. As Jim Woolsey and Chelsea Sexton point out in chapter 1, oil is a "strategic commodity"—one on which vehicle fleets and therefore modern economies depend. The near-total dependence of U.S. cars and trucks on petroleum confers vast wealth and power on leaders of oil-exporting nations, including Mahmoud Ahmadinejad and Hugo Chavez, who wish the United States ill. U.S. oil dependence played an important role in the rise of al Qaeda and continues to constrain the United States in the fight against Islamic extremism.

If hundreds of millions of cars and trucks ran on electricity, oil's status as a strategic commodity would be threatened. The influence of unfriendly oil producers would sharply diminish. The United States would gain new flexibility and authority in the fight against al Qaeda and other Islamic extremists. Many geopolitical relationships would be transformed.

Yet caution is warranted. As Irving Mintzer explains in chapter 6, electric motors and batteries depend on several minerals with limited or nonexistent domestic supplies. Could we end up trading our current dependence on imported oil for dependence on imported lithium, cobalt, or neodymium? At present that risk seems small, but the supply chain for key minerals, as well as potential substitutes, will need to be continually evaluated as the electric car industry grows.

A second important benefit is that PEVs can reduce pollution. Vehicles are currently the largest source of pollution in many U.S. cities. Plug-in electric vehicles emit nothing when running on their electric motors. As a result, PEVs would dramatically improve air quality in many urban areas, leading to fewer cases of asthma among children, greater worker productivity, and improved quality of life. With tens of millions of PEVs on the road, air quality in some cities would return to levels not experienced for more than fifty years.

Plug-in electric vehicles also can play an important role in fighting global warming, as Deron Lovaas and Luke Tonachel explain in chapter 3. The extent of the benefit depends on the technology used to generate electricity. When PEVs are recharged from wind, solar, or nuclear power, emissions of heat-trapping gases from driving are reduced almost to zero. Even when PEVs are recharged with electricity generated by an old-fashioned coal plant, emissions are still less than those of today's average U.S. car running on oil, because the electric motor in a PEV uses energy much more efficiently than an internal combustion engine. Yet reducing heat-trapping gases by driving PEVs is likely to be less cost-effective than many alternatives (such as driving conventional hybrids or improving the energy efficiency of buildings), as Daniel Kammen, Samuel Arons, Derek Lemoine, and Holmes Hummel caution in chapter 9. PEVs are at best one part of a much broader strategy needed to fight global warming.

Third, PEVs can cut driving costs and help transform the struggling U.S. auto industry. As Bracken Hendricks and Benjamin Goldstein point out in chapter 10, surveys consistently demonstrate strong interest in the technology among car buyers. The innovative approach of Better Place, explained by Tom Collina and Ron Zucker in chapter 11, has captured the imaginations of national leaders in several countries. Someday utilities may even pay drivers for the value of reserve power stored in car batteries, as Jon Wellinghoff explains in setting forth his vision of a "CashBack" car in chapter 4. PEVs can be a central feature of a longer-term transformation toward a clean energy economy.

How quickly could plug-in vehicles deliver the anticipated benefits? That depends on many factors, but changes in the U.S. vehicle fleet will not happen overnight. Today, more than 240 million cars are on U.S. roads, almost all of which depend entirely on petroleum. These cars last an average of more than ten years. In the United States, only 5 to 7 percent of the cars on the road each year are new. That means new technologies such as plug-in electric motors enter the fleet slowly, taking a decade or more to make up a substantial fraction of the vehicle fleet.

The authors in this volume offer different projections of the rate at which plug-in vehicles will enter the fleet. In chapter 5, Alan Madian, Lisa Walsh, and Kim Simpkins assume a 15 percent compound annual growth rate for PEV sales, noting that that rate is higher than the 8 percent compound annual growth rate in SUV sales since 1988. They calculate that at that rate, PEVs would still make up only about 25 percent of new sales and less than 8 percent of the light-vehicle fleet in 2030. Saurin Shah offers a more aggressive deployment scenario in chapter 2, noting that many recent innovations in automotive technology have reached 50 percent penetration in new car sales within seven to nine years. Shah sees electrification dominating road transport within thirty years.

What should the federal government do to promote the transition to plug-in electric vehicles? It already has taken some steps. The Energy Policy Act of 2005 (EPAct), for example, specifically authorized some modest research and development on PEVs, along with demonstration programs. The Energy Independence and Security Act of 2007 authorized additional research and development, further demonstration programs, loan guarantees for conversion of domestic manufacturing facilities, and more. Perhaps most significant, the Emergency Economic Stabilization Act of 2008 included a tax credit of $2,500 to $7,500 for up to 250,000 plug-in electric vehicles. In chapter 7, Dean Taylor presents a comprehensive summary of the history of federal support for plug-in vehicles.

Federal tax policy offers a potentially important tool for promoting plug-in vehicles. Targeted tax credits—of the kind enacted for plug-ins in fall 2008—can sometimes gain support across a broad ideological spectrum, bringing together those who support the cause being promoted and those eager to see taxes cut more generally. However, research suggests that consumer tax credits are most effective when applied at the point of sale, not when they must be claimed in connection with annual filings such as federal income tax returns. In chapter 8, Ben Harris suggests these principles to guide Congress in shaping any tax credit for plug-in vehicles: the tax credit should be large enough to make PEVs competitive with traditional cars; the credit should be simple; the credit should be refundable; and the credit should be based on the efficiency of the vehicle, not its purchase price.

Federal procurement policy also offers an important tool. The federal government buys more than 65,000 vehicles each year. A federal commitment to purchase large quantities of plug-in vehicles could help reduce battery costs and help manufacturers finance expansion of their capacity to produce vehicles. Yet providing government procurement officers with the resources and incentives to sharply increase purchases may present challenges. Bracken Hendricks and Benjamin Goldstein explore these issues and suggest development of a federal fleet purchasing agreement as part of the answer.

Federal guarantees can help remove barriers to commercialization. For example, some auto manufacturers have expressed concern that the batteries likely to be installed in many plug-in vehicles will not last for ten years or 100,000 miles—a standard warranty period expected by many car purchasers. Nevertheless, there is strong public interest in manufacturers selling plug-in electric vehicles. Hendricks and Goldstein suggest creation of the "Federal Battery Guarantee Corporation," designed to prevent concerns about battery life from stifling growth in the plug-in vehicles market.

Federal regulatory programs can play a role as well. The state of California, for example, has adopted a "low carbon fuel standard" requiring carbon emissions from fuel used in vehicles to decline over time. Tom Collina and Ron Zucker propose establishment of a federal low carbon fuel standard that would provide incentives for manufacturing plug-in vehicles recharged with electricity from renewable sources.

A related topic is utility regulation. Electric utilities can play an important role in the transition to plug-in vehicles by adopting time-of-day pricing, installing smart meters, and expanding charging infrastructure. Yet, as Steve Marshall points out in chapter 12, many utilities currently have only modest incentives to take such steps. Federal action may be needed to ensure that regulated utilities both support and are able to profit from sales of plug-in electric vehicles. Alternative business models in the utility sector could also make a big difference, as Peter Fox-Penner, Dean Murphy, Mariko Geronimo and Matthew McCaffree explain in chapter 13.

Finally, federal research and development can play an important role, with programs aimed at reducing the cost and improving the performance of the batteries on which plug-in electric vehicles depend. Energy R&D in the United States lags badly behind historical levels. Public sector R&D is well below levels from the 1970s and has dropped sharply in recent years. Federal R&D programs could help unlock important innovations in energy storage, with the potential to spark explosive growth in electrification of the vehicle fleet. Further work is needed to chart the best ways to expand federal programs in this area.

I conclude with a prediction. Some day one of my grandchildren will look at one of my children (now teenagers) and say, "You mean you couldn't plug in cars when you were a kid?" That will seem as odd to children twenty-five years from now as a world without cell phones seems to my children today.

Electrification will transform vehicle fleets in the decades ahead. Yet the pace of the change is uncertain. Plug-in vehicles could enter the fleet slowly, starting with a few test models and then growing only gradually because of expensive batteries, old business models, outmoded regulations, and other factors. Or plug-ins could quickly become an important segment of the auto market as sales grow quickly, cutting costs in the process. Federal policies can have an important impact on—though by no means control—the speed of growth.

Plug-in electric vehicles are coming. How soon? Federal policies in the years ahead will help answer that question.

Note

1. Ryan Fulcher, quoted in "TreeHugger TV: Plug-In Hybrids" (www.treehugger.com/files/2006/06/treehuggertv_plug_in_prius.php [December 8, 2008]).

PART I

Benefits

CHAPTER ONE

Geopolitical Implications
of Plug-in Vehicles

R. JAMES WOOLSEY and CHELSEA SEXTON

There are many aspects of our dependence on oil for 97 percent of our transportation needs that affect both our national security in a traditional sense and, through the contribution of oil to climate change, our security in a broader sense as well. Yet the oil industry continues to enjoy a monopoly on transportation, receiving over the years the support of substantial subsidies and maintaining a close working relationship with the auto industry. So successful is this partnership that whole categories of transportation and fuel technologies have fallen victim to its interests, from streetcars in the 1960s to electric vehicles in the 1990s. Population and industrial growth around the world promises to add more and more people to the driving population—at a time when, given the current geopolitical climate, we can least afford it.

We do not believe that this country will achieve a sound energy policy if it ignores any of three key needs: to have a long-term supply of transportation fuel that is as secure as possible, as clean as possible (in terms of global warming gas emissions as well as other pollutants), and as inexpensive as possible. Today oil meets none of these three criteria. The reason that this is important to us is that oil is not merely a commodity; today, insofar as we are in near-total dependence on it for transportation, it is a strategic commodity. Until a little over a century ago, as Anne Korin has pointed out, salt also was such a strategic commodity.[1] Wars were fought and national strategies driven in part by the demand for salt, because it was the only generally available means of preserving meat, a major portion of our food supply.

Today we have not stopped using salt, but no part of our national behavior is driven by the need for it—it has a market, and it is shipped in commerce. But because it has affordable and effective competitors for meat preservation—refrigeration, among other technologies—its dominant role is over. No nation sways world events because it has salt mines.

For a number of reasons we must strive to set oil on a similar path of decline in influence—away from being a strategic commodity and toward being simply a commodity. Oil will still be useful and valued for its high energy content and its relative ease of shipment for a long time. It will also be used in heating and in the production of some chemicals, although in those uses it is already, in a sense, no longer a strategic commodity because it has competitors. Doubtless it will be used for many years to produce transportation fuel as well. But in the interests of our national security, our climate, and our pocketbooks, we should now move together as a nation to destroy, not oil of course, but oil's strategic role in transportation as quickly and as thoroughly as possible.

National Security

Our problems with oil derive in no small measure from the fact that more than two-thirds of the world's proven reserves of conventional oil lie in the turbulent states of the Persian Gulf, as does much of the oil industry's international infrastructure. Increasing our dependence on this part of the world for our transportation needs is subject to a wide range of perils.

In February 2006, in response to Osama bin Laden's many calls in recent years for attacks on oil infrastructure, al Qaeda attacked Abcaiq, the world's largest oil production facility, in northeastern Saudi Arabia. Had it succeeded in destroying—say, with a simple mortar attack—the sulfur-clearing towers there, through which about two-thirds of Saudi crude passes, it could have driven the price of oil to well over bin Laden's goal of $144 a barrel, for many months. Another major al Qaeda attack on oil infrastructure in the Gulf region was thwarted in April 2007.

Royal succession in Saudi Arabia could also bring major problems. King Abdullah is a sponsor of some reforms in the Saudi system and sometimes works toward cordial relations with us and other oil importers, but he is in his eighties, as is Crown Prince Sultan. Prince Nayef, the interior minister, is one possible successor to the throne. His views are famously close to those of the members of the extremely reactionary Wahhabi religious movement in the kingdom. Cordial relations with the United States may not be at the top of his agenda.

Iran's President Ahmadinejad is radical even by Iranian post-1979 standards. The efficacy of deterrence and containment in dealing with Iran's nuclear weapons development program is not clear when Iran's leaders talk of the desirability of Iran's becoming "a martyr nation" and shrug at the possibility of millions of deaths by saying "Allah will know his own."

In response to Iran's nuclear program, six Sunni Arab states, including Egypt and Saudi Arabia, announced in the winter of 2008 that they too would have "peaceful" nuclear programs. But since a number of those states have very plentiful supplies of oil and gas, it seems unlikely that all the programs will be limited to electricity generation. We may be seeing the beginning stages of a nuclear arms race in the Gulf region between Sunni and Shia, funded by our oil purchases.

Oil prices ranged in 2008 from $35 to nearly $150 per barrel, forcing the United States to borrow between $1 billion every few days to $2 billion per day to import oil. That contributes heavily to a weakening dollar and to upward pressure on interest rates (our annual oil debt is well above our trade deficit with China). If the IOUs we send abroad put a strain on our economy, the world's wealthiest, think what they do to the economies of developing countries—in, say, Africa—that have no oil themselves. Debt is the central inhibitor of economic development—importing expensive oil is helping to bind hundreds of millions of the world's poor more tightly in poverty.

A share of our payments for oil, along with a share of the payments of others, finds its way to Saudi Arabia. The Saudis contribute billions of dollars annually to their Wahhabi sect, which establishes religious schools and institutions throughout the world. In his book *The Looming Tower,* Lawrence Wright notes that with only a little more than 1 percent of the world's Muslim population, the Saudis support through the Wahhabis

"90 percent of the expenses of the entire faith, overriding other traditions of Islam."[2]

Wahhabi teachings, if one reads the fatwas of their imams—as set forth, for example, in Shmuel Bar's *Warrant for Terror: Fatwas of Radical Islam and the Duty of Jihad*—are murderous with respect to the Shia, Jews, homosexuals, and apostates and horribly repressive with respect to everyone else, especially women.[3] They are essentially the same basic beliefs as those expressed by al Qaeda. The Wahhabis and al Qaeda do not disagree about underlying beliefs but, a bit like the Stalinists and Trotskyites of the 1920s and 1930s, about which of them should be in charge. The hate-filled underlying views of both, however, point in the same general direction. Many Wahhabi-funded madrassahs worldwide echo and perpetuate those views and thus promote their effects. Thus, as has often been said, when we pay for Middle Eastern oil today, the "Long War" against terrorism in which we are engaged becomes the only war, other than our Civil War, that we have ever fought in which we pay for both sides.

Finally, as Tom Friedman of the *New York Times* put it, "the price of oil and the pace of freedom always move in opposite directions."[4] The work of various scholars has pointed out the link between commodities that command huge amounts of economic rent, such as oil (or the gold and silver brought from the New World by Spain in the sixteenth century), and political autocracy. Such a commodity, unless it is acquired by a mature democracy such as Norway or Canada, tends to concentrate and enhance its associated power in the hands of a ruler. Observing that Americans believe that there should be no taxation without representation, Bernard Lewis pointed out that the converse also is true: there is no representation without taxation.[5] If a country is so oil rich that it does not need taxes, it does not need, and often does not have, any real legislative body to levy them—and thus no alternative source of power in the state. And as for enhanced power from oil wealth, note the behavior in recent years of Messrs. Ahmadinejad, Chavez, and Putin.

So the national security reasons to move against oil as a strategic commodity are substantial. Shifting the trade patterns for oil does nothing to alleviate the problem in the grand scheme. There will always be someone else who will buy from these countries if we do not; all oil-importing nations are to a certain extent caught in the same net. Oil should thus be an early candidate for public policy decisions to speed its strategic demise.

Because there is no way to allow transportation to be dependent on oil and not ourselves be dependent, by extension, on the countries that have it, moving our vehicles off petroleum is the most significant step we can take toward breaking free.

Climate Change

Today the clear weight of scientific opinion—for example, the views of the U.S. National Academy of Sciences—is on the side of the proposition that global climate change is in part anthropogenic and that it is related to the release of carbon dioxide (CO_2) and other gases such as methane. And although critics are right to point out that earlier global predictions by others have not occurred—global cooling, massive famine from population increase—that should not affect our judgment about CO_2 and global climate change (except to give all of us a reasonable reminder of the importance of always holding scientific theories tentatively).

Oil contributes more than 40 percent of the global warming gas emissions caused by fossil fuels. Extrapolating from that, we might conclude that our purchases today of gas-guzzling SUVs can contribute, some decades hence, to sinking portions of Bangladesh and Florida beneath the waves. That possibility might once have been seen as a tangential issue to this chapter, were it not for the fact that more and more members of the defense and intelligence communities are recognizing that climate change is a national security issue. As certain resources become scarcer, as disease spreads, and as property is subjected to flooding and extreme weather events, we are likely to see increased migration from the affected areas, causing global tension and destabilization of trade. As a society, we are hesitant to examine our own choices, but they will leave us vulnerable nonetheless—pretending that this is not true because we cannot see the impact immediately does not change that fact.

Strategic Investments

Certainly, individuals become interested in moving the United States (indeed the world) away from oil dependence for a number of reasons. Some are interested in protecting the environment, including from the effects of climate change. Some are especially worried about our increasing dependence on the Middle East for oil and resentful of the use of oil revenues to spread doctrines that bolster terrorist ideology. But many are simply average Americans who are worried about how much it will cost to get to work tomorrow. Whether gasoline is $2 or $4 per gallon, the evolution of the collective discussion of independence from oil—from one of "if and when" to one of "how and now"—must continue. However, we cannot responsibly discuss the economics of the solution without considering the investment required to get there.

We have, as a country, made some substantial mistakes with regard to affordability in the past. Ignoring cost in attempting to destroy oil's strategic role in transportation is not only expensive, it is self-defeating. For example, in the aftermath of war, revolution, and oil crises in the Middle East in the 1970s, the United States initiated the very expensive Synfuels Corporation. It promptly went bankrupt in 1986 after the Saudis increased production from their reserves and drove the price of oil down to near $5 per barrel. Something similar happened to various expensive petroleum alternatives in the late 1990s when, for a number of reasons, oil prices sank to around $10 per barrel.

If we insist on seeking expensive single solutions (hydrogen comes to mind) as a silver bullet—ignoring completely the technological, economic, and infrastructure challenges—we will fail. That is in part because while oil is a strategic commodity for transportation for us, the importers, it also is a strategically manipulable commodity for those who control it. Chinese and Indian demand—and the possibility that the peak oil theory will prove true and the major Middle Eastern fields will see declining production capability—may move oil prices to high levels. But many investors will still be worried about a repeat of the sharp drops in oil prices of the mid-eighties and late nineties. The world changed in important ways in the early 1970s when the Railroad Commission of Texas was in effect replaced by OPEC as the arbiter of the world's oil prices.

We must make clear to all concerned that we will not allow our economy to be manipulated by others because they think that we are too aggressive in developing alternatives to oil or too determined in supporting the existence of Israel or for any other reason. Instead, we should develop a portfolio of approaches to breaking oil's strategic hold on us, building on existing transportation capabilities whenever possible and keeping in mind cost, carbon emissions, and national security.

Solutions

By far the most promising path to the trifecta of cleaner, cheaper, domestic fuel is through electrification of transportation. As modern battery technology has developed in response to the markets for electronics, communications, power tools, and a host of other uses, it has brought with it the opportunity to substitute electricity for oil products in transportation. Promisingly, gasoline-based hybrid cars have now been provided with advanced batteries—such as lithium-ion—with improved energy and power densities.

Dozens of vehicle prototypes are now demonstrating that "plug-in hybrids" can more than double conventional hybrids' overall gasoline mileage. With a plug-in, charging your car overnight from an ordinary 120-volt outlet in your garage can provide twenty miles or more of electric range before the car lapses into its normal hybrid mode, using the liquid fuel in the tank as insurance when your trip exceeds that electric range. Other automakers are developing fully electric vehicles with ranges of 100 to 250 miles, well more than enough to meet most drivers' daily needs. And because electricity, at off-peak rates, can cost as little as a penny per mile while gasoline costs at a minimum will be several times higher, the average family will save a significant amount of money.

Even better for some drivers, the vehicles themselves require no compromise in the driving experience—any size or body style of vehicle can be electrified without affecting performance or safety, resulting in cars that are just as compelling as those that inspired the American love affair with the automobile in the first place. In the face of rising legacy costs, dwindling market share, and consumer demand for more efficient cars, many automakers have come around to accepting the notion of plug-in vehicles, and their development is fast becoming a horserace.

It should be noted that shifting to electricity is not completely without potential national security concerns. The electric grid in this country is woefully vulnerable to both accidents and terrorist attack on key physical or cyber components and to electromagnetic pulse attack with a nuclear weapon. A key mechanism to minimize the threat—in addition to the much-needed step of enhancing the security of our infrastructure against such attacks—is to encourage distributed generation of electricity.

Most people are familiar with the idea of distributed generation through the deployment of renewable technologies such as small-scale solar and wind power. Plug-in vehicles also serve the effort, through "vehicle to grid" (V2G) and "vehicle to home" (V2H) models, in which the vehicle is enabled to discharge electricity from its batteries back to the grid or to the home at peak times. V2G takes advantage of the often surprising fact that today's light-vehicle fleet has twenty times the power capacity of our electric power system and less than one-tenth its utilization. A relatively few vehicle batteries can thus store much larger amounts of energy relative to the grid's needs than most people realize. Others discuss this concept and its economic advantages in greater detail in other chapters dealing with grid capacity. But the role that vehicles can play in facilitating a distributed and more secure electric grid should not be understated. Encouraging such self-sufficiency at the local level makes us far more societally resilient.

In our view, even if the nation moves toward plug-in hybrid gasoline-electric vehicles and expected improvements in battery technology are made, there will be a substantial market for liquid fuels for some time. Some drivers will simply exceed the driving range afforded by the electric capacity of a plug-in hybrid. Others will want the psychological comfort of knowing that they have a liquid fuel safety net. Larger fleet vehicles and those used in moving goods are beginning to be electrified to a certain extent, but liquid fuels remain an important component for now. In addition to reductions in the cost of batteries, wide availability of public charging infrastructure may reduce the demand for liquid fuels over time. Meanwhile, it is crucial to shift our liquid fuel needs away from oil.

Cellulosic-based fuels—ethanol, methanol, and butanol—will in time exhibit cost advantages over corn-derived ethanol. For example, production of cellulosic ethanol is likely to be simplified by perfecting consolidated bioprocessing. That would permit multiple steps in deriving and fermenting sugars from cellulose and hemi-cellulose to take place together. Production costs may be lowered by crop yield improvements resulting from new genetic techniques, possibly but not necessarily including genetic engineering of feedstocks themselves. For example, this would simplify the breakdown of lignin in grasses or other feedstocks. And shipping costs may be lowered by locating small facilities near markets. Switch grass, for example, will grow in more parts of the country than corn, and it avoids the food-for-fuel arguments that corn can face. Bio-butanol may exhibit similar advantages and also may profit from the fact that it is both more energy intensive and more pipeline friendly than ethanol.

Renewable diesel and other fuels, made by thermal or algae processes from many types of carbon-based waste—from turkey offal to rice straw to used tires—and P-Series fuels, made from waste and biomass, may exhibit cost advantages by charging tipping fees for environmental cleanup. Conversion of only a portion of agricultural, municipal, and animal wastes—using such processes now coming into commercial operation—appears to be able to yield several million barrels a day of diesel, or with modest further processing, methanol, and even aviation fuel.

In short, there is a good deal of promise that we may be able to shift our liquid fuel consumption toward renewable fuels that radically reduce our reliance on oil products. A key policy step to allow for a choice of liquid fuels is to ensure that virtually all new cars are flexible-fuel vehicles—cars that can run on any combination of gasoline and alcohols such as ethanol and methanol. Every car sold in the United States is required to have seatbelts and airbags; similarly, every internal combustion car should enable fuel flexibility, a feature that adds less than $100 to the manufacturing cost of a vehicle and provides a platform on which fuels can compete.

Notably, for each of the billions of dollars a week that we can avoid borrowing for oil—and that we can figure out how to spend productively in producing domestic fuels for our transportation needs—we can create 10,000 or more jobs in the United States. Net U.S. farm income is in the range of $80 billion a year. So by replacing about $1 billion a week of our imports with domestic alternatives, we create value in this country about equal to a two-thirds increase in net farm income. At a time when auto plants are closing at an alarming rate and entire communities are suffering from seemingly instant and extensive unemployment, moving quickly to new propulsion systems and fuels for conventional vehicle models is the most promising strategy for the automotive industry.

Once plug-ins start appearing in showrooms, it is not only consumers and utility shareholders who will be smiling. If cheap off-peak electricity supplies a portion of our transportation needs, that will help insulate alternative liquid fuels from OPEC market manipulation designed to cripple oil's competitors. Future Indian and Chinese demand and peaking oil production may make it much harder for OPEC to use any excess production capacity to drive prices down and destroy competitive technology. As plug-ins come into the fleet, low electricity costs will stand as a substantial further barrier to such manipulation. Since OPEC cannot drive oil prices low enough to undermine our use of off-peak electricity, it is unlikely to embark on a course of future radical price cuts at all because such cuts would be painful for its oil-exporting members. Plug-ins thus may well give investors enough confidence to back alternative liquid fuels without any need for new taxes on oil or subsidies to protect those fuels.

Even when the solution has been identified, incumbent companies have not always been good at getting out of their own way. As a result, the major automakers of the last century are being challenged by eager upstarts based in Silicon Valley, and it no longer is assumed that cars of the future will be sold by car companies at all. New business models for using batteries in cars are emerging almost as fast and in as many flavors as the batteries themselves. Advance purchase agreements will ensure that at the end of their useful life in cars, batteries will enjoy a second life in energy storage before finally being recycled a decade or two after they were first produced. Each of those factors contributes to our overall independence from oil as a society, as we climb on the wagon for good.

The role of consumers cannot be overlooked either. Much is made of the fuel price at which people will change their behavior: "At $3 a gallon, people will stop driving their SUVs . . . OK, at $4 a gallon," and so forth. But consumers will change their behavior only if they have a reasonable alternative to switch to—and obviously, each person has to decide for himself or herself what is reasonable. What we know for sure is that the best way to get people to use less oil is to give them the chance to use none, even for a portion of their daily driving. We can educate people to make better choices, but we have to give them those choices in the first place.

The principal effort of the federal government on these issues should be to remove market barriers to entry for alternative transportation fuels so that oil sees vigorous competition as a strategic commodity. That step will, if undertaken wisely, help introduce Americans and others sooner rather than later to practical alternatives in their daily lives—the ability to choose rather than being forced to take what OPEC decides to give us. There is no reason not to use our capacity for technological innovation to reduce our dependence on oil decisively—while avoiding fantasies of finding a single perfect solution. The audacity of the challenge is rivaled only by the capacity of American ingenuity to meet it—luckily for us all, it is exactly the sort of challenge that can most engage the human spirit.

Notes

1. Anne Korin, testimony before the House Committee on Foreign Affairs, *Rising Oil Prices, Declining National Security,* May 22, 2008 (http://foreignaffairs.house.gov/110/kor052208.htm); and R. James Woolsey and Anne Korin, *Turning Oil into Salt,* National Review Online, September 25, 2007 (http://article.nationalreview.com/print/?q=OTlmMjFjYWRjOWI3ZGI0MzUxZDJjYTBlMmUzOTc2Mzc=).

2. Lawrence Wright, *The Looming Tower: Al-Qaeda and the Road to 9-11* (New York: Knopf, 2006), p. 149.

3. Shmuel Bar, *Warrant for Terror: The Fatwas of Radical Islam and the Duty of Jihad* (Lanham, Md.: Rowman & Littlefield, 2006).

4. Thomas Friedman, "As Energy Prices Rise, It's All Downhill for Democracy," *New York Times,* May 5, 2006 (http://select.nytimes.com/2006/05/05/opinion/05 friedman.html).

5. From an interview on C-SPAN's *Booknotes* program, December 30, 2001, by host Brian Lamb with Lewis regarding his book *What Went Wrong?: Western Impact and Middle Eastern Response*: "You know, there's this old American dictum: no taxation without representation. What is sometimes overlooked is that the converse is also true: no representation without taxation" (www.booknotes.org/Transcript/?Program ID=1657).

CHAPTER TWO

Electrification of Transport and Oil Displacement:
How Plug-Ins Could Lead to a 50 Percent Reduction in U.S. Demand for Oil

SAURIN D. SHAH

With global oil consumption exceeding 85 million barrels a day and the price of oil about $50 a barrel, the cost of the world's "oil addiction" now runs over $1.5 trillion a year.[1] U.S. consumption accounts for about 25 percent of total global volume. Most oil in the United States is used in transportation, particularly road transportation; therefore, under any scenario, achieving a meaningful reduction in the country's dependence on oil requires radically reducing our vehicles' consumption of petroleum.[2] Hybridization (combining an internal combustion engine with an electric motor) and electrification (connecting the motor in a vehicle to the electric grid) are the two most promising ways to do that. Plug-in hybrids, which combine both elements, will be a critical enabling technology for a future in which petroleum consumption is substantially reduced.

Hybrid passenger vehicles have been commercially available in the United States for nearly a decade,[3] and hybrid buses and trucks are starting to be been seen on roads across the country. These vehicles and their underlying technologies represent an important first step toward reducing our use of oil. However, much greater reductions are possible when vehi-

This chapter reflects solely the personal views of the author and does not necessarily represent the views, positions, strategies, or opinions of Neuberger Berman or Lehman Brothers.

cles are connected to the grid. Indeed, all-electric vehicles require zero petroleum in the tank. While all-electric vehicles are close to commercialization for certain niche markets, they are likely to be many years away for the U.S. mass market. Plug-in hybrids, which will likely offer an electric drive range of ten to forty miles between charges, are within sight. Several major OEMs (original equipment manufacturers) have announced plans to manufacture these vehicles in volume over the next few years.

Plug-in vehicles are likely to be an integral part of a profound paradigm shift in which electrons displace significant amounts of hydrocarbons, enabling fuel flexibility to finally emerge in large parts of the transportation sector. Since the electrons needed can be generated from a variety of domestically available energy sources—such as coal, nuclear energy, and wind and solar power and other renewable sources—our dependence on foreign oil will fall while overall emissions from the transportation sector will decline.

This chapter discusses current oil consumption and the assumptions behind a mainstream forecast for consumption in 2030—focusing on light-duty vehicles, the largest contributor to oil use in the United States—and illustrates how a 50 percent reduction in consumption could be achieved largely through full-scale hybridization and electrification of road transport. It also examines the historical record to see what it would take for the United States to break free from oil—not entirely, but sufficiently—and how long such a transition would take. Why this paradigm shift is likely to occur and what its costs could be are also discussed.

Current Consumption

According to the U.S. Department of Energy's Energy Information Administration (EIA), the United States consumed about 20.7 million barrels of oil a day in 2007; almost 60 percent of that oil, or 11.6 million barrels a day, was used for road transport (see table 2-1).[4] Light-duty vehicles, the single largest category within road transport, accounted for nearly 76 percent of road transport consumption, using 8.8 million barrels a day, or 42 percent of total U.S. oil consumption. The figure of 8.8 million barrels a day can be approximated by multiplying the stock of light-duty vehicles (231 million) by the average number of miles each vehicle travels per year (11,600 miles) and dividing the product by the average fuel efficiency of the vehicle stock (20 miles per gallon on a gasoline-equivalent basis).[5]

TABLE 2-1. U.S. Oil Consumption in 2007 and the EIA's 2030 Forecast

| Year | Transportation use | | | Nontransportation use (residential/ commercial and industrial uses)[b] | Total consumption |
	Light-duty vehicles	Other road transport[a]	Other transport		
2007					
Million barrels per day	8.8	2.8	3.0	6.1	20.7
Percent total	42	14	14	30	100
2030					
Million barrels per day	9.7	3.6	3.9	5.6	22.8
Percent total	43	16	17	25	100
CAGR[c] (percent)	0.5	1.0	1.2	−0.4	0.4

Source: EIA, *Annual Energy Outlook 2008*.

a. "Other road transport" includes two- and three-wheelers, buses, and medium- and heavy-duty trucks; "other transport" includes air, ship, train, and military travel.

b. "Nontransportation use" includes all uses for homes, businesses, factories, and power plants.

c. CAGR = Compound annual growth rate.

Future Consumption

While many forecasters have projected U.S. oil consumption in 2030, each forecast inevitably suffers from the biases underlying its assumptions. EIA forecasts have two advantages favoring their use: first, because the EIA projections are widely followed, studied, and cited, they anchor many public and private sector forecasts and hence are a reasonable proxy for consensus thinking; second, they are published annually and in sufficient detail that changes in bias are clear to see.

In its most recent report, the EIA projects that in 2030 the U.S. need for oil will reach nearly 23 million barrels a day, with road transport still accounting for nearly 60 percent of total consumption and light-duty vehicles for about 43 percent of total consumption.[6] In terms of the number of barrels consumed each day, the EIA estimates that road transport will consume about 13.3 million barrels in 2030, with light-duty vehicles accounting for 9.7 million barrels. The latter figure is based on the agency's forecasts of the stock of light-duty vehicles in 2030, estimated at about 295 million vehicles; average annual miles driven per vehicle, estimated at nearly 13,800 miles; and average fuel efficiency of the vehicle stock, estimated at 27.9 miles per gallon on a gasoline-equivalent basis. For our pur-

TABLE 2-2. EIA's 2008 Forecast of the U.S. Light-Duty Vehicle Stock in 2030, by Type

Type	Cars (millions)	Light trucks (millions)	Total cars (percent)	Total trucks (percent)	Total (percent)
Gasoline	113.4	78.6	38.5	26.7	65.1
Diesel	4.7	20.3	1.6	6.9	8.5
Ethanol	13.2	31.4	4.5	10.7	15.1
Other (natural gas, fuel cell)	0.08	0.04	0.03	0.01	0.04
Full hybrids (gasoline)	15.0	18.1	5.1	6.1	11.23
Full hybrids (diesel)	0.03	0.000	0.01	0.00	0.01
Full hybrids (plug-ins)	0.02	0.000	0.01	0.00	0.01
Electrical vehicles	0.003	0.001	0.001	0.000	0.001
Total	146.4	148.5	49.7	50.3	100.0
Total	294.9				

Source: EIA, *Annual Energy Outlook 2008.*

poses, the key forecast variable is the last factor, the average fuel efficiency of the vehicle stock, which is a function of the types of vehicles likely to constitute the stock in 2030 and their associated fuel consumption profiles.

As shown in table 2-2, the EIA anticipates that vehicles powered by petroleum (gasoline and diesel) will continue to dominate the vehicle stock, although their combined share (74 percent) will be lower than it was in 2007 (94 percent). Nonconventional vehicles will account for the remaining 26 percent. Full hybrids (gas- and diesel-based) are forecast to account for 11 percent of the vehicle stock in 2030; plug-in hybrids and all-electric vehicles together for just 0.01 percent; and flex-fuel ethanol vehicles for the remaining 15 percent.[7]

EIA's projections of the fuel efficiency of new vehicles sold in 2030 (see table 2-3) appear to be quite conservative when evaluated in light of the advanced technologies that already have been commercialized in the United States and other countries, upcoming vehicle launches planned by existing OEMs and new entrants into the hybrid and electric vehicle market, and current innovations in the research and development pipeline of the auto industry. For instance, EIA's projections of forward penetration rates are relatively low for a range of new technologies now available and capable of significantly improving the fuel efficiency of conventional internal combustion engines, even as far out as twenty-plus years.[8]

TABLE 2-3. EIA's Fuel Efficiency Assumptions for New Light-Duty Vehicles Sold in 2030

Miles per gallon

Fuel type	Passenger cars	Light trucks	Weighted average[a]
Gasoline	40.3	29.8	36.0
Diesel	51.0	37.0	39.6
Ethanol	40.6	30.2	33.3
Other (natural gas, fuel cell)	52.8	28.1	44.5
Full hybrids (gasoline)	53.7	39.5	45.9
Full hybrids (diesel)	57.3	45.4	57.3
Full hybrids (plug-ins)	72.9	56.5	72.9
Electric vehicles	103.2	81.9	97.9

Source: EIA, *Annual Energy Outlook 2008*.

a. Weighted average miles per gallon reflects the miles per gallon of cars and light trucks for each type weighted by the assumed percentage of cars and light trucks in the vehicle stock, shown in table 2-2.

In addition, the EIA forecast does not factor in the substantial changes in fuel efficiency that are likely to result from the introduction of lithium-ion and other advanced batteries in plug-in vehicles; the potential use of lighter-weight materials and/or second-generation biofuels with hybrid electric drive vehicles; and possible breakthroughs in battery chemistry and/or design that would make much greater electric drive ranges feasible for plug-ins and all-electric vehicles. Interestingly, the EIA assumes that plug-in hybrids will achieve an electric drive capability of only ten miles over the forecast period, when General Motors (GM) already has announced plans to commercialize the Chevy Volt with a forty-mile all-electric drive by 2010 and Fisker Automotive and Audi are developing plug-ins with electric drive ranges of fifty and sixty miles, respectively.[9]

In fact, the average electric drive range for all announced plug-in and all-electric vehicles and retrofit kits is about 42 miles and 110 miles, respectively.[10] The reason that this metric matters is that the EIA's assumption that plug-ins achieve an electric drive range of only ten miles results in an average fuel efficiency of 72.9 miles per gallon for the vehicle type over the anticipated drive cycle. However, plug-in conversion kits such as those offered by A123System's Hymotion and others already deliver thirty to forty miles of electric drive range, resulting in 93.5 miles per gallon (and more) on average over the many drive cycles tested.[11] It is important to note that in the case of plug-in and all-electric vehicles, drivers who travel less than the maximum electric drive range on a daily basis are not likely to use any petroleum at all, so their mileage per gallon of petroleum-based fuel would be, in effect, infinite.

The EIA also is especially conservative in its forecast of the potential share of the vehicle stock that hybrid and plug-in electric vehicles can capture considering that there are nearly twenty hybrid models available in the United States today and more than thirty new models anticipated over the next few years alone. There also are more than seventy efforts under way by incumbent OEMs and many new entrants to commercialize plug-in or all-electric vehicles or both.[12]

Other Consumption Scenarios

What would oil demand be if hybrids and electric vehicles collectively accounted for 80 percent of the vehicle stock in 2030—with plug-in hybrids, at 35 percent of the vehicle stock, representing the single-largest share (see table 2-4)?[13] To answer that question, let's assume that the fuel efficiencies that EIA projects for new vehicles in 2030 will actually be reached for the vehicle stock as a whole in 2030. That would require those efficiencies to be introduced in new vehicles ten to fifteen years earlier than they are in the EIA forecast. If that is the case—and using the same vehicle stock, miles driven, and respective shares of cars and light trucks in the vehicle stock as used by EIA for 2030—the resulting average fuel efficiency for the entire future stock is 59 miles per gallon (see table 2-4). An average fuel efficiency of 59 miles per gallon yields a reduction in oil use by light-duty vehicles in 2030 of roughly 53 percent and a decline in total oil consumption of 23 percent if all else stays the same as in the EIA forecast. If other road transport vehicles (for example, buses and medium- and heavy-duty trucks) are similarly hybridized or electrified so that their average fuel consumption also is reduced by 50 percent, the annual reduction in total U.S. demand for oil would be more than 30 percent less than 2030 EIA forecast levels of 22.8 million barrels a day.[14] At a price of $100 a barrel, the economic savings would be upward of $260 billion a year.

If plug-ins could achieve greater electric drive ranges and plug-ins or all-electrics capture a higher share of the light-duty stock, the reduction in oil demand would be even greater. For instance, if the average fuel efficiency of the entire vehicle stock was 100 miles per gallon (mpg) by

TABLE 2-4. Electrification Scenario, 2030 Assumptions

Fuel type	Vehicle stock (percent)[a]	EIA's weighted average (mpg)
Gasoline	10	36.0
Diesel	5	39.6
Ethanol	5	33.3
Other (natural gas, fuel cell)	0	44.5
Full hybrids (gasoline)	30	45.9
Full hybrids (diesel)	5	57.3
Full hybrids (plug-ins)	35	72.9
Electric vehicles	10	97.9
Total	100	59 (New average mpg)

Source: EIA, *Annual Energy Outlook 2008*.

a. Percentages of the vehicle stock for each vehicle type (column 2) are assumed by the author to reflect a scenario of full-scale electrification by 2030. The miles per gallon (mpg) figures reflect EIA's projections for the fuel efficiency of new vehicles sold, by type, in 2030. These projections are applied to the entire vehicle stock in 2030, yielding a forecast of 59 miles per gallon—the new average mpg. The actual EIA projection for the fuel efficiency of vehicle stock in 2030 is 27.9 miles per gallon.

2030, the reduction in oil demand from light-duty vehicles would be more than 70 percent. If other road transport vehicles also saw efficiency gains of 50 percent, total U.S. oil demand would be reduced by nearly 40 percent.

Total U.S. oil consumption could decline by almost 40 to 50 percent from projected levels in 2030 if non–road transport uses of oil concurrently experience greater substitution (as with natural gas in home heating) or see efficiency gains from fuel-saving airplanes and ships and less oil-intensive industrial processes that collectively result in an additional 10 percent reduction in oil consumption.[15] If the reductions achieved in non–road transport uses are greater than 10 percent, total consumption could fall by 50 percent or more.

If such outcomes materialize, the age of oil, as we know it, will be over. Oil is the largest source of energy in the United States, accounting (on a BTU basis) for 40 percent of our total energy use, and because 97 percent of our transport fuels are petroleum based, it has a stranglehold on transportation.[16] Plug-in hybrids and all-electric vehicles promise to break our dependency by significantly boosting efficiency and making electricity a viable substitute fuel—and thus enabling meaningful fuel flexibility in transportation for the first time since the turn of the twentieth century. With the transformation of road transport through hybridization and electrification and modest improvements in other sectors, oil's share of total energy use could be reduced dramatically, to about 20 percent, on par with coal's share today, significantly enhancing our economic and energy security. Moreover, such a reduction would represent a profound structural change, a paradigm shift with the potential to reshape the automotive, energy, and transportation industries and to alter the geopolitics of oil and the Middle East.

One might ask whether the electrification of transport would increase our reliance on electricity so significantly that it will somehow set us back. It will not, for several reasons. First, greater reliance on electricity should not affect our energy security since electric power can be generated from a wide variety of domestically available sources. Second, several research studies indicate that much of the U.S. vehicle stock could be converted to plug-in electrical vehicles with minimal impact to the U.S. grid, principally because of the tremendous excess capacity it has during off-peak hours, which would likely be the primary charge times.[17] Indeed, using that excess capacity may enhance the grid's overall efficiency and thereby lower electricity costs. Third, the use of electricity as a transport fuel will lower operating costs for drivers, particularly if they charge at night. The estimated difference in the per-mile cost is dramatic: $0.02 to $0.04 per mile for electricity versus $0.16 per mile for gasoline.[18]

Last, there also are potential benefits on the emissions side from moving transport from oil to electricity. Recent studies show that plug-in electric vehicles—even with the current power generation infrastructure, which is highly reliant on coal-fired power plants—would be less harmful to the environment than conventional vehicles in terms of greenhouse gas emissions and that the reduction would be on par with that achieved with today's hybrids.[19] However, since over time a greater proportion of our power generation will come from much cleaner sources, such as nuclear plants, solar panels, and wind turbines, the use of electric drive vehicles will result in much larger reductions in greenhouse gases in the years ahead. Indeed, the shift to plug-in hybrids and all-electrics will give utilities additional revenue that can be used to make the grid cleaner and more efficient.

Is Such a Transition from Oil Possible?

History suggests that a transition from oil is possible. As figure 2-1 illustrates, in the past the United States has successfully transitioned twice: once from wood to coal and then from coal to oil. Neither transition was made because we ran out of a resource; both were made following innovations in technology and processes. Those innovations used new feedstocks that led to higher efficiencies; more convenience, power, or speed; and (frequently) lower cost. For instance, society gained tremendous efficiency and convenience by moving from wood-burning to coal- and kerosene-fired stoves. Tremendous efficiencies also were gained by moving from natural gas stoves to microwaves in more recent times (see figure 2-2). A similar pattern emerges in other applications, such as steam engines and lighting, supporting the view that society has been on a long quest for higher efficiency and convenience and that it is unable to go backward. Historically, innovation begot innovation in a virtuous circle that allowed for forward progress. It is hard to imagine, therefore, that anyone would want to use paraffin candles or kerosene lanterns for lighting again or would opt for wood over natural gas for cooking, even if doing so were cheaper, because those methods are much less efficient and convenient to use. Indeed, as figure 2-3 illustrates, society has moved forward, innovating engines with both more efficiency and more power or speed.

It is interesting to note that while each energy transition resulted in a greater amount of energy being consumed, our relative dependency on each feedstock has declined. For instance, in the age of wood, we consumed about 3 quadrillion BTUs of energy in the form of wood and we were essentially solely reliant on it (80 to100 percent); today we rely on it for just 3 percent of our energy (see figure 2-4). During the coal era, we consumed about 15 quadrillion BTUs in the form of coal and we were dependent on it for up to 75 percent of our energy; today coal's share of our energy consumption is 20 percent. Currently, we consume about 40 quadrillion BTUs of oil, which represents about 40 percent of our total energy use; however, at its peak, in 1979, oil accounted for 49 percent of our total energy use. Thus, we are relatively less dependent on oil today than we were on other energy sources in the past. Moreover, as the figure implies, the age of oil will likely end when oil constitutes about 20 percent of our total energy mix, making it equal in importance to coal.

FIGURE 2-1. Estimated Primary Energy Consumption in the United States, by Select Fuels

BTUs, quadrillions

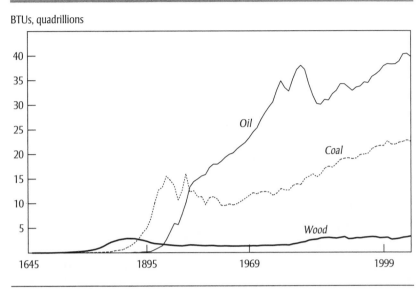

Source: EIA, *Annual Energy Review 2007*.

FIGURE 2-2. Efficiency of Stoves, by Fuel Source

Percent

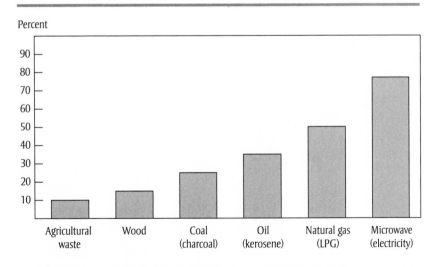

Sources: United Nations, World Energy Assessment: Energy and the Challenge of Sustainability; and R. U. Ayres, L. W. Ayres, and B. Warr, "Energy, Power, and Work in the U.S. Economy," INSEAD 2002.

FIGURE 2-3. Efficiency and Speed of Engines

Efficiency, percent

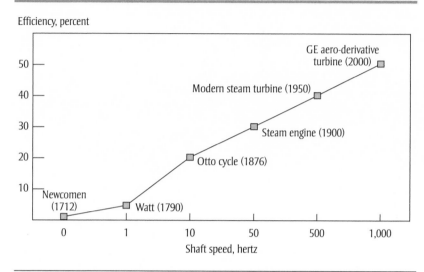

Source: Peter Huber and Mark Mills, *The Bottomless Well: The Twilight of Fuel, the Virtue of Waste, and Why We Will Never Run Out of Energy* (New York: Basic Books, 2006).

FIGURE 2-4. Share of Total Energy Consumed in United States, by Source

Percent

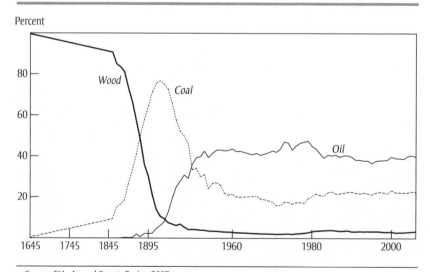

Source: EIA, *Annual Energy Review 2007.*

FIGURE 2-5. **Share of U.S. Manufacturing Capacity, by Energy Source**

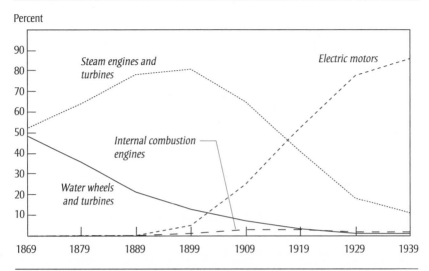

Percent

Sources: Warren Devine, "From Shaft to Wires: Historical Perspective on Electrification," *Journal of Economic History* (June 1983); and Samuel Baldwin, "The Materials Revolution and Energy-Efficient Electric Motor Drive Systems," *Annual Review of Energy* 13 (November 1988): 67–94.

How Long Will Electrification of Transport Take?

Four analogs are helpful in considering how quickly the vehicle stock can be hybridized or electrified or both. First is the rate of electrification of the manufacturing sector at the turn of the twentieth century. As shown in figure 2-5, it took electric motors approximately forty years from introduction to displace steam engines, water wheels, and other technologies, thereby capturing 80 percent of the market for power in U.S. manufacturing. Second, diesel electric locomotives—arguably the world's first hybrids since they use diesel engines to power electric motors to move the wheels—came to dominate rail transport in a span of just thirty years by displacing the incumbent steam locomotives, which had been in use for nearly a hundred years (see figure 2-6). In both cases, electric motors displaced steam engines because they ran more efficiently, they were more convenient or practical to deploy, they were easier or cheaper to maintain, and they were able to generate greater power or speed and less exhaust. In addition, while their capital costs were higher, their operating costs

FIGURE 2-6. Locomotives in Service on U.S. Railroads, by Type

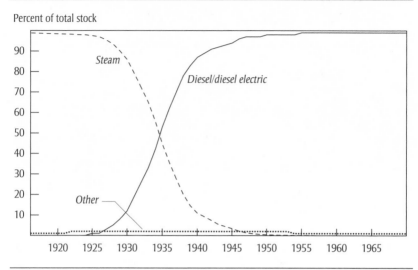

Percent of total stock

Source: U.S. Census Bureau, *Historical Statistics of the United States: Colonial Times to 1970.*

were significantly lower, leading to favorable economics over the life of the motor. Third, in China today the two-wheeler market, which consists of petrol-powered scooters, mopeds, power bikes, and motorcycles, is witnessing rapid adoption of battery-operated electric alternatives. If the trend continues, within a span of twenty to thirty years from introduction, these alternatives may displace enough of the traditional petrol-powered two-wheelers to constitute 80 percent of the future stock of two-wheelers (see figure 2-7).

Fourth, the penetration rates of new technologies in U.S. car sales in the postmodern era show that it has taken roughly seventeen years on average for various innovations to reach 80 percent or more penetration (see table 2-5). That suggests that it takes about twenty-seven to thirty-seven years to capture an 80 percent share of the vehicle stock.

If history is a guide, these analogs suggest that it would take roughly thirty years for hybridization/electrification to dominate road transport. Since hybrid cars were first introduced in the United States in 1999, we can reshape the stock of light-duty vehicles by 2030.

FIGURE 2-7. **Electrification of China's Two-Wheeler Market**

Units sold, millions

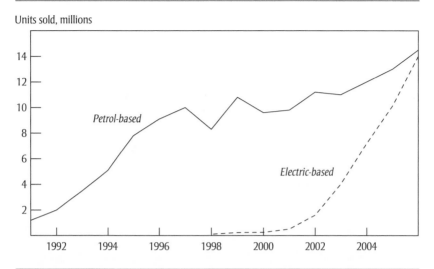

Source: Jonathan Weinert and others, "The Future of Electric Two-Wheelers and Electric Vehicles in China," *Energy Policy* 36, no. 7 (July 2008): 2544–55.

TABLE 2-5. **Achievement Time for Penetration of New Automotive Technologies from Introduction (in Years)**

Technology	Year introduced in United States[a]	Years to achieve × percent penetration of new car sales		
		20 percent	50 percent	80 percent
Air conditioning	1958	8	12	25
ABS (advanced)	1978	11	14	20
Airbags[b]	1974	16	19	21
Radial tires	1972	3	4	4
Front wheel drive	1975	6	9	13
Lockup transmission	1978	4	5	18
MultiValve engine[c]	1986	3	10	21
Electronic fuel injection	1967	17	21	23
Disk brakes	1966	4	5	7
Average		8.0	11.0	16.9

Sources: Wards *Automotive Yearbook*, select years. Charles Wessner, *The Advanced Technology Program: Assessing Outcomes* (Washington: National Academies Press, 2001); EPA, "Light-Duty Automotive Technology and Fuel Economy Trends: 1975 through 2005" (www.epa.gov/otaq/fetrends.htm); and Wikipedia.

a. Introduction reflects availability in new cars sold, except for ABS, which reflects introduction in new cars and light trucks sold.

b. Driver's side airbag; mandated.

c. More than two valves in engine.

What Would Be the Reasons for Such a Transition?

The transition from petroleum-powered vehicles to electric vehicles is likely to occur for ten principal reasons.

First, the internal combustion engine is relatively inefficient at converting fuel energy to a propulsion force. Only 15 percent of the gasoline pumped into a conventional automobile is used to move it or to power accessories. The vast majority is wasted as heat, and the rest is dissipated in idling and drive line loss.[20] The performance of diesel-powered automobiles is slightly better, with on-board efficiencies of about 20 percent. Conversely, all-electric vehicles have on-board efficiencies of about 80 percent, a five- to sixfold improvement over those of conventional vehicles. Some hybrids like the Toyota Prius have comparable efficiencies in the range of 30 to 35 percent. The efficiencies of plug-in hybrids are even higher, depending on the percentage of miles driven in electric mode.[21] As noted earlier, society has been on a long march to higher efficiency, and the question is when, not if, the inefficient combustion engine will be displaced by a better alternative.

Second, electric drive offers much lower operating costs than conventional petroleum-based drive—the higher the price of oil, the greater the difference.

Third, electric drive also offers a more compelling user experience, with enhanced performance from the instantaneous torque of the electric motor as well as greater safety and control through the increase in on-board electronics made possible by the enhanced capacity of a vehicle's battery.[22]

Fourth, maintenance costs should be lower, since electronic systems break down much less often than their mechanical counterparts, and the more optimal use of the engine allows the fewer mechanical systems on board in a hybrid, plug-in, or all-electric vehicle to last longer.

Fifth, hybrids and plug-ins should allow for considerable product choice since vehicles of all sizes can be hybridized or electrified or both. That means that consumers will not have to sacrifice space or other cabin comforts or switch to a smaller car to see meaningful efficiency gains.

Sixth, the cost and technology improvement curves for electrical systems are much steeper than for mechanical systems. Electric drive vehicles can get better and cheaper faster. For instance, in the span of just six years, Toyota improved the gas mileage and acceleration of the Prius by more than 30 percent while enlarging it from a subcompact into a family sedan—and also reduced production costs by 50 percent in the process.[23]

Seventh, electric drive vehicles enhance overall convenience because they do not require fluid changes and other routine checks, and they need fewer trips to the gas station and repair shop.

Eighth, battery-powered electric drive vehicles do not require massive new infrastructure, in contrast to hydrogen-powered fuel cell vehicles, nor do they tax existing infrastructure and resources, as biofuels may do with respect to land and water resources. In fact, plug-ins and all-electric vehicles may help boost the efficiency and quality of the existing electric grid by helping with load balancing. That is especially important in regions whose baseloads are reliant on coal or nuclear power. Over time, these vehicles may even help with load leveling and peak shaving if a vehicle-to-grid infrastructure is developed, which permits unused capacity in a vehicle's battery to be injected back into the grid. This notion appeared to be "science fiction" several years ago, but several institutions are now actively studying its potential and evaluating the requisite technologies.[24]

Ninth, electric drive has a natural sponsor in the utility industry to help nurture its existence and push for its acceptance. Utilities stand to see a whole new source of revenue and profit opening up for them if electric drive takes off; therefore they are increasingly likely to work for its success. Already, GM and Ford have announced collaborations with the Electrical Power Research Institute (EPRI) and a large number of utilities to study technical issues related to plug-ins in the United States. Toyota is collaborating with France's EDF (Électricité de France) and Japan's Tokyo Electric to develop recharging stations for plug-in hybrids in Europe and Japan, and to establish appropriate standards and work on other related issues. EDF has also agreed to work with PSA Peugeot Citroen to support the development and marketing of plug-in hybrids. In addition, Austin Energy in Texas has announced a $1,000 credit for customers who purchase plug-ins when they become available and has signed a pledge to purchase forty plug-in hybrids for its own municipal fleet. Such incentives and fleet purchases by utilities (and other interested parties) will help reduce costs for the mass market. On the all-electric front, Daimler is working with Germany's RWE Energy AG, Nissan with the Tennessee Valley Authority, Mitsubishi and Fuji Heavy Industries with Tokyo Electric, Renault with EDF, and Better Place with Danish energy company

DONG to build charging stations and infrastructure in a variety of pilot projects to demonstrate the viability of electric drive.

Tenth, governments around the world are likely to respond to concerns about climate change with more legislation to curb emissions. Since transportation accounts for 20 percent of global emissions, mandates to reduce fuel consumption and hence vehicular emissions from the transport sector are likely to be more stringent. Electric drive vehicles offer the potential to substantially reduce CO_2 emissions more than the alternatives while also reducing other pollutants such as nitrogen oxides (NOx) and particulate matter (PM), which other technologies like common rail diesel still have a hard time achieving. On that point, the Japanese government has recently concluded that at least 50 percent of Japan's vehicle stock will have to consist of plug-ins with a substantial electric drive range or all-electric vehicles to achieve the required CO_2 reductions by 2030.[25] In addition, the Spanish government has indicated that it would like to promote the use of 1 million electric vehicles by 2015, and the Israeli and Danish governments are actively working with Better Place to import electric vehicles in mass quantities. The latter governments have offered significant tax incentives to accelerate their adoption.

Hybrids are the first step on the road to electrification. Plug-ins are more compelling than hybrids due to the larger displacement of oil and the potential for enhanced emissions reductions from their use. Moreover, plug-ins will cost less than all-electrics and may get us a considerable distance to the goal of meaningfully reducing our oil dependence. Also, they afford more flexibility than all-electric vehicles because drivers can use the existing petroleum refueling infrastructure for long trips.

The biggest question in determining the timing and scale of the transition to electric drive is the rate of improvement in price, performance, and life of the battery. For example, if the goals of the U.S. Advanced Battery Consortium (USABC) can be met, overall penetration would be very high because consumers could then pick the electric drive option best suited for their average drive cycle.[26] Plug-ins should lead the pack since they are likely to produce high petrol displacement per incremental cost for most drivers, while delivering a compelling drive experience and affording drivers the convenience of not having to rely on a charging network for long trips.

Past evidence from Toyota suggests that the USABC goals can be met because the company has been able to improve battery performance and reduce weight (and hence cost) at a rate of 8 to 10 percent a year. Moreover, several battery chemistries already meet USABC's goals for plug-in hybrid batteries on two important criteria: power density and energy density. The USABC's goals for all-electric vehicle batteries on power and energy are more onerous to meet today. However, that too is likely to change, considering that nearly fifty companies are actively pursuing energy storage and related technologies. While the majority are focusing on lithium-based batteries as the next-generation solution, a number of them are actively pursuing other approaches, such as ultra capacitors, which will free the battery from having to deliver both energy and power.[27] Others are seeking fundamental breakthroughs with new chemistries or materials. We also are likely to see considerable progress with respect to cost and other performance dimensions including battery safety and life.

Skeptics of electrification often argue that gasoline will always be superior to batteries in storing energy. Hence, they argue, either the move to electric vehicles will never happen or, if it does, it will only be a stepping stone to a future based on hydrogen, which also naturally stores a great deal of energy.

A recent paper from Stuart Licht of the U.S. National Science Foundation and other researchers from the University of Massachusetts debunks that mode of thinking.[28] The team of scientists has found that while gasoline has a practical energy storage capacity of about 2.7 kWh/liter and current state-of-the-art lithium-ion batteries have a capacity of 0.5 kWh/liter, their new electrochemical energy system, a vanadium boride (VB_2) air cell, has a practical energy storage capacity of 5 kWh/liter, or nearly twice the capacity of gasoline. In addition, the research team also has found hydrogen's practical energy capacity to be about 2 kWh/liter, and although that is much greater than the 0.3 kWh/liter capacity of nickel metal hydride (NiMH), the predominant electrochemistry in today's hybrid batteries, it is in line with the energy capacity of zinc air batteries and is still much lower than that of their VB_2 cell.

The research by Licht and his team indicates that the future can belong to batteries.[29]

The VB_2 cell that they have developed is a long way from being commercialized, but it suggests that society should move ahead and support hybridization, opening the path to electrification with plug-in hybrids. Eventually breakthroughs will come in zinc air, vanadium boride air, or other metal air batteries to enable either plug-ins with a substantial electric drive range or all-electric vehicles with ranges comparable to today's petroleum-based vehicles, or both.

What Will the Transition to Electric Drive Cost?

While it is difficult to estimate the cost of hybridization and electrification of the entire road transport sector, the costs of transforming the U.S. light-duty vehicle stock of 2030 appear to be in the range of $325 billion to $1 trillion. The USABC has estimated the battery cost for a conventional gasoline hybrid at $500 to $800; for plug-in hybrids at $1,700 to $3,400, with 10 to 40 miles of electric drive range; and for all-electric vehicles at about $4,000 in scale production (defined as 20,000 to 100,000 units). Over the past few years, battery costs have represented about half of the total incremental cost of hybrids (for example, the battery comprises $2,500 of the $5,000 incremental cost to Toyota to build the Prius). Assuming that the relationship holds and applying the resulting total incremental costs to the electrification scenario mentioned above, in which plug-ins account for 35 percent of the stock in 2030, yields a cost of about $940 billion.[30]

However, between now and 2030, the estimated costs may fall by at least 50 percent. The historic cost curve has featured 8 to 10 percent declines each year. That would mean the forward costs for vehicle conversion would be in the range of $225 to $940 billion, depending on when the vehicles were commercialized, how fast the technology was adopted, how rapidly economies of scale were achieved, and the magnitude of the resulting cost reductions.[31] Assuming that plug-in and all-electric vehicles take a combined 45 percent share of future miles driven[32] and factoring in the cost of electricity at a rate of 0.25 kWh per mile and a charge of $0.10 per kilowatt leads to an additional cost of about $50 billion. Let's further assume that making plug-ins and all-electrics widely available in the United States requires a modest buildup of the charging infrastructure at a cost of an additional $50 billion. That brings the total societal cost of electrification into the range of $325 billion to $1 trillion.

Given that the annual cost savings from oil displacement is projected to be $260 billion, of which light-duty vehicles account for $180 billion, the payback period for the transformation of passenger cars and light trucks would be between two to six years.[33] There also is likely to be an additional carbon benefit, which we have not quantified, because the electricity to fuel those miles will be increasingly supplied by cleaner sources. That benefit may further reduce the payback period if the United States adopts a tax (direct or indirect) on carbon. Although these costs are large, they are manageable given the size of the economy, current spending on oil, and the historic costs of several programs that the nation has undertaken in the past, such as developing the interstate highway system.

Conclusion

In the United States, the paradigm shift to electric drive is occurring and will accelerate. That shift is likely to lead to a dramatic 50 percent reduction in demand for oil over the next twenty to thirty years. Society has transitioned from one energy source to another before, and it will do so again, with innovation leading the way. Internal combustion engines are relatively inefficient, expensive to operate and maintain, and dirty from the perspective of CO_2 emissions. Conversely, plug-in hybrids and all-electric vehicles are efficient, they are cheap to operate and maintain, and they have low CO_2 emissions. The continuing success of conventional hybrids will pave the way for plug-ins and all-electric vehicles as automobile manufacturers and suppliers achieve economies of scale and thus are able to lower costs on many of the vehicles' shared components, offering greater drive ranges as battery and other technology breakthroughs occur.

Notes

1. While the $1.5 trillion sum is no doubt large, it is less staggering than the costs faced in the summer of 2008, when oil prices peaked at $140 a barrel. Had those record high prices been sustained, the economic charge for global oil consumption would have been more than $4.3 trillion a year. BP Statistical Review of World Energy 2008 (www.bp.com).

2. Energy Information Administration (EIA), *Annual Energy Outlook 2008* (www.eia.doe.gov). Road transport includes light-duty vehicles (passenger cars and trucks), buses, medium- and heavy-duty trucks, motorcycles, and three-wheelers.

3. The first hybrid to be sold in the United States by a major automobile manufacturer was the Insight by Honda Motor Company in 1999. Toyota Motor Corporation first launched the Prius in Japan in 1997; it was sold in the United States as a 2001 model beginning in late 2000.

4. EIA, *Annual Energy Outlook 2008*.

5. The calculation used to derive the 8.8 million barrels a day is simplified; the EIA's actual methodology uses conversion factors to put non–gasoline-based fuels on a

gasoline-equivalent basis in order to more precisely estimate the average fuel efficiency of the vehicle stock.

6. Forecast from Reference Case, EIA, *Annual Energy Outlook 2008*.

7. Nearly all of the hybrids sold today use a gasoline engine as the primary source of power, and many have an electric motor that provides additional power when needed. How much additional power the motor supplies determines whether a hybrid is considered a full, mild, or micro hybrid. Full hybrids can use their electric motor as the sole source of propulsion for certain applications, such as low-speed, low-acceleration driving (in stop-and-go traffic) or backing up.

8. These new technologies include advanced engines (for example, direct injection or HCCI/CAI) and transmissions (for example, CVT or dual clutch); camless actuation; cylinder deactivation; variable valve timing and lift; electric pumps and steering; and stop/start, launch assist, and regenerative braking.

9. The EIA's assumption that plug-ins achieve only a ten-mile range was confirmed in a June 2008 telephone conversation that I had with John Maples, a transportation demand analyst at EIA.

10. Using information from trade publications and websites, industry conferences, analyst reports, Automotive X Prize, and company press releases, I tabulated more than seventy plug-in and all-electric initiatives under way with incumbent auto manufacturers and new entrants as of August 2008. Plug-in initiatives include the AFS Trinity XH 150 (40 miles), Audi Sportsback A1 (62 miles), BYD F6 DM (62 miles), Fisker Automotive Karma (50 miles), GM Chevy Volt (40 miles), and Volvo C30 Recharge (30 miles). All-electric initiatives include AC Propulsion ebox EV (120 miles), BYD E6 (186 miles), Electrovaya Maya 300 (120 miles), Hybrid Technologies EV (120 miles), Lightning Car Company GT (250 miles), Mitsubishi I-MIEV (75–95 miles), Nissan EV (60–70 miles), Phoenix Motorcars (130 miles), Renault EV (approximately 100 miles), Reva G Wiz (75 miles), Tesla Motors Roadster (220 miles), Think City (112 miles), and Venturi Fetish (155 miles).

11. See "RechargeIT Driving Experiment" (www.google.org/recharge/ [October 20, 2008]) for results of drive tests of converted plug-ins (for example, a Prius hybrid retrofitted to be a plug-in) conducted by the RechargeIT program of Google.org; see www.a123systems.com for data on Hymotion's conversions/retrofits.

12. See note 10.

13. The scenario depicted, with 80 percent of the vehicle stock hybridized and/or electrified by 2030, is broadly consistent with forecasts by other entities such as Alliance Bernstein, Electric Power Research Institute (EPRI), General Electric, Global Insight, and the Natural Resource Defense Council (NRDC), among others.

14. A number of companies already are working on the electrification of such vehicles—Eaton, Enova, and Odyne for medium- and heavy-duty trucks and GM, Daimler, and ISE for municipal buses.

15. Higher efficiencies in road transport provide reductions of 30 to 40 percent, and efficiency gains in non–road transport uses provide an additional 10 percent reduction, for a total reduction of 40 to 50 percent.

16. Oil use as a percentage of total energy use and oil's share of fuels consumed in transportation are on a BTU basis; see EIA, *Annual Energy Outlook* (2008) and www.eia.doe.gov. The data cited reflect 2006 figures.

17. Michael Kintner-Meyer, Kevin Schneider, and Robert Pratt, "Impacts Assessment of Plug-in Hybrid Vehicles on Electric Utilities and Regional U.S. Power Grids," Pacific Northwest National Laboratory, November 2007; P. Denholm and W. Short, "An Evaluation of Utility System Impacts and Benefits of Optimally Dispatched Plug-In Hybrid Electric Vehicles," National Renewable Energy Laboratory, October 1, 2006; Stanton W. Hadley and Alexandra Tsvetkova, "Potential Impacts of Plug-in Hybrid Electric Vehicles on Regional Power Generation," *Oak Ridge National Laboratory Review* 41, no. 1 (2008); Robert Graham, "Plug-in Hybrid Electric Vehicles: Changing the Energy Landscape," Electric Power Research Institute, May 2005. According to the EIA, nearly 50 percent of U.S. electricity is generated by coal, 20 percent by natural gas, 19 percent by nuclear fuel, 7 percent by hydropower, 2 percent by petroleum, and 2 percent by renewable sources of energy.

18. Toyota's plug-in hybrid is believed to use a three-kilowatt-hour (kWh) battery, which—assuming a three-hour charge time and a electricity charge of $0.10/kWh— would cost $0.30 to fully charge. Assuming that the vehicle has an electric range of ten miles, its operating cost would be $0.03 per mile. Several Prius plug-in retrofits have a similar cost. The Chevy Volt plug-in hybrid will have an operating cost of $0.02 since it is seen as using eight kilowatt-hours of battery capacity to travel forty miles; a cost of $0.20/kWh for electricity would make the cost $0.04 per mile. The operating cost of a conventional vehicle with assumed gas mileage of 25 miles per gallon at $4.00 per gallon would be $0.16 per mile, or four to eight times the cost. These costs are for operation only; the cost of the battery as well as the costs of other electronics and components reflected in current premiums of about $5,000 per full hybrid (gasoline) and as much $10,000 to $15,000 for plug-in hybrids are not considered in operating costs.

19. C. Samaras and K. Meisterling, "Life-Cycle Assessment of Greenhouse Gas Emissions from Plug-in Hybrid Vehicles: Implications for Policy," *Environmental Science Technology* 42, no. 9 (2008); Luke Tonachel and Roland Hwang, "The Next Generation of Hybrid Cars: Plug-in Hybrids Can Help Reduce Global Warming and Slash Oil Dependency," Natural Resources Defense Council, April 2007; Electric Power Research Institute and Natural Resources Defense Council, *Environmental Assessment of Plug-In Hybrid Electric Vehicles*, vol. 1, *Nationwide Greenhouse Gas Emissions* (2007); David Talbot, "Plug-In Hybrids: Tailpipes vs. Smokestacks," *Technology Review* (March-April 2008).

20. See Amy Raskin and Saurin Shah, "The Emergence of Hybrid Vehicles: Ending Oil's Stranglehold on Transportation and the Economy," Alliance Bernstein, June 2006. This paper was widely distributed to clients and the media; it can be found at www.calcars.org and www.alliancebernstein.com.

21. Plug-in hybrids and electric vehicles also have the potential to achieve higher efficiencies than conventional vehicles and other alternative technologies, such as hydrogen and biofuels, over the entire cycle (also referred to as well-to-wheel efficiency), which accounts for the energy needed to get from point of origin to point of use, in addition to the energy actually used in propulsion. See Sherry Boschert, *Plug-in Hybrids: The Cars That Will Recharge America* (Gabriola Island, British Columbia: New Society Publishers, 2006).

22. See Raskin and Shah, "The Emergence of Hybrid Vehicles" for a discussion of how hybrids compare with other drivetrains, particularly on horsepower versus torque, and a list of the additional features that larger batteries make possible.

23. The gas mileage data are based on the prior EPA test criteria. The vehicle also reduced its emissions by 90 percent in the same time period. Source: Toyota Motors.

24. These institutions include the University of Delaware, U.S. Department of Energy, Federal Energy Regulatory Commission, several U.S. national laboratories, Electric Power Research Institute, Pacific Gas and Electric (PG&E) and a few other utilities, Ford, and Google.

25. Dave Paterson, Mitsubishi, in a presentation at Plug-In 2008, San Diego, California.

26. USABC is an arm of the U.S. Council for Automotive Research, a consortium comprising Ford, General Motors, and Chrysler that works closely with the Department of Energy, national laboratories, educational institutions, and suppliers to support and direct cooperative research on and development of advanced automotive technologies in the United States. USABC has established goals for advanced batteries for hybrids, plug-ins, and all-electric vehicles; details are available on its website (www.uscar.org/guest/article_view.php?articles_id=85).

27. The family of lithium-based battery chemistries for automotive applications currently includes lithium cobalt oxide (LCO), lithium nickel cobalt and aluminum (NCA), lithium iron phosphate (LFP), lithium nickel cobalt manganese (NCM), lithium manganese spinel (LMS), lithium titanium (LTO), and manganese titanium (MNS or MN).

28. Stuart Licht and others, "Renewable Highest Capacity VB2/Air Energy Storage," *Chemical Communications,* June 17, 2008.

29. Alliance Bernstein predicts that the automotive battery market could reach $150 billion if electrification of transport materializes. See Amy Raskin, Saurin Shah, Nils Mellquist, and Brett Winton, "Abating Climate Change," Alliance Bernstein, January 2008. The report can be found at alliancebernstein.com.

30. The $940 billion figure is derived by multiplying $1,300 by the hybrid share (30 percent) of the stock of 295 million vehicles, plus $2,300 multiplied by the diesel hybrid share (5 percent) since we assume that diesel hybrids will cost about $1,000 more than gasoline hybrids, plus $5,100 multiplied by the plug-in share (35 percent), plus $8,000 multiplied by the all-electric share (10 percent).

31. The $225 billion figure is calculated by assuming that the scale costs leading to the $940 billion estimate are achieved in 2013 and by applying an annual cost reduction rate of 8 percent from 2014 to 2030.

32. According to the EIA, total miles driven in 2030 by the entire stock of light-duty vehicles will be 4,069 billion.

33. The cost savings assumes a future price of oil of $100 per barrel.

CHAPTER THREE

Pluggable Cars:
A Key Component of a
Low-Carbon Transportation Future

DERON LOVAAS and LUKE TONACHEL

Plug-in electric vehicles are an essential element of any strategy for fighting global warming. Other elements—such as improved fuel efficiency, sustainable biofuels, and public transportation alternatives—also are important. But to achieve the needed reductions in emissions of heat-trapping gases, we must power a growing number of vehicles with clean, renewable electricity. That requires an aggressive, farsighted plan to transform our electrical grid and vehicle fleet to better fit into a carbon- and oil-constrained world. Bridging the chasm between the fossil fuel–dependent present and a better future will generate good jobs, insulate our economy by making it less oil intensive, and spare consumers countless trips to the gas station.

The threats facing the nation are real, and calls for consideration of new vehicle technologies are backed by glaring and alarming events. Petroleum reaches unheard-of price levels in the global marketplace and stays at what seems to be a plateau that is several times higher than the previous one. Household budgets, already strained by housing costs and income growth outpaced by inflation, groan under the added burden of energy costs. Nations such as Iran and Venezuela rattle their modern-day equivalent of sabers: the oil that lies in abundance under their sand and soil.

Linked with economic and security concerns is the growing awareness that we have filled the sky with carbon dioxide pollution. Concentrations are more than 30 percent higher than in pre-industrial times, and they are rising. It once seemed that stabilizing concentrations at 450 parts per million (ppm) would forestall the most dire consequences of climate change. But now scientists say that that figure is too high, and NASA scientist Jim Hansen, the Paul Revere of climate change, states that we should aim instead for 350 ppm.[1] And then there are the low-probability consequences that we cannot ignore. If one or more rapid "positive feedback loops"—such as a massive release of methane from ice under the ocean floor or the shutdown of the global ocean conveyor belt due to dropping salinity at its origin—are triggered, then the consequences would not be just damaging, they would be catastrophic.

While combustion of coal, as Hansen states, is the biggest contributor to global warming pollution, transportation is a part of the challenge too. And looking upstream to the sources of energy for the transport sector, it is clear that it is at risk of drifting to a dangerous, high-carbon future. High oil prices have made it economically feasible for Canada, for example, to produce more than 1 million barrels a day of crude oil from diffusely deposited bitumen in the province of Alberta. The carbon intensity of the production and refining of this stuff means that its carbon footprint is several times that of conventional oil.[2] Interest also is growing in producing oil from shale in the arid western United States and in liquefying coal through the Fischer-Tropsch process. The high-price scenario in the Energy Information Administration's 2008 projection is telling: by 2030, it projects that the United States will be producing 1.5 million barrels a day of unconventional oil, the vast majority of it from coal and 140,000 barrels a day from shale.[3]

Biofuels are a promising low-carbon alternative. However, the bloom is off the rose—or the corn stalk. Most biofuels in the United States are derived from corn, and studies find that under some circumstances the carbon footprint of the production process can be the same as or higher than that of gasoline.[4] Whether that is the case is contingent on the resource intensity of the feedstock, the biofuel yield per acre, and the direct and indirect land use changes caused by cultivation.[5] The picture will change substantially once one or more techniques for creating fuel from cellulose are commercially viable.[6]

What else is to be done? A burst of efficiency—the "first fuel," as the Alliance to Save Energy dubs it—is the first, fastest, and cheapest way to cut both oil and carbon use in light-duty vehicles. Even the National Petroleum Council has agreed that fuel economy for light-duty vehicles could double by 2030, and in the Energy Independence and Security Act of 2007 Congress mandated at least a 40 percent increase by 2020.[7] Other assessments find that there is even more technical potential for fuel economy increases.[8]

But in the coming decades, no matter how efficiently we use conventional gasoline and diesel fuels, substitutes will be necessary to improve energy security and cut carbon dioxide emissions. Electricity generated from renewable sources should be one of those substitutes.

Climate Change: The Challenge

The United States has about 5 percent of the world's population, but it is responsible for about one-quarter of oil consumption and one-fifth of carbon dioxide emissions. To stabilize carbon dioxide emissions, global pollution would have to be cut by half of current levels by 2050.[9] Due to its outsized role as a polluter, the United States would have to slash pollution 60 to 80 percent by 2050.[10]

Most reductions would come from the coal-dependent electricity sector, which is responsible for nearly 40 percent of U.S. emissions.[11] A burst of efficiency, particularly through improvements in U.S. building stock and appliances, is the quickest and most cost-effective way to cut pollution. As a recent report from the McKinsey consulting firm found that a whopping 710 to 870 megatons of carbon dioxide could be abated by making our building stock and appliances more efficient; retrofitting lighting; improving heating, ventilation, and air conditioning systems; switching to higher-performance office electronics and appliances; and other measures.[12]

Beyond that, fast development and deployment of technology to capture and safely dispose of carbon dioxide emissions, coupled with rapid scale-up of renewable technologies (specifically solar and wind energy), is a key to pushing down pollution from the electricity sector. And, of course, that becomes doubly important should the private light-duty vehicle fleet become pluggable.

Plug-in vehicles also can be part of a strategy to reduce the transportation sector's impact on local air quality. According to the American Lung Association, ground-level ozone (smog) and particle pollution continue to threaten the health of 42 percent of the U.S. population.[13] Plug-in vehicles operating solely on electricity have zero tailpipe emissions, so where these vehicles displace high numbers of dirtier conventional vehicles, ozone and particle pollution can be reduced. Charging plug-ins with renewable electricity also prevents pollution at the electricity source, making plug-ins truly a zero-emissions energy source over their full fuel cycle.

A Strategy for Transforming Our Fossil Fuel–Dependent Vehicle Fleet

Transportation is the most oil-dependent sector (at least 96 percent of the energy that it uses comes from oil), it is responsible for the lion's share of U.S. oil consumption (nearly two-thirds, 60 percent of which goes into light-duty vehicles), and it contributes more than one-quarter of U.S. carbon dioxide pollution.[14] Reducing the oil intensity of the sector and lowering its carbon profile are the sine qua non for achieving energy security and stabilizing the climate. Our transportation system and vehicle fleet must undergo a radical transformation. How do we achieve such a dramatic shift?

We have a three-pronged strategy for cutting the oil consumption of vehicles. The first step is to boost the efficiency of conventional vehicles by combining a number of proven improvements to engines, bodies, and drivelines.[15] A bigger change would be driven by higher penetration of hybrid electric vehicles, which range from "mild" to "strong" versions, providing a large boost of as much as 50 to 60 percent in fuel economy.[16] Such a leap in efficiency could get us nearly halfway to near-freedom from gasoline.[17]

The second step is to shift to low-carbon alternatives: next-generation biofuels (grown in the right places) and electricity generated from low-carbon sources. Pluggable hybrids are a crucial part of the strategy. The third and last step is to decrease road traffic through a combination of investments in transportation alternatives, land use policy reforms, and road pricing measures. Figure 3-1 shows one scenario for turning the oil dependence of light-duty vehicles on its head: instead of relying on gasoline for more than 90 percent of their energy, light-duty vehicles would get

FIGURE 3-1. Scenario for Displacement of 240 Billion Gallons of Gasoline Demand for Light-Duty Vehicles in 2050, by Source[a]

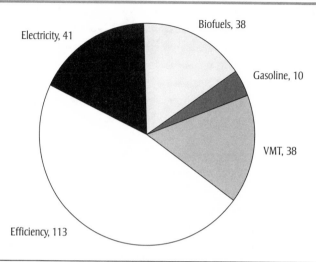

Source: Analysis by Luke Tonachel, included in testimony of Deron Lovaas, Natural Resources Defense Council, before the Senate Environment and Public Works Committee, *Future Federal Role for Surface Transportation*, 110 Cong., 2 sess., June 25, 2008.

a. In billions of gallons of the gasoline equivalent of each fuel displacing the expected demand in 2050 of 240 billion gallons of gasoline.

a mere 10 percent from gasoline. Another recent scenario found that just the combination of pluggable hybrids (with an electric range of twenty miles) and high-blend cellulosic ethanol (E85) could cut per-vehicle emissions and oil consumption to a mere 10 percent of current levels.[18]

Low-Carbon Vehicle Fleet Scenario

To reemphasize the importance of the demand-side components of this program, substitution of biofuels and electricity for fossil fuel liquids is not a viable proposition without large decreases in the baseline consumption of fossil fuel liquids due to an increase in vehicle efficiency and a decrease in vehicle miles traveled (VMT). A host of conventional and advanced technologies are available for that purpose, including vehicle components such as fuel-efficient tires, aerodynamic vehicle designs, continuously variable transmissions, and other modes of transportation, including bus rapid transit for intracity travel and high-speed rail for travel between cities. The International Energy Agency finds that the cumulative effect of vehicle technologies alone could save 14 to 27 percent (conventional vehicle technologies) on the low end and 28 to 45 percent (advanced vehicle technologies, such as hybrids) on the high end.[19] And a sketch analysis commissioned by the Natural Resources Defense Council (NRDC) finds that VMT could be reduced by 31 percent by 2050 from a combination of land use reforms, pricing measures (such as high-occupancy vehicle toll lanes, which charge vehicles a higher rate if they do not include a designated number of occupants), and investments in public transportation.[20]

Demand must be moderated, but substitutes for oil must be produced by low-carbon methods. For biofuels, that requires taking a hard look at feedstocks and the land where crops are cultivated as well as the process for producing the fuel. That is especially important for plug-in and all-electric vehicles, which compete with improved conventional vehicles and hybrid electric vehicles. In order for pluggable vehicles to contribute substantially to meeting pollution reduction goals, decarbonizing the electricity sector is imperative.

Basically, for the U.S. light-duty vehicle sector to achieve its share of the reductions in global warming pollution needed to meet climate stabilization targets (80 percent below the level in 1990), a transformation of the on-road fleet from today's conventional cars and light trucks to a fleet of flex-fuel (that is, capable of running on E85) plug-in hybrids is necessary. About half of annual vehicle mileage would be powered by cleaner and cleaner grid electricity, and the other half would be powered by very-low-carbon biofuels that would achieve an 80 percent reduction in the level of global warming pollution caused by gasoline. Advancements in battery storage that improve energy density and cycling life and lead to reduced ownership costs can enable a further shift of annual mileage from biofuels to electricity. With continuous improvement in vehicle efficiency, the demand for both electricity and biofuels can be reduced.

The good news is that the Energy Independence and Security Act of 2007 was a good start toward weaning surface transportation from fossil fuels. The new fuel economy standards for cars and trucks will raise the bar for fuel economy by at least 40 percent for new vehicles by 2020.[21] For the first time, similar standards must be set for heavy trucks.[22] The new law also contains dramatic increases in the renewable fuels standard, including more and more production of cellulosic biofuel, and a sustainability standard to address the growing list of concerns about the environmental effects of direct and indirect land use changes spurred by rising production of biofuels.[23] The bill also contained some important new investments and programs supporting pluggable hybrid technology, summarized in table 3-1.

The bad news is that Congress balked at adopting a national "renewable portfolio standard," which would have required that 15 percent of power come from renewable sources by 2020.[24] In addition, while the increase in fuel economy standards is laudable, it is shamefully overdue. There was an initial leap in fuel efficiency pursuant to implementation of the fuel economy program under the Energy Policy and Conservation Act in the 1970s, but progress has been nonexistent in the past two decades, with automakers improving efficiency only enough to stay at the same fuel economy level while increasing vehicle weight, power, and accessories.[25] Turnover of stock—for electricity generation or vehicles—takes decades; we cannot afford more delays from policymakers.

New Load Requirements: The Role of Efficiency and Renewable Energy Sources

Shifting a large portion of our vehicle fleet to electric power will put pressure on a grid already in need of modernization and improvement. New capital investments to serve plug-in vehicles can be minimized through adoption of aggressive efficiency measures. Vehicle charging is a new load to be supplied by electrical utilities, but when it is coupled with efforts to improve the efficiency of other electrical loads, such as household appliances and industrial machines, utilities can avoid the need for additional fossil fuel–based energy generation.

The success of policies that reduce energy use is well documented. California's energy efficiency standards and programs have been critical in keeping per capita electricity use roughly constant, while in the United States as a whole per capita electricity consumption has increased by nearly 50 percent since the mid-1970s.[26] Over the past three decades, California's energy efficiency efforts have avoided the need to build twenty-four large power plants.[27]

For load increases that cannot be offset through intelligent load management and increased efficiency, new energy generation should come from renewable resources. Renewable, low-carbon sources of electricity are critical for maximizing the emissions benefits of plug-in hybrids, which, if

TABLE 3-1. **Provisions of Energy Independence and Security Act of 2007 Regarding Plug-In Electric Vehicles**

Issue	Energy Act provisions	Authorization and timeline
Commercialization of plug-in hybrid vehicles	Plug-In Hybrid Electric Drive Vehicle Program: federal grants to governments, NGOs, and private entities to encourage widespread use of plug-in vehicles and advance their production.	$95 million a year authorized for FY2008–13.
	Domestic Manufacturing Conversion Program: grants and loan guarantees to auto manufacturers and suppliers to retool domestic factories to produce hybrid plug-in vehicles and advanced diesel vehicles.	Authorization of such sums as necessary to carry out the program
Fleet fuel consumption	Inclusion of electric drive in Energy Policy Act of 1992: fleets can meet alternative vehicle purchase requirements of EPAct 1992 by purchasing plug-in electric drive vehicles.	Authorization of such sums as necessary to carry out the program for FY2008–13.
	Federal fleet conservation requirements: federal fleets must achieve a 20 percent reduction in annual petroleum consumption and a 10 percent increase in alternative fuel consumption relative to FY2005 baseline levels. Commercially available plug-in electric drive vehicles can be purchased to meet the requirement.	Targets to be met by October 1, 2015
Battery cost	Advanced Battery Loan Guarantee Program: loan guarantees for U.S.-based advanced vehicle battery and battery system manufacturing facilities.	Authorization of such sums as necessary to carry out the program.
Battery cost, recycling, and disposal.	Competitiveness in energy storage technology: research, development, and demonstration to support U.S. global competitiveness in energy storage for electric vehicles. Establishes energy storage research centers at several national laboratories. Includes RD&D into secondary use, materials recycling, and final disposal of batteries.	$290 million a year authorized for FY2008–18; $5 million authorized for secondary use, recycling, and disposal for FY2009.
Integration of vehicles and electric power grid	Smart grid technology research, development, and demonstration: includes promotion of the use of underused electricity production capacity and establishment of grid-to-vehicle communication protocols to intelligently manage vehicle charging demands and to access electricity stored by vehicles to help meet peak power demand.	Authorization of such sums as necessary to carry out the program.

Source: Authors' compilation.

charged using renewable sources such as wind, solar, biomass, and geothermal energy, can be driven emissions free. The electricity grid therefore must continue to transition to the cleanest sources as plug-in hybrids penetrate the fleet. Of course, a plug-in hybrid relies on petroleum when not running on electricity, but when it is charged with a renewable source of electricity, a mere twenty miles of electrical range means that the vehicle emits only as much global warming pollution as a car that gets 74 miles per gallon. As the electricity sector cleans up by shifting to renewables and other zero- or low-carbon technologies (such as fossil fuel power plants that capture and dispose of carbon underground), the vehicles powered by that electricity will become even cleaner than today's electric vehicles.

Figure 3-2 provides a simplified view of the impact of a cleaner grid on plug-in hybrids.[28] The simplifying assumption is that plug-in vehicles are charged by an electricity grid that gradually meets a climate stabilization target calling for an 80 percent reduction in the level of current emissions by 2050.

Manufacturers' Commitment to a Future with Pluggable Vehicle Choices

To envision the primary vehicle of 2050, consider the plug-in hybrids that will be hitting the roads in the next few years. General Motor's Chevy Volt is touted to run approximately forty miles on electricity, which for the average driver means using grid electricity as the main energy source for 60 percent or more of annual driving. Shorter-range plug-in hybrids such as GM's Saturn Vue and offerings from Toyota also are expected to hit the market within three years. Because the average car is driven only twenty to thirty miles a day for commuting and routine errands, electric drive capability of just twenty miles can cover a substantial portion of annual mileage.

The two largest automakers, General Motors and Toyota, have announced their intention to produce plug-in hybrids starting in 2010.[29] Other manufacturers are likely to follow, both to capture market share and to fulfill requirements of the California Zero Emission Vehicle program. The program was recently modified to give manufacturers more flexibility in meeting the required volume of zero-emissions vehicles by allowing them to substitute multiple plug-in hybrids for one zero-emissions vehicle. If carmakers take maximum advantage of the flexibility offered, more than 133,000 plug-in hybrid vehicles (with an all-electric range of twenty miles) could be put on U.S. roads from 2012 through 2014.

FIGURE 3-2. Global Warming Pollution in 2020 and Beyond: Plug-In Hybrids Compared with Other Mid-Sized Cars[a]

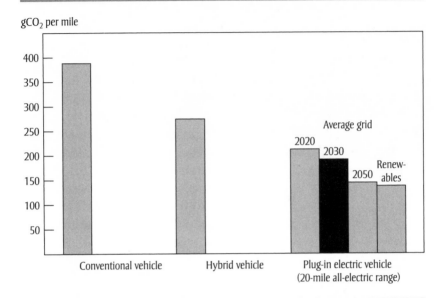

Source: Analysis by Luke Tonachel, presented at the National Environmental Partnership Summit, Washington, D.C., May 18, 2008.

a. Measured in grams of carbon dioxide per mile (gCO_2/mi). Since conventional vehicles and hybrid electric vehicles run only on gasoline, their emissions (grams of carbon dioxide per mile) do not change as the electricity grid gets cleaner. Conversely, plug-in hybrids use electricity from the power grid for some of their energy. As the electricity sector cleans up, plug-in hybrid emissions decrease. The figure shows potential emission rates for plug-in hybrids as the grid gets cleaner, using the average emissions of the electricity sector (since they are one component of the plug-in hybrid's emissions) for the years 2020, 2030, and 2050. The cleanest electricity comes from renewable sources, which effectively have no CO_2 emissions for electricity production. The figure shows renewables compared with the average grid. No timeframe is associated with the renewables because we do not assume that the whole grid will be supplied by them in any particular year.

Emissions Benefits of Large-Scale Use of Plug-in Vehicles

The Natural Resources Defense Council partnered with the Electric Power Research Institute (EPRI) to study the impact on emissions of large-scale adoption of plug-in hybrids in the continental United States.[30] The joint study looks broadly at the pollution impacts of electrified transportation considering both global warming pollution and criteria pollutants emitted by power plants and vehicles. In contrast to the simplified approach shown in figure 3-2, the NRDC-EPRI study evaluates the emissions associated with the charging resources brought on line to serve vehicles after electricity has supplied preexisting electrical loads. In other words, the study's emissions results reflect the marginal electricity production required for vehicles. The study also considered scenarios in which the grid was constrained by climate policies that required reductions in power plant emissions from 2010 to 2050. The analysis is presented in two volumes.

Volume 1: Nationwide Greenhouse Gas Emissions. The results of the analysis of greenhouse gas emissions show that wide-scale adoption of plug-in hybrids leads to a reduction in global warming pollution that is significant compared with the reduction from a fleet without plug-in hybrids. Not surprisingly, the largest reductions in global warming pollution are achieved when the highest penetration of plug-in hybrids is coupled with the cleanest electricity grid. Reductions of 612 million metric tonnes of CO_2-equivalent ($MMTCO_2e$)—the equivalent pollution from about 111 million of today's on-road vehicles—are achieved when nearly 80 percent of the on-road fleet is plug-in hybrids and the electricity sector has reduced annual emissions by 85 percent from 2010 to 2050. The large savings are calculated by comparing that fleet to a baseline fleet without plug-in hybrids that is made up of 25 percent conventional gasoline-only vehicles and 75 percent nonpluggable hybrids.

In all, nine different scenarios with varying levels of plug-in hybrid penetration and electric sector greenhouse gas intensities were included in the analysis. As shown in table 3-2, significant reductions in annual greenhouse gas (GHG) emissions are achieved in 2050 under all scenarios.

Plug-in hybrid adoption results in reductions in global warming pollution from the vehicle fleet in all regions of the country. The study assumes that plug-in hybrids are distributed across the country, consistent with today's vehicle distribution, displacing a significant percentage of both conventional and nonpluggable hybrid vehicles. The plug-in hybrids have an all-electric capability that ranges from ten miles to forty miles, and the on-road fleet is divided between a fleet of plug-ins that have a range of ten to twenty miles in the early years and a fleet dominated by plug-ins that have a forty-mile range beyond 2030 as battery costs decrease.

Plug-in hybrids' battery-charging load is considered a new power generation requirement, and the electricity emissions rate is determined by the marginal charging sources. Charging is done predominantly during off-peak periods, with 74 percent occurring between 10:00 p.m. and 6:00 a.m. In the scenario with medium plug-in hybrid penetration and medium reduction in the carbon intensity of electricity generation, the total increase in energy demand from the electricity sector is estimated at

TABLE 3-2. Annual GHG Reduction in 2050

Million metric tonnes of CO_2 equivalent

Plug-in hybrid fleet penetration (percent of new vehicles that are plug-in hybrids)	Electric sector CO_2 intensity (2050 annual emissions change from 2010)		
	High (+25 percent)	Medium (–41 percent)	Low (–85 percent)
Low (20 percent)	163	177	193
Medium (62 percent)	394	468	478
High (80 percent)	474	517	612

Source: Data in the table are from EPRI and NRDC, *Environmental Assessment of Plug-In Hybrid Electric Vehicles*, vol. 1, *Nationwide Greenhouse Gas Emissions* (July 2007) (www.epri-reports.org).

4.8 percent (282 million megawatt-hours) in 2030 and 7.6 percent (598 million megawatt-hours) in 2050. The corresponding reduction in oil use is 2 million barrels a day in 2020—a saving of more than 12 percent in oil use by vehicles projected by the Department of Energy in a business-as-usual (basically no plug-in hybrids) scenario[31]—and 3.7 million barrels a day in 2050.

Volume 2: U.S. Air Quality Analysis Based on AEO-2006 Assumptions for 2030. Volume 2 evaluates the emissions of criteria pollutants and mercury that result from large-scale plug-in hybrid adoption in 2030. The analysis focuses primarily on emissions of nitrogen oxides (NOx), a principal contributor to ground-level ozone or smog; sulfur dioxide (SO_2), a major acid rain pollutant; particulate matter (PM), which causes soot; and mercury (Hg), which becomes a potent neurotoxin in the human body. The results of the study show widespread, small, but significant improvements in air quality with large-scale plug-in hybrid use.

The approach to modeling the electric sector taken in the air quality analysis is different from that used in the greenhouse gas analysis discussed above. No policies are assumed in the air quality study that would force reductions in global warming pollution. Only the criteria pollutant and mercury rules in place or near enactment at the time of the study were included. Therefore, the study examines a case of high electric sector emissions in which nearly all the additional electricity needed to power an aggressive market penetration of plug-in hybrids is assumed to come from an increase in the use of current coal-fired generation technology, with only currently required environmental controls.[32] That is consistent with the U.S. Department of Energy's *2006 Annual Energy*

Outlook, which assumes no national greenhouse gas policies or constraints and a sizable increase in coal-fired generation.

The study evaluates the pollutant emissions from U.S. power plants as load is increased to charge plug-in hybrids; the results are then run through a complex air quality model to evaluate impacts on regional air quality. The increase in emissions from plug-in hybrids is determined from the difference in two scenarios: a base case without any penetration of plug-ins and a plug-in hybrid case in which plug-in hybrids penetrate the market at the same rate as in the medium case in the volume 1 greenhouse gas analysis, attaining shares of 50 percent of new-vehicle sales and 40 percent of on-road vehicles by 2030. In the plug-in hybrid case, the overall fraction of vehicle miles traveled by the U.S. vehicle fleet using electricity is 20 percent.

The air quality benefits derived from using plug-in hybrids are primarily the result of two factors: one, electric drive displaces a significant amount of the tailpipe emissions that would occur from burning gasoline and diesel fuel; two, regulatory caps on the electric power sector for NOx and SO_2 prevent increases in those pollutants even when electricity demand increases. The NRDC-EPRI study summarizes the air quality results as follows:

> Because of these two factors, the study finds that in many regions deployment of plug-in hybrids would reduce exposures to ozone and particulate matter, and reduce deposition rates for acids, nutrients, and mercury.
>
> On the other hand, because of assuming no further controls beyond existing regulations for the power sector, ozone levels would increase locally in some areas.[33] Similarly, the direct emissions of particulate matter and mercury would increase somewhat and some regions and populations would experience marginal increases in exposures to those pollutants.[34]
>
> Overall, the air quality benefits from plug-in hybrid vehicles are due to a reduction of vehicle emissions below levels required by current regulation (due to their non-emitting operation in all-electric mode), and because most electricity generation emissions are constrained by existing regulatory caps. Any additional increase in the amount of all-electric vehicle miles traveled or further emissions constraints on the electric sector would tend to magnify these benefits.

Accelerating toward a Pluggable Vehicle Future: The Role of Fleet Managers

The first and easiest steps toward creating robust market demand for plug-in hybrids can be taken by the nation's public and private fleet owners. Specifically, government and private vehicle fleets can help jump-start the market for plug-in hybrids by ensuring that fleet purchasing requirements give priority to the most efficient vehicles; by charging vehicles with low-carbon electricity to the maximum extent possible; by testing vehicle use, collecting data, and establishing a central data repository for analysis of various use patterns and vehicle designs; and by becoming a test bed for the best charging practices to ensure intelligent management of charging loads outside of periods of peak demand for electricity.

Fleets also are ripe for plug-in hybridization because the driving range of fleet vehicles often is modest, allowing the vehicles to run entirely on electricity most days. And they often are parked at a central location where recharging can occur overnight.[35] Large fleets that require daytime charging should consider installation of solar arrays for vehicle charging.

New Policy: Getting Cars on the Road and Transforming the Electricity Sector

In addition to funding approved in the Energy Independence and Security Act of 2007, funding should be directed to a national research and demonstration program to advance electric vehicle technology by reducing battery cost, ensuring battery safety, evaluating plug-in hybrid performance under different electric drive scenarios, and educating the public on the costs and benefits of electric vehicles. Serious and sustained consumer purchase incentives should be offered to offset the higher upfront costs of the necessarily large plug-in batteries.

Policymakers also must cap emissions from all economic sectors so that the grid becomes cleaner as plug-in hybrids are deployed in large numbers. Such policies can be designed to help spur large-scale commercial production of a pluggable fleet. For example, the climate bill debated by the 110th Congress—the Lieberman-Warner Climate Security Act—would have instituted a declining cap on global warming pollution and established a system for trading carbon allowances under that cap. Both electricity and fuels were included in the program, and nearly $70 billion of the revenue from the sale of allowances would have been invested in constructing and retrofitting auto manufacturing facilities to produce advanced vehicles, including plug-in hybrids.[36] An analysis of the likely effects of such a policy on the vehicle fleet commissioned by the NRDC found that by 2050 it would help transform the fleet to the extent that electricity and ethanol would overwhelm gasoline and diesel as the largest sources of energy for cars and trucks.[37] Figure 3-3 compares two scenarios for implementation of the bill to a business-as-usual approach, showing the remarkable shift that it would prompt.

Of course, complementary and technology-neutral performance standards can accelerate such changes even further. Specifically, Congress and federal agencies should continue increasing vehicle fuel economy standards and enact standards for low-carbon fuels and electricity portfolios. Putting such policies into place and ratcheting them up expeditiously will help transform both the transportation and the electricity sector.

Charging an increasing number of vehicles inevitably will require expansion of power generation capacity. However, off-peak battery charging and smart load management can maximize the use of excess capacity that sits idle at night. For example, one study found that in California, 1 million pluggable vehicles would not substantially increase system peak power use but that "[l]arger fleets could require the expansion of system capacity if not charged during the hours of lowest demand."[38] To forestall the need for new capacity, particularly since there will be a time lag between enactment of policies to decarbonize electricity and actual decarbonization, policymakers should provide incentives for smart load management and off-peak charging. As mentioned earlier, the McKinsey study and California's experience show that there are ample opportunities to reduce loads from appliances and buildings. Policy must also include charging practices, through rate structures and vehicle-to-grid interconnection technology and protocols that encourage and automate off-peak charging. Policymakers also should create programs and requirements for battery recycling. Even after its useful life in a vehicle, a battery is likely to have sufficient capacity for secondary, likely stationary, applications in which available energy and cycling requirements are less severe.

Conclusion: Ground Rules for a New Marriage

As other authors have noted, after a century of marriage, the time for a divorce between the oil and auto industries may be fast approaching, followed by "a transition to plug-in hybrids [that] would begin to couple the

FIGURE 3-3. Projected Light-Duty Vehicle Fuel Use under the Lieberman-Warner Climate Security Act

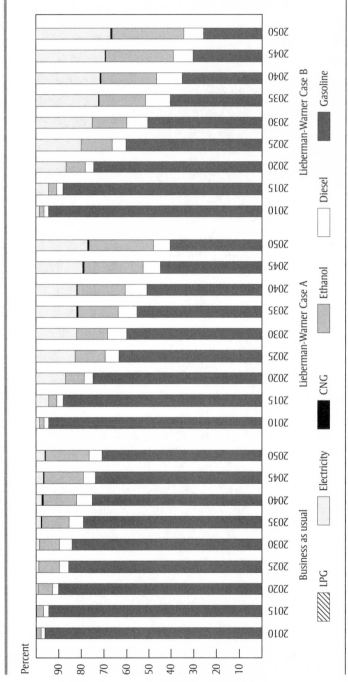

Source: MARKAL analysis by International Resources Group for NRDC: International Resources Group, "U.S. Technology Choices, Costs, and Opportunities under the Lieberman-Warner Climate Security Act: Assessing Compliance Pathways," PowerPoint presentation, May 2008. For more information, see www.nrdc.org/media/ 2008/080513.asp.

transportation and electric power generation sectors."[39] Engineers at the two largest automakers are studying the benefits of such an arrangement, including the crucial issue of battery durability and performance.[40]

But in order for this new marriage to work out, at least three important issues must be resolved. First is the question of whether plug-in hybrids can compete with other means of increasing efficiency in the light-duty vehicle fleet. Conventional improvements in efficiency can cut both global warming pollution and oil consumption by around 40 percent, and hybridizing vehicles can cut both by 50 to 60 percent.[41] Those technologies are not standing still, which means that pluggable hybrids have to continually improve as well in order to compete in a marketplace that is now embracing a host of efficient vehicle technologies.

Second, the time gap between slow infrastructure changeover and the urgent need for cuts in oil use and carbon dioxide emissions must be addressed. Turnover of power generation and the vehicle fleet will consume years, if not decades. Policy must play a key role in speeding up deployment of new renewable generation capacity and pluggable vehicles.

Third and last, but certainly not least, is the related issue of low-carbon power generation. While electric motor efficiency gives pluggable vehicles a pollution-reduction advantage over conventional autos, the main advantage lies in the potential to power the vehicle fleet with electricity from clean sources such as wind and solar energy. To make this important technology a highly effective part of a climate strategy, the United States must adopt policies that transform the electricity sector into a low-carbon system.

Notes

1. Andrew C. Revkin, "Back to 1988 on CO2, Says NASA's Hansen," dotearth blogs.nytimes.com, March 18, 2008.

2. Dan Woynillowicz, Chris Severson-Baker, and Marlo Raynolds, "Oil Sands Fever: The Environmental Implications of Canada's Oil Sands Rush," Pembina Institute, November 23, 2005.

3. Energy Information Administration, *Annual Energy Outlook 2008* (www.eia.doe.gov).

4. Most notably Timoth Searchinger and others, "Use of U.S. Croplands for Biofuels Increases Greenhouse Gases through Emissions from Land use Change," *Science* 319, no. 5867 (February 29, 2008): 1238–40.

5. Statement of Nathanael Greene, National Resources Defense Council, before the Senate Committee on Environment and Public Works, Subcommittee on Clean Air and Nuclear Safety, 110 Cong., 2 sess., July 10, 2008.

6. Ibid.

7. National Petroleum Council, *Hard Truths: Facing the Hard Truths about Energy* (2007); Energy Independence and Security Act of 2007, P.L. 110-140, December 19, 2007.

8. See, for example, Jim Kliesch, "Setting the Standard: How Cost-Effective Technology Can Increase Vehicle Fuel Economy" (Cambridge, Mass.: Union of Concerned Scientists, April 2008).

9. "Climate Change 2007: Synthesis Report. Contribution of Working Groups I, II, and III to the Fourth Assessment Report of the Intergovernmental Panel on Climate Change," edited by R. K. Pachauri and A. Reisinger (Geneva, Switzerland: IPCC, 2007).

10. Ibid.

11. Energy Information Administration, *Annual Energy Outlook 2008*.

12. Jon Creyts and others, "Reducing U.S. Greenhouse Gas Emissions: How Much at What Cost?" U.S. Greenhouse Gas Abatement Mapping Initiative Executive Report, McKinsey & Company and the Conference Board, December 2007.

13. American Lung Association, "State of the Air: 2008" (www.stateoftheair.org/2008/key-findings/ [July 22, 2008]).

14. Energy Information Administration, *Annual Energy Outlook 2008*.

15. National Petroleum Council, "Topic Paper 2: Social/Cultural/Economic Trends," in *Hard Truths: Facing the Hard Truths about Energy*.

16. Matthew Kromer and John B. Heywood, "A Comparative Assessment of Electric Propulsion Systems in the 2030 U.S. Light-Duty Vehicle Fleet," SAE Technical Paper 2008=01-0459 (Massachusetts Institute of Technology, 2008); also see Energy Information Administration, *Energy Technology Perspectives 2008*.

17. Deron Lovaas, Natural Resources Defense Council, testimony before the Senate Environment and Public Works Committee, *Future Federal Role for Surface Transportation*, 110 Cong., 2 sess., June 25, 2008.

18. Ronald E. West and Frank Kreith, "A Scenario for a Secure Transportation System Based on Fuel from Biomass," *Journal of Solar Energy Engineering* 130 (May 2008).

19. Energy Information Administration, *Energy Technology Perspectives 2008*.

20. Bill Cowart, "Sketch Analysis of Measures for Addressing Travel Activity Patterns," presented to the Natural Resources Defense Council, 2007.

21. Energy Independence and Security Act of 2007.

22. Ibid.

23. Ibid.

24. Proposed in section 9611 of Housing and Economic Recovery Act of 2008 (H.R. 3221), 110 Cong.

25. Nicholas Lutsey and Daniel Sperling, "Energy Efficiency, Fuel Economy, and Policy Implications," *Transportation Research Record* 1941 (2005): 8–17; Lee Schipper, "Automobile Fuel Economy and CO_2 Emissions in Industrialized Countries: Troubling Trends through 2005/6" (Washington: World Resources Institute Center for Sustainable Transport, 2007).

26. California Energy Commission, "Integrated Energy Policy Report 2007," CEC-100-2007-008-CMF (December 2007), p. 2.

27. California Green Innovation Index, 2008 Inaugural Issue, November 2007, p. 5. The index is published by Next 10, an independent, nonpartisan, educational organization.

28. Assumes that a conventional vehicle achieves 35 mpg (in the lab) and 28 mpg on the road. Hybrid electric vehicles and plug-in hybrid electric vehicles have 43 percent better fuel economy with respect to gasoline use than conventional vehicles. Electric drivetrain efficiency, measured in kilowatt-hours per mile, improves from 2020 to 2050 by 14 percent, per EPRI modeling. Grid CO_2 intensity (g CO_2/kWh) follows trend needed from electricity sector to meet 80 percent reduction in GHG emissions by 2050 according to NRDC modeling.

29. David Shepardson, "GM Plans to Build 'Tens of Thousands' of Chevy Volt Plug-Ins, Official Says," *Detroit News*, January 31, 2008 (www.detnews.com/apps/pbcs.dll/article?AID=/20080131/BIZ/801310505); Margarita Bauza and Mark Phelan, "Saturn Turns Up the Volume with Hybrids," *Detroit Free Press*, January 14, 2008; Tom Stricker, "Toyota's Hybrid Vehicle Strategy," testimony before the House Appropriations Committee, Subcommittee on Energy and Water, 110 Cong., 2 sess., February 14, 2008.

30. EPRI and NRDC, *Environmental Assessment of Plug-In Hybrid Electric Vehicles,* vol. 1, *Nationwide Greenhouse Gas Emissions,* and vol. 2, *United States Air Quality Analysis Based on AEO-2006 Assumptions for 2030* (July 2007) (www.epri-reports.org).

31. Energy Information Administration, *Annual Energy Outlook 2008.*

32. EPRI and NRDC, *Environmental Assessment of Plug-In Hybrid Electric Vehicles,* vol. 2: "Participation in this study does not imply that NRDC endorses the power plant emission control assumptions in the air quality report. . . . NRDC firmly believes that stronger emissions controls are necessary to protect human health. This study does not attempt to determine the adequate level of power plant controls or adequate levels of ambient air pollution and strives only to determine the specific impacts of large-scale plug-in hybrid penetration given the assumptions of the study."

33. Ibid.: "NRDC does not support trading off pollution benefits in some regions for pollution increases in others regions. NRDC believes that no areas or populations should be allowed to experience increases in air pollution exposures and that further emission controls from all sources are needed in order to protect public health. Consequently, NRDC supports more stringent emissions control requirements for the electric and transportation sectors, as well as other economic sectors. NRDC supports the introduction of plug-in hybrids accompanied by substantial additional improvements in power plant emission rates. In areas where there are potential adverse impacts from air pollution as a result of plug-in hybrid charging, NRDC believes it is not appropriate to promote introduction until the public can be assured that air pollution will not increase. . . . [C]onsidering the electric and transportation sector together, total emissions of VOC, NOx, and SO_2 from the two sectors decrease due to use of plug-in hybrid vehicles. Ozone levels decreased for most regions but increased in some local areas. When assuming a minimum detection limit of 0.25 parts per billion, modeling estimates that 61 percent of the population would see decreased ozone levels and 1 percent of the population would see increased ozone levels."

34. Ibid.: "Primary emissions of particulate matter (PM) increase by 10 percent with the use of plug-in hybrid electric vehicles primarily because of the large increase in coal-powered generation assumed in the study. Mercury emissions increase by 2.4 percent with the increased need for generation to meet plug-in hybrid charging loads. The study assumes that mercury is constrained by a cap-and-trade program, with the option for using banked allowances, as proposed by EPA during the execution of the study. Modeling of the electric sector indicates that utilities take advantage of the banking provision to realize early reductions in mercury that result in greater mercury emissions at the end of the study timeframe (2030)."

35. Chris O'Brien and others, *Responsible Purchasing Guide for Fleet Vehicles* (Responsible Purchasing Network, 2007).

36. Lieberman-Warner Climate Security Act of 2007 (S. 2191).

37. MARKAL analysis by International Resources Group for NRDC: International Resources Group, "U.S. Technology Choices, Costs, and Opportunities under the Lieberman-Warner Climate Security Act: Assessing Compliance Pathways," PowerPoint presentation, May 2008. For more information, see www.nrdc.org/media/2008/080513.asp.

38. Derek Lemoine, Daniel K. Kammen, and Alexander Farrell, "Effects of Plug-In Hybrid Electric Vehicles in California Energy Markets" (Transportation Research Board, 2007).

39. Constantine Samaras and Kyle Meisterling, "Life Cycle Assessment of Greenhouse Gas Emissions from Plug-in Hybrid Vehicles: Implications for Policy, Environmental Science, and Technology" (American Chemical Society); and Iain Carson and Vijay Vaitheeswaran, *Zoom: The Global Race to Fuel the Car of the Future* (2007).

40. Masayuki Komatsu and others, Toyota Motor Corporation, "Study on the Potential Benefits of Plug-in Hybrid Systems," SAE Technical Paper 2008-01-0456 (2008); E. D. Tate and others, General Motors Corporation, "The Electrification of the Automobile: From Conventional Hybrids, to Plug-in Hybrids, to Extended-Range Electric Vehicles," SAE Technical Paper 2008-01-0458 (2008).

41. Matthew Kromer and John B. Heywood, Massachusetts Institute of Technology, "A Comparative Assessment of Electric Propulsion Systems in the 2030 U.S. Light-Duty Vehicle Fleet," SAE Technical Paper 2008-01-0459 (2008); also see Energy Information Administration, *Energy Technology Perspectives 2008*.

CHAPTER FOUR

The CashBack Car

JON WELLINGHOFF

You're out for a Sunday afternoon drive, enjoying the open road and the feeling of freedom that comes with that great American institution, the automobile. As you pull back into your driveway, you notice that the fuel gauge is nearing empty, so you do what is necessary for your local distributor to fill it up at home. Yes, they now make deliveries. They deliver at a convenient time when the price of fuel is the lowest, and the delivery is made without interruption or intrusion. At the end of the month you open the statement for the fuel that you had delivered, and included with the statement is a check made out to you. Yes, they paid you to fuel your car. And they delivered at home. They also deliver at work, at the supermarket, at the mall, and even at your hotel while you are on vacation. In fact, delivery points are everywhere. And, better yet, it's automatic. No scheduling and no phone calls

Does that sound incredible? It's not. Automatic delivery of virtually free fuel for your car wherever you are is close at hand. The potential exists today, in current technology and infrastructure. That potential can be realized by shifting vehicles to electric power as the primary source of energy and enabling them to use that energy not only to move people from home to work and back but also to support and enhance the nation's electric grid.

The challenge is to make that capability commercially available to everyone. The first task is powering a car electrically. The second is using the car's electric system and battery to assist the electric grid to operate more efficiently. You will have a car for your transportation needs for the typical hour a day that you drive it; for the other twenty-three hours of the day, you'll have an electric storage, charging, and grid communication system to use to "refuel" the car and provide grid support services.[1] One task, providing you with transportation, will cost about $.04 per mile for fuel instead of the $.16 per mile for fuel for a gasoline-powered automobile.[2] That is equivalent to buying gas at about $1.00 per gallon. The second task pays you to charge the car by using it as a distributed energy resource to provide grid stabilization services, which will pay you back most, if not all, of the $.04 per mile cost to charge the car. But both tasks must be incorporated into the vehicle to realize the full value from electric-based transportation. The merging of the two functions will create the "CashBack" car.

Electrification of transportation is something that everyone seems to be talking about. From President Barack Obama, to prominent members of Congress, to respected statesmen such as George Schultz, former secretary of state, and James Woolsey, former director of the CIA, all are advocating moving from oil to electricity for our transportation needs.[3] Even the auto industry is recognizing this imperative. Rick Wagoner, CEO of General Motors, recently conceded, "The auto industry can no longer rely almost exclusively on oil to supply the world's automotive energy requirements."[4] Andy Grove, former CEO of Intel and another proponent of electric transportation, has concluded that we are at a "strategic inflection point" where "the drumbeat of electrical transportation is accelerating like nothing I've ever seen in my life. Electricity in transportation has to be done. It is urgent."[5]

Feeding the growing consensus is the fact that oil was recently priced well over $100 per barrel, driving gasoline to more than $4.00 per gallon. The first $60 to $80 fill-up is the kind of shock to the wallet that will propel anyone to contemplate alternatives. Even though prices for oil and gasoline have again fallen, that kind of volatility and uncertainty is one factor driving consumers to seek more stable transportation fuel sources. An electric-powered vehicle that could be "filled up" for less than $20 and then could "pay back" that fill-up the following week by providing services to the grid would get the attention of most consumers, despite its higher initial cost.[6]

Other compelling reasons to move rapidly from oil to electricity for our transportation needs include the potential to significantly reduce greenhouse gas emissions, reduce urban pollution, and improve national security. It is a myth (often repeated) that moving from gas-powered transportation to electric transportation does not reduce greenhouse gases, that it only moves the pollutants from the tailpipe to the smokestack.[7] But in fact, national studies from well-respected independent research institutions have concluded that changing the U.S. vehicle fleet to primarily electric drive could reduce greenhouse gas emissions by as much as 27 percent and reduce oil imports by as much as 52 percent.[8] That is because even coal plants are more efficient than the internal combustion gasoline engine and our total stock of power plants for generating electricity is becoming cleaner as we continue to add more renewable resources to the mix. In addition, any pollution that emanates from the stack of a generating plant is easier to control and clean than pollution from millions of tailpipes.

Finally, the need to reduce greenhouse gases is driving the need to incorporate more renewable energy into the total energy resource pool. One of the most abundantly available renewable resources in North America is wind. A recent U.S. Department of Energy study concluded that we could derive 20 percent of our total energy needs from wind power by 2030.[9] But because of the variability of wind, to integrate this clean energy resource into the electric grid requires a substantial increase in grid stabilization services. Those services can be supplied by the systems in electric vehicles when the vehicles are connected to the grid.

The Challenge of Electric-Based Transportation

So how do the economic and environmental benefits of using electric power in transportation become reality in the United States? Auto manufacturers and other entrepreneurs need to be encouraged through the appropriate government and regulatory agencies to aggressively move forward with the production and marketing of vehicles that use primarily electricity for drive power. They can take the form of a battery electric vehicle (BEV) or a plug-in hybrid electric vehicle (PHEV). A BEV is a car that is driven by an electric motor instead of an internal combustion engine. On-board batteries power the electric motor; the batteries are recharged through a plug much like the familiar small rechargeable batteries in power tools and other household appliances. Mrs. Henry Ford drove an electric car—no getting out and cranking.[10] The PHEV is a variant of the BEV in that in addition to the electric motor and batteries, it has an internal combustion engine (ICE) that can be used either to charge the batteries while the vehicle is under way (called a series PHEV) or to drive the vehicle directly as is currently done in a conventional gasoline-powered car (called a parallel PHEV).[11] The advantage to a PHEV is that it may have a longer range than a BEV and somewhat more flexibility due to its ability to run on gasoline (or diesel or other alternative fuel) in addition to electricity.

Despite widespread popular support for the production of BEVs and PHEVs, car manufacturers are moving very cautiously. Currently no PHEVs are in production for the mass market. Demonstration conversions of hybrid electric vehicles (HEVs) to PHEVs have been successfully tested, and commercial aftermarket converters have established conversion facilities to provide HEV owners with the opportunity to drive a PHEV.[12] The number of these conversions to date, including manufacturer demonstrations, is in excess of 150. There is limited production of BEVs (less than 1,000 units a year) by some small manufacturers; one major manufacturer is producing BEVs (on a limited basis) for lease only.[13] Although speculation continues in the auto industry, only two companies, China's BYD Auto and General Motors (GM), have announced commercial production of PHEVs for consumer purchase, in 2009 and 2011, respectively.[14] Toyota has announced limited production of PHEVs for fleet sales only in 2010.[15]

Admittedly, there are barriers to overcome and issues to understand before manufacturers accelerate production of such vehicles, including retooling existing production lines, improving battery reliability and cost, and integrating batteries with the electric grid. Of these, grid integration and interface is the issue that has been most ignored and misunderstood by auto manufacturers. Yet it is this unique aspect of the new variants that has the greatest potential to increase consumer acceptance and alleviate the single-biggest market barrier, the increased cost of vehicle production due to the high cost of the batteries required. The U.S. Department of Energy (DOE) in its 2007 R&D plan for PHEVs determined that "cost is the primary impediment" to producing PHEVs.[16] Yet in the same

R&D plan, DOE dismissed any immediate interest in developing vehicle-to-grid (V2G) capabilities for the PHEV that would enable it to interact with the grid as a distributed resource and to receive revenues to offset the incremental first costs. DOE concluded that "other aspects of PHEV-utility interface, such as vehicle-to-grid power flow, could have system-level benefits as well, but it requires more sophisticated communication and a more complex relationship between the customer and utility. It is not considered an enabler for vehicle technology in the short term."[17] This decision by DOE fails to consider the substantial synergies that would result from the use of a PHEV as both a means of transportation and as a distributed resource for the grid. The benefits for both uses would be substantial, but use as a grid resource would enable PHEVs to be effectively marketed for transportation by reducing the first cost to the consumer.

Many assume that the precursor to full production of PHEVs or BEVs by mainstream auto manufacturers is the hybrid electric vehicle (HEV) and that a PHEV is simply an incremental step up from the HEV. The Toyota Prius has been the most successful HEV to date.[18] Despite its success, auto manufacturers are discovering that the move from an HEV to a PHEV or BEV is not simply incremental; it is, in fact, disruptive.[19] Switching from gasoline to electricity for drive power would have profound disruptive impacts on how consumers and society view and use the device now commonly known as the "car." Those impacts would be a function of the interface of the PHEV or BEV system with the world's largest system, the U.S. electric grid. They would be the same impacts that could make the PHEV and BEV not only a superior transportation option for the nation from the perspective of the environment and oil security but also an affordable option that would enable rapid integration of large quantities of new, clean renewable resources such as wind power into the national grid.

The Grid

In order for auto manufacturers, government policymakers, and consumers to understand the full implications and potential benefits of a car that plugs into the electric grid, it is necessary to consider the grid's engineering, economic, and regulatory characteristics. From an engineering perspective, the grid must be operated as a large integrated system. It consists first and foremost of multiple, ever-changing loads that require power.

Loads range from the load from a cell phone charger, which may draw a few watts, to the load from an electric arc furnace in an aluminum smelter, which may draw tens of megawatts. Loads come on and off at all times of the day and night; the sum of all loads on a given system over a period of time is called a load duration curve. The loads are interconnected by a distribution system composed of local electric distribution wires and distribution transformers to regulate flows and reduce voltage to loads as required. Beyond the local distribution system are transmission lines that operate at higher voltages than the distribution system in order to transmit bulk power for longer distances at lower losses from neighboring electric systems and central generating plants (see figure 4-1).[20]

The generating side of the electric system is composed primarily of large coal-fired plants (about 50 percent), natural gas generators (about 20 percent), nuclear power plants (nearly 20 percent), and hydroelectric facilities (about 7 percent); facilities using oil and distributed renewable resources such as solar, wind, geothermal, and biomass energy make up the remainder.[21] The last category of resources typically is smaller than central station coal, gas, or nuclear plants, but facilities can range from 50 megawatt geothermal or biomass plants to 1 kilowatt (kW) solar photovoltaic systems on homes.

For the entire system to work and not spin out of control and cause a blackout, the loads and generation to meet the loads must match exactly all the time—twenty-four hours a day, seven days a week. In the United States, there are three major segments of the grid: the Western Interconnect, from Colorado to California, Oregon, and Washington; the Eastern Interconnect, from Kansas to the East Coast from Maine to Florida, excluding Texas; and the Texas Interconnect, which is an independent system (see figure 4-2). Within each of those segments there are numerous control areas with separate control area operators who are responsible for keeping their area in balance by controlling loads and generation.[22]

To keep the grid functioning over the short term, grid operators typically have three concerns. The first is day-ahead scheduling, wherein the operator forecasts the expected loads on the grid for the next day and schedules the resources to meet those loads. The second concern is real time during the next day, when the grid operator must "follow" the load. That is, as the load ramps up or down over ten-minute to one-hour increments—usually in a relatively gradual incline or decline—new resources

FIGURE 4-1. U.S. Transmission Grid

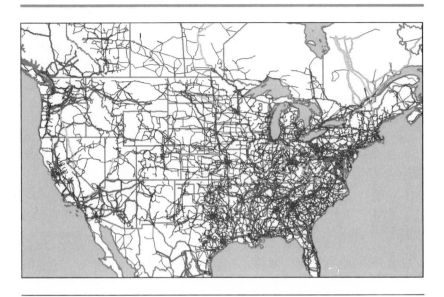

FIGURE 4-2. Major Segments of the U.S. Transmission Grid

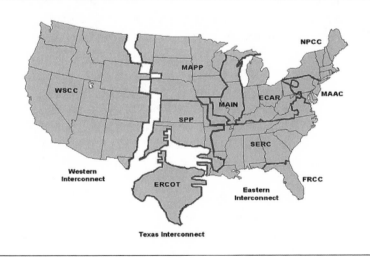

must be called up to meet increasing loads or resources must to taken off the system to match declining loads. Variances over the day are the result of both human activity (such as employees arriving for work in the morning and leaving in the afternoon) and external events like the weather (such as hot summer afternoons that cause an increase in air conditioning loads and mild days that require neither heating nor air conditioning). Third, in order to keep the grid within its frequency tolerances, it is necessary to provide what are known as regulation services, through which rapid-response maneuverable resources deliver bursts of power on short time scales (seconds to minutes), allowing operators to maintain system balance and frequency. These services typically are provided by generators using automatic generation control (AGC), whereby grid operators communicate through Internet connections with the generators in real time to signal them to provide regulation services.

The first of these three operational parameters, day-ahead scheduling, is designed to deliver the power to operate the loads on the system—lights and air conditioners and everything else that runs on electricity. The other two—load following and regulation—do not deliver power per se, but they are necessary for the stable operation of the grid; they are called ancillary services. Historically, ancillary services have been provided by generating resources that have the capability to rapidly respond to the grid operator's communication signal within hours, minutes, or even seconds to keep the grid in balance. The type of generating resources capable of providing such services are rapid-response units like natural gas–fired combustion turbines, which can spin up and down quickly. This type of operation is not possible with a coal plant or a nuclear unit because they are too slow to respond.

Over the past several years it has been demonstrated that loads as well as generators can provide some types of ancillary services. The ideal ancillary service provider would respond virtually instantaneously to the communication signal of the grid operator, either adding or reducing power to the grid as required. A load can effectively perform the same function by turning on or off, if it can be signaled to do so by the grid operator. That has been demonstrated to be feasible for all loads—from the largest, such as an industrial electric furnace, to the smallest, such as a home dishwasher. In fact, Pacific Northwest National Laboratories (PNNL) conducted a test at 112 residential sites on the Olympic Peninsula in Washington, in which ordinary appliances like water heaters and dryers were retrofitted with electronic chips that could actually sense the frequency on the grid.[23] The appliances could thereby automatically determine whether ancillary regulation services were required; they then either shut off or turned on as required, but they did so within limited parameters set by resident participants. Thus, residents were not inconvenienced; their clothes got dried and their water was heated. But the grid was made more stable by the regulation services that the appliances provided. No grid operator intervention was required.

Data from that demonstration verified that the appliances provided regulation services faster and more smoothly than a generator. In addition, the grid was made more efficient because regulation services that were usually provided by less efficient generating units were provided by a nonpolluting controlled load. And the generators that were operating were allowed to do so more efficiently, without having to ramp up and down constantly to match loads and keep the grid in balance. Thus generators could operate at their optimum efficiency and burn less fuel. Finally, consumers in the demonstration benefited in two ways. First, as just discussed, the grid was operated more efficiently, so overall electric costs were reduced for all electric customers on that grid. But second, the residents in the PNNL demonstration benefited directly and immediately in that they received direct payments for the grid regulation services that their appliances provided.

The use of loads to provide ancillary services has been so well established that several grid operators now pay controlled loads, generally called "demand response," or "DR," to provide services comparable to those of generators. In addition, to further the effort to make the grid more efficient, the Federal Energy Regulatory Commission (FERC) has found that the sale of ancillary services by demand response and other load resources should be permitted where appropriate on a basis comparable to service provided by generation resources.[24] Thus, under FERC rules, both generators and controlled loads have the opportunity to receive compensation for providing regulation services.

Electric Vehicles and the Grid

So what does the provision of regulation services to the grid have to do with PHEVs and BEVs? A 2006 research paper by two investigators from the National Renewable Energy Laboratory (NREL) and a university professor from Green Mountain College reviewed the potential for PHEVs or BEVs to provide regulation services to the grid and to be compensated for them.[25] That paper looked at two of the largest grid control areas in the country, PJM and ERCOT. PJM, the largest grid operator in the United States, encompasses an area from New Jersey to Illinois that serves more than 51 million people in thirteen states and the District of Columbia. It operates the grid independently under the jurisdiction of FERC.[26] ERCOT encompasses most of Texas, including the two largest load centers, around Houston and Dallas, and functions as an independent grid operator under the jurisdiction of the Texas Public Utilities Commission.

The paper investigated a number of issues related to electric-based transportation but focused on the economic viability of providing payments to a PHEV or BEV for supplying regulation services to the grid. The investigators chose regulation services for analysis because they are required twenty-four hours a day, every day of the year, and the PHEV or BEV would be available to provide such services 90 percent of the time—the amount of time the average vehicle is not being driven. Under FERC's mandatory reliability rules, grid operators are required to maintain regulation reserves approximately equal to 1.5 percent of the control area peak load for a given day. In addition, regulation services are the most valuable ancillary service provided. It is estimated that they constitute more than a $5 billion market in the United States, and they are growing as additional wind resources are added to the grid, thus requiring more regulation services.

The high value of regulation services relative to other ancillary grid services is demonstrated by the variance in the price of these services on the grid in relationship to other ancillary services, such as spinning reserve services. For example, in the New York Independent System Operator (NYISO), regulation services commanded prices from $50 to $70 per MWh during 2007–08 while spinning reserve services rarely exceeded $15 per MWh and usually averaged below $10 per MWh during the same period.

This magnitude of payments for regulation services for NYISO is consistent with that found by the researchers in the PJM and ERCOT study discussed above. The PJM and ERCOT average market prices for regulation services in 2005 (the year used in the study) ranged from $38 per MWh for ERCOT to $50 per MWh for PJM. The analysis then took the average market prices for regulation services and applied them to two hypothetical electric vehicles: one capable of plugging into a 120 volt, 20 amp standard electric circuit and providing 2 kW of reverse power flow and one capable of connecting to a 240 volt, 50 amp electric circuit (such as would be used for an electric dryer) and providing 10 kW of reverse power flow.

The results were astonishing. The owner of a PHEV or BEV providing 2 kW of power for regulation services could have received payments of approximately $500 for the year in ERCOT and $650 for the year in PJM, if we assume that grid services were provided 75 percent of the time in a given year. If the vehicle was capable of delivering 10 kW of regulation services, then the owner would receive a substantial increase in payments—approximately $2,500 for the year in ERCOT and $3,300 for the year for PJM. At 2007–08 NYISO compensation levels for regulation service, those payments could be 20 to 30 percent higher. One key parameter making that level of payment possible was that the vehicle could deliver both regulation-up and regulation-down services. That means that the charger in the vehicle was assumed to be capable of both taking power from the grid for charging and delivering power to it through discharge.

But in order to realize such payments for providing regulation services, several things are required. Primary among them is that the vehicle would have to be capable of receiving an automatic generation-control signal from the grid operator, just as a generator is, and responding to that signal within seconds to provide regulation services. The authors of the study admitted that that question had been analyzed "primarily from a theoretical perspective."[27] But concurrent with their theoretical analysis, other researchers were undertaking an effort to demonstrate in real time with a real electric vehicle its ability to deliver regulation services to the grid.

Real Time Demonstration of the CashBack Car

Willett Kempton leads a team of electric vehicle researchers at the University of Delaware. Over the past eleven years he has published numerous articles on the potential of electric vehicles, both PHEVs and BEVs, to provide support to the electric grid and to assist in integrating new wind sources into the grid.[28] In 2007 he formed a group called the Mid-Atlantic Grid Interactive Car consortium (MAGIC). MAGIC is composed of partners from the University of Delaware, PJM, the regional utility (PHI), an electric transportation propulsion system manufacturer (AC Propulsion), and a provider of demand response services to grid operators and utilities (Comverge). The objective of the consortium is to demonstrate at scale the delivery of grid support and support for the integration of additional wind resources into the grid by electric vehicles. Those vehicles would be equipped with the electronic control and communications devices necessary for them to receive signals from the grid operator and to respond by delivering grid support services.

On October 23, 2007, Kempton drove from his research lab at the University of Delaware to FERC in Washington. He made the trip at my behest in a converted Toyota Scion in order to demonstrate the provision of regulation services by an electric vehicle. The vehicle had been converted to an eBox BEV by the MAGIC consortium partner AC Propulsion.[29] The converted Scion eBox has a range of more than 120 miles and will go from 0 to 60 mph in less than seven seconds. It has a 20 kW charger. Most important, an automatic generation-control system module was installed in the vehicle, enabling it to communicate in real time to the grid operator at PJM. The car was brought to FERC and connected to a 240 volt outlet through a standard mechanical electric meter, and the meter started to move as the charger drew power from the grid to charge the car.

As part of the demonstration, the senior engineer from PJM, Kevin Komara, brought his laptop computer and connected through a wireless Internet connection to his grid control center at PJM headquarters in Pennsylvania. He then accessed the PJM regulation control screen, where he was able to see the generation resources that were available to PJM to provide regulation services. Among those resources was an 35 kWh Scion eBox ready to be dispatched, just like any other regulation service generator. With a few strokes on the keyboard, Komara called on the eBox to provide regulation-up service (to stop charging and provide power to the grid), and instantaneously the meter stopped and then reversed, pushing power back into the grid. Kevin signaled again, and the meter reversed again, in the charging direction, now providing regulation-down services. This demonstration established—in real time, with a real vehicle—that it is possible to charge a PHEV or BEV and at the same time get paid to do so by providing electric services to the grid. And what is astounding is the fact that at the same time that this demand resource is providing regulation services, the grid is operating more efficiently because a nonpolluting passive load is being controlled and dispatched instead of a polluting active generator. That allows generators that would otherwise be rapidly ramping up and down to operate instead at optimum levels, thus reducing fuel use and producing fewer emissions while lowering overall grid system costs. Questions by auto manufacturers and battery manufacturers regarding the process focus on the effect on battery life. But provision of regulation services by controlling the charging of a PHEV or BEV likely will not significantly affect the battery life in any material way because there is no deep cycling of the battery during the regulation control cycle. And as discussed below, a one-way regulation charging scheme for the provision of regulation service also could be implemented that would have no effect on battery life.

The next step for the MAGIC consortium is to conduct a demonstration at a scale of 300 to 500 vehicles to provide regulation services to the PJM grid.[30] A demonstration of that size would more closely match PJM's minimum requirements for providing compensation for regulation services. The consortium is actively seeking sponsors to conduct the demonstration at scale. Once at-scale regulation services are proven, the economic benefits of providing such a service becomes real for auto manufacturers and prospective purchasers of PHEVs and BEVs. At that point, the remaining barriers to the rollout of the CashBack car would lie primarily in issues of economics, logistics, and regulatory requirements and communications protocols.

Economics

The economics and marketability of a CashBack car to consumers would depend on its sales price and associated benefits and the incentives that consumers receive for purchasing it. With gas prices at $4.00 per gallon, the cost increment barrier of approximately $4,000 to $6,000 between an internal combustion engine, gasoline-powered car and an HEV seems to be falling.[31] But while the ability to purchase fuel at a gasoline equivalent price of $1.00 per gallon for a PHEV may now be more attractive, the expected price differential of the PHEV would appear to still be a barrier to widespread consumer acceptance. Figure 4-3 analyzes the economics of owning various types of cars in today's environment. The figure shows the initial cost for the car and the lifecycle cost of fuel (excluding maintenance, depreciation, insurance, and discount rate factors), assuming that

FIGURE 4-3. **Economics of Ownership of Various Types of Cars Today**

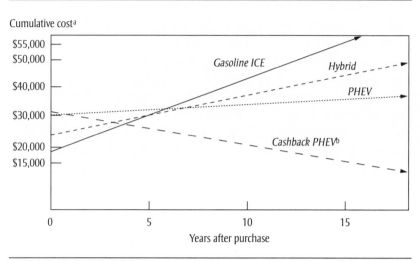

Cumulative cost[a]

a. $4.00/gallon; $0.084/kWh (off-peak rate); maintenance costs not included, no discount rate applied.
b. Payments to CBH owners for regulation services. Assume $1,500/year.

gasoline is $4.00 per gallon and electricity is $.08 per kWh. The internal combustion engine vehicle selected was a Chevrolet Cobalt, which had a manufacturer's suggested retail price (MSRP) of $18,000.[32] Estimated EPA mileage was 24 miles per gallon. Average yearly mileage driven for all vehicles analyzed was estimated at 15,000 miles per year. You can see that in less than ten years, the owner of this vehicle would pay more for gasoline than the original purchase price of the car.

The next vehicle analyzed was a Toyota Prius HEV with an MSRP of $24,000, or a $6,000 premium over the Chevy Cobalt. Estimated mileage was 42 miles per gallon. Given the higher gas mileage of the Prius, it would overcome its cost premium and become less expensive to operate than the Cobalt in approximately five years. The next vehicle on the chart is the PHEV. This PHEV cannot provide grid regulation services and does not incorporate the automatic generation-control communication module necessary for such services. It was estimated to have a cost premium of $12,000 over the Cobalt, or an MSRP of $30,000, the price initially estimated by GM for its PHEV Volt to be available in 2010.[33] More recent estimates by GM have revised the price to be the range of $40,000 to

$45,000.[34] The analysis in figure 4-3 shows that even at the $30,000 price point and a fuel cost advantage equivalent to $1.00-per-gallon gasoline, this PHEV with no CashBack services overtakes its cost premium over the ICE vehicle only in the sixth year and does not overcomes its cost premium over the Prius until at least the seventh year of ownership.

The CashBack PHEV analyzed last in the figure was identical to the PHEV except that it could provide regulation services. It would at least have a 240 volt connection and could have a charger with two-way power flow capability. As can be seen from the PJM and ERCOT study discussed previously and the estimates of future levels of compensation for regulation services, the $1,500 yearly compensation estimate for the provision of regulation services may be conservative. On the other hand, if the charger is 120 volts and is capable only of one-way power flow (to charge the battery), the compensation level may be overestimated. The incremental premium for the controller hardware, software, and communications module to make the PHEV capable of providing grid-compatible regulation services is estimated at $200. That is really no more sophisticated than the electronics that will be in the new Apple iPhone 3G. As figure 4-3 shows, adding payments for regulation services, the CashBack car will better the cost premium over the ICE vehicle in a little over three years; that is within the financing period for many vehicles. That means that if the grid regulation payments could be bundled with the original purchase price of the vehicle, it may be possible to structure payments for the CashBack car that are less than those of an ICE vehicle.

Logistics

Auto manufacturers are very uncertain of the benefits of incorporating vehicle-to-grid CashBack characteristics into the PHEVs that they plan to manufacture in the near future. The manufacturers, primarily GM, are on an accelerated schedule to have a PHEV on the market by 2010, and stopping to consider, design, and implement the incorporation of vehicle-to-grid technology into the first round of PHEVs could delay that schedule. Recent discussions were conducted between representatives of FERC and the automotive industry at a board meeting of the Electric Drive Transportation Association to describe the benefits of the Cash-Back car for the auto manufacturer representatives present.[35] During the discussions several things became apparent. First, auto manufacturers are still largely uninformed about the ability of demand resources, including properly equipped PHEVs, to provide services to the grid and receive payments for those services. Second, once informed of the progress in this area, they are interested and enthusiastic about the prospect of such benefits to assist in marketing the vehicles. Third, manufacturers do not have the scheduling flexibility to fully incorporate 240 volt, two-way power flow charger technology with vehicle-to-grid communication-and-control modules into the first round of PHEVs that they manufacture and market.

Despite that limitation there was discussion at the meeting of the possibility of a "CashBack Lite" solution for the first round of PHEV vehicles that would entail incorporating only one-way control (on/off only) capability, similar to that demonstrated by the PNNL residential appliance test in Washington state. This simplified control strategy would allow the grid operator to switch the charger off or on to provide regulation services for the grid. Because the flow of power would be only one way, the level of payment would be reduced, but there also would be no effect on battery life.[36] Discussions revealed that that was possible because the currently contemplated communication-and-control technology to be incorporated into the first PHEV production run will provide for off-peak charging and can easily be adapted to the CashBack Lite scheme.

From a logistics perspective, it would be useful next to schedule a series of meetings between key auto manufacturers and selected large grid operators to determine the common interfaces necessary to initiate regulation services from this first group of PHEVs. It is contemplated that the services would be provided by an aggregator, who would bundle scale-size groups of vehicles to bid for regulation services in the grid operators' regulation markets. The MAGIC consortium could assist in developing the business plan for such aggregated services. Regulatory issues also need to be considered and potential changes in tariffs and regulations evaluated. FERC representatives are working with the ISO/RTO Council (IRC), the Electric Power Research Institute (EPRI), automotive industry representatives, and others to schedule meetings to discuss those issues. FERC and the IRC met in November 2008 to initiate discussions on PHEV and BEV grid integration issues. As a result, an IRC working group will be formed to develop policies and procedures for the provision of fast-response regulation services by PHEVs and BEVs to ISO/RTO grid operators, including necessary communication protocols and economic settlement procedures. Meetings with EPRI and other electric and automotive industry representatives are scheduled for January 2009 at PJM headquarters.

Policy Implications and Conclusions

Moving to an electric-based transportation system has many benefits for this country and for the world. Those benefits multiply significantly when the move incorporates the synergies of both electric fuel for transportation and electric storage and systems for grid support and enhancement. The CashBack car can be driven more efficiently at less cost with less pollution and less dependence on foreign oil. But it also can provide for more efficient operation of the grid while helping to incorporate more clean wind energy into the grid.

Both the states and the federal government are considering incentives or requirements for lower-emissions vehicles such as PHEVs. For example, California's zero-emissions vehicle program mandates that nearly 60,000 plug-in cars be sold in the state between 2012 and 2014. Connecticut, Massachusetts, Maine, Maryland, New Jersey, New Mexico, Oregon, Rhode Island, and Vermont have adopted similar requirements, and other states will follow. At the federal level, several bills have been introduced to provide tax credits for PHEVs and BEVs.[37] Yet none of those initiatives directly addresses the desirability of ensuring that any PHEVs or BEVs produced include CashBack capabilities.

In *Freedom from Oil*, policy analyst David Sandalow made a number of solid policy recommendations for the next president regarding PHEVs.[38] They include the following:

—Buying 30,000 PHEVs for federal fleets at an $8,000 premium and agreeing that half the vehicles purchased by the federal government thereafter will be PHEVs

—Issuing consumer tax credits of $8,000 for the first million PHEVs and $4,000 for the second million

—Replacing CAFE standards with Fuel Reduction and Energy Efficiency (FREEdom) standards

—Creating a Federal Battery Guarantee Corporation to help manufacturers provide ten-year battery warranties for the first million cars.

The book ends with a proposed speech by the president-elect to the nation calling for "new ways of doing business that create jobs, cut pollution, and make us stronger" and "proposing a grand bargain with American automakers. If you invest in advanced technologies, we'll invest in you."

As demonstrated by the economic analysis in figure 4-3, all of that is needed. This chapter demonstrates, however, that any such incentive programs, state or federal, should also require all new PHEVs or BEVs to incorporate vehicle-to-grid CashBack capability into their electronic architecture if they are to receive the incentives. By insisting on this standard for the vehicles, the nation will gain substantial benefits at relatively little cost.

Notes

1. From home to work, the average commute is 26.4 minutes. Bureau of Transportation Statistics (BTS) Omnibus Household Survey, *OmniStats* 3, no. 4 (October 2003) (www.bts.gov/publications/omnistats/volume_03_issue_04/).

2. Assume a mid-sized sedan averaging 21 miles per gallon, gasoline at $4.00 per gallon, and electric rates of $.10 per kilowatt-hour. Note that the fuel cost difference of $.12 per mile is enough to allow you to afford an additional $150 per month in car payments. Gasoline prices have dropped by more than $2.00 a gallon recently, but most analysts concede that the drop is likely to be a short-lived phenomenon. But even with gasoline at $2.00 a gallon, electric transportation is more economical.

3. The California Cars Initiative (www.calcars.org/endorsements.htm).

4. "As Oil Prices Rise, Carmakers Look to Electric Future," *NewsHour with Jim Lehrer*, June 25, 2008 (www.pbs.org/newshour/bb/transportation/jan-june08/electric cars_06-25.html).

5. Ken Thomas, "Ex-Intel Head Pushes Electric Cars," *Chicago Tribune*, June 27, 2008 (www.chicagotribune.com/news/chi-ap-grove-plug-ins,0,1749993.story).

6. Assume electricity at $1.00 per gallon equivalent ($.08 to $.10 per kilowatt-hour) for the equivalent of fifteen to twenty gallons of drive power.

7. David Sandalow thoroughly debunks this myth in his recent book, *Freedom from Oil: How the Next President Can End the United States' Oil Addiction* (New York: McGraw-Hill, 2007), pp. 64–65.

8. Scott Kintner-Myer, Warwick Pratt, and Elliot Schiedner, *Impacts Assessment of Plug-In Hybrid Electric Vehicles on Electric Utilities and Regional U.S. Power Grids* (Pacific Northwest National Laboratory, January 2007). Also see Electric Power Research Institute and Natural Resources Defense Council, *Environmental Assessment of Plug-In Hybrid Electric Vehicles* (July 2007).

9. U.S. Department of Energy, *20 Percent Wind Energy by 2030: Increasing Wind Energy's Contribution to U.S. Electric Supply*, prepublication version, May 2008.

10. Henry Ford Estate, "Inside Henry Ford's Garage–1914 Detroit Electric" (www.henryfordestate.org/claracar.htm).

11. It is possible to have a combined serial/parallel PHEV that can both charge the batteries through the internal combustion engine and drive the car's wheels.

12. Currently there are at least eight conversion companies in Europe and North America. One company, Hymotion (www.hymotion.com) of Ontario, Canada, retrofits the Toyota Prius, as do many of the other converters. Hymotion was recently acquired by battery maker A123Systems (www.a123systems.com) of Hopkinton, Massachusetts. Crash-tested Prius conversions can now be ordered for $9,950 plus $400 delivery (with a $1,000 deposit) from Hymotion distributors at several cites.

13. Tesla Motors is the most well-known entrant in the BEV sphere in the United States, producing a $100,000-plus battery-powered sports car built on a Lotus frame. The chairman of Tesla, Elon Musk, stated at the roll out of Tesla's first commercial production car on February 1, 2008, "I want to be very clear; we are going to put thousands of vehicles out there." See the Tesla Motors website (www.teslamotors.com). BMW is producing a BEV version of its popular Mini Cooper. But first-year production is limited to 500 vehicles, for lease only. See EV World, "Mini E: AC Propulsion Inside" (www.evworld.com/EVWORLD_TV.CFM?storyid=1595).

14. "Plug-in hybrid," *Wikipedia*, November 14, 2008 (http://en.wikipedia.org/w/index.php?title=Plug-in_hybrid&oldid=251735441). A comprehensive listing of each auto manufacturer's current position on producing PHEVs or BEVs can be found on the CalCars site (www.calcars.org/carmakers.html).

15. Irv Miller, "Plug-in Hybrid Fleet Coming, Toyota Chief Says," *Toyota Open Road Blog*, January 13, 2008 (http://blog.toyota.com/2008/01/plug-in-hybrid.html).

16. U.S. Department of Energy, *Plug-in Hybrid Electric Vehicle R&D Plan*, external draft, February 2007, p. 3 (www1.eere.energy.gov/vehiclesandfuels/pdfs/program/phev_rd_plan_02-28-07.pdf).

17. Ibid., p. 32.

18. The HEV has a gasoline-driven engine plus an electric motor that runs in parallel (or for very short periods in series) for added mileage and performance. Its extra batteries, which run the electric motor, are charged by the gasoline engine and are not recharged from the grid. Toyota says cumulative worldwide sales of the Prius hit 1,028,000 in April 2008. See http://blog.wired.com/cars/2008/05/prius-sales-top.html.

19. *Disruptive technology* is a term describing a technological innovation, product, or service that uses a "disruptive" strategy, rather than a "revolutionary" or "sustaining" strategy, to overturn the existing dominant technologies or status quo products in a market. "Disruptive Technology," *Wikipedia* (http://en. wikipedia. org/w/index.php? title=Disruptive_technology&oldid=25211 7278). See also Graeme Pietersz, "Disruptive Technology," Moneyterms Guides (http://moneyterms.co.uk/disruptive-technology/).

20. Transmission efficiency is improved by increasing the voltage using a step-up transformer, which reduces the current in the conductors while keeping the power transmitted nearly equal to the power input. The reduced current flowing through the conductor reduces the losses in the conductor since the losses are proportional to the

square of the current. Thus halving the current makes the transmission loss one-quarter of the original value. See "Electric Power Transmission," *Wikipedia*, November 16, 2008 (http://en.wikipedia.org/w/index.php?title=Electric_power_transmission &oldid= 252240357). See also Edward Oros and Bob Cocco, "Determine the Efficiency of Your Transmission Line" (www.qsl.net/w4sat/lineeff.htm).

21. Energy Information Administration, "Electricity InfoCard 2006," November 2007 (www.eia.doe.gov/bookshelf/brochures/electricityinfocard/elecinfocard2006/elecinfocard.html).

22. There are approximately 150 control area operators in the United States and seven major independent control areas; see note 26 below.

23. "Department of Energy Putting Power in the Hands of Consumers through Technology," Pacific Northwest National Laboratory, January 9, 2008 (www.pnl.gov/topstory.asp?id=285).

24. For a complete discussion of FERC's consideration of demand response to provide ancillary services in wholesale electric markets see Jon Wellinghoff and David Morenoff, "Recognizing the Importance of Demand Response: The Second Half of the Wholesale Electric Market Equation," *Energy Law Journal* 28, no. 2 (2007): 389–419.

25. Steven Letendre, Paul Denholm, and Peter Lilienthal, "Electric and Hybrid Cars, New Load or New Resource?" *Public Utilities Fortnightly*, December 2006, p. 28.

26. There are six independent grid operators in the United States under the control and jurisdiction of FERC: PJM (grid operator for the Mid-Atlantic states), Mid-West Independent System Operator (MISO), California ISO (CAISO), New York ISO (NYISO), New England ISO (ISO-NE), and Southwest Power Pool (SPP). The Texas grid is independently operated by the Electric Reliability Council of Texas (ERCOT). In other regions of the county, the interstate grid is also under the jurisdiction of FERC, but the grid is operated by the owners of the transmission system or in some instances by other federal, state, or municipal agencies.

27. Letendre, Denholm, and Lilienthal, "Electric and Hybrid Cars, New Load or New Resource?" p. 30.

28. See "V2G: Vehicle to Grid Power," Center for Carbon-Free Power Integration, University of Delaware, April 2007 (www.udel.edu/V2G/).

29. See "About the eBox," AC Propulsion (www.acpropulsion.com/ebox/).

30. Willett Kempton, "Vehicle to Grid Power," briefing for the Federal Regulatory Commission, October 23, 2007 (www.ferc.gov/news/media-alerts/2007/2007-3/10-22-07-v2g.pdf).

31. Eoin O'Carroll, "Hybrid Availability Plunges as Demand Rises," *Christian Science Monitor Bright Green Blog*, June 11, 2008 (http://features.csmonitor.com/environment/2008/06/11/hybrid-availability-plunges-as-demand-rises).

32. Manufacturer's suggested retail prices and EPA mileages were obtained from *Consumer Reports*. Models and prices may vary.

33. Ralph Hanson, "GM Expects Volt to Cost Less Than $30,000," *Motor Authority*, May 24, 2008 (www.motorauthority.com/news/concept-cars/gm-expects-volt-to-cost-less-than-30000).

34. "Volt Could Spark GM Bailout," *Newser*, July 2, 2008 (www.newser.com/story/31427.html).

35. I made a presentation summarizing the material in this chapter and had discussions regarding the material with the board of directors of the Electric Drive Transportation Association in Washington, D.C., on June 18, 2008.

36. Regulation service payments for one-way power flow would be one-quarter the level of payments for two-way power flow.

37. See "Legislation, Tax Credits, Funding, and Other News," Electric Drive Transportation Association (www.electricdrive.org/index.php?tg=articles&topics= 127& new=0&newc=0).

38. Sandalow, *Freedom from Oil.*

PART II

Barriers

CHAPTER FIVE

The Impact of Plug-In Hybrids on U.S. Oil Use and Greenhouse Gas Emissions

ALAN L. MADIAN, LISA A. WALSH, and KIM D. SIMPKINS

All models are wrong; some are useful.
George Box

We estimate that plug-in hybrids could become the dominant technology for light vehicles sometime between 2030 and the second half of the twenty-first century.[1] With or without government intervention, we expect economics to have a significant role in determining whether and when it happens. From the economic perspective, buyers can be expected to select their vehicles on the basis of a comparison of costs and performance of plug-in hybrids, hybrids, and nonhybrid alternatives. With government intervention, the cost calculation will change. The change could well be the result of cost increases from policy-driven carbon or emission charges and cost reductions due to government incentives to purchase vehicles with alternative fuels and lower emissions.

Purchase considerations will almost certainly broaden from prestige and performance, including vehicle speed, size, and maneuverability, to include increased emphasis on fuel consumption and environmental performance. Convenience is also likely to be important. Environmental performance will be assessed using community standards that only now are emerging but that could gradually lead to significant changes in consumer preferences. Sophisticated analyses of environmental performance will consider all of the emissions associated with light vehicles and the fuel they consume, not just the emissions that emerge from the tailpipe, and these analyses can be expected to gradually affect community standards.

This essay focuses on two questions: First, how long will it take for plug-in hybrids to have a significant impact on oil usage and greenhouse gas emissions in the United States? The estimates will vary significantly, depending on the assumptions of the estimators. The outcome is highly uncertain, notwithstanding supportive government policies and significant investments in plug-in vehicle technology.

But, despite the uncertainty, the short answer is quite a long time. This is true even if a significant impact is defined as a reduction of only 10 percent of U.S. light-vehicle fuel consumption.[2] The short answer results from the constraints imposed by the time it will take to complete development of the required technologies, particularly battery technologies, and the necessary production capacity. Incentives will also take time to develop and implement.

Limitations on the all-electric distances (or driving distances attained on batteries alone) that can be attained with reasonably priced batteries have been the single greatest technological constraint and challenge to widespread deployment of electric cars and plug-in hybrids for over a century.[3] That challenge has yet to be overcome. For example, battery manufacturers are not yet prepared to warrant even very high-priced batteries for plug-in vehicles for a period longer than three years. Given the high replacement costs, batteries will probably have to have at least ten-year warranties for plug-in hybrid vehicles to gain widespread acceptance. Once the battery challenge has been overcome, supply chains will need to be established along with facilities for mass production.

The current size and replacement cycle of the vehicle fleet means that replacement by new vehicles takes a long time. At present, only about 5 to 6 percent of the light-vehicle fleet is replaced each year, and that rate has been slowing in recent years as vehicle durability improved.

Second, what should we do until plug-ins or vehicles powered by other new fuel consumption–reducing technologies, such as fuel cells, are widely deployed? The short answer is that there are a number of options that can contribute to reduced petroleum consumption and greenhouse gas emissions.

There have been significant gains in internal combustion–powered vehicle fuel efficiency in the United States over the past four decades.[4] As discussed later, such gains can be expected to continue. However, for at least two decades, efficiency gains have not led to reduced fuel use. Recent gains have been primarily allocated to increased vehicle performance and size. Changing the way that future efficiency gains of all technologies are allocated so that the focus becomes reduced fuel consumption can significantly improve fleet fuel efficiency.

Reducing vehicle weight may be the single most important short-term opportunity to reduce oil consumption and greenhouse gas emissions. There are also near-term opportunities to deploy existing technologies to increase vehicle efficiency and fuel economy. For example, increased deployment of turbochargers with smaller gasoline and biofuel engines and with diesels, as has already occurred in Europe, could contribute significantly. These are established technologies that can rapidly replace less efficient engines in existing vehicle models. Greenhouse gas emissions can also be reduced by substituting cellulosic ethanol and other biofuels and natural gas for petroleum-based fuels for the existing vehicle fleet.

The Near-Term Forecast (2008–20)

The potential short-term contribution of any technology to fuel efficiency and emissions reduction of the light-vehicle fleet is necessarily constrained. The most important constraint for deployment of any new vehicles is the slow rate of replacement of the light-vehicle fleet.[5]

Cars are classified as consumer durables for good reason. They typically last for well over a decade, and the average time between purchase and obsolescence has increased steadily in recent years. This means that transformation of the light-vehicle fleet to new internal combustion technologies or to hybrid and plug-in hybrid technologies will take decades from the time such vehicles are widely available at competitive prices. The time to transform the fleet could be reduced if there are effective incentives to scrap less efficient vehicles, particularly if the incentives are focused on less efficient vehicles with long life expectancies.

At least for the short term, plug-in hybrids face unresolved technological challenges, the most important concerns batteries that are limited in their all-electric range and that are, many believe, too expensive.[6] Productive capacity for the manufacture of innovative drivetrain components is another constraint that particularly affects plug-in hybrids. To estimate the expected timing of widespread deployment of plug-in hybrids requires that each of these constraints be taken into account.

For at least a decade, internal combustion–powered vehicles likely will continue to compete in total cost per mile with hybrids and plug-in hybrids.[7] There are a number of existing technologies being deployed in small quantities in the United States that have been widely deployed in Europe and that significantly reduce light-vehicle petroleum consumption and greenhouse gas emissions. Smaller vehicles; turbocharged four-cylinder gasoline engines, instead of six- and eight-cylinder engines; and turbocharged diesels make up a far larger proportion of the light-vehicle fleet in Europe than they do in North America. Fuel economy is far superior as a direct result. There also are significantly more natural gas– and liquefied petroleum gas–fueled light vehicles in Europe.

Wide deployment of these technologies in the United States and reduction in the size and weight of vehicles could significantly reduce fuel consumption and greenhouse gas emissions per mile traveled in the next decade and make these vehicles potential competitors to hybrids and plug-in hybrids even among the environmentally conscious.

Of course, plug-in hybrids promise greater reduction in oil consumption per vehicle mile, which to the extent there is a policy to diversify vehicle transportation fuels may lead to government incentives.

The all-electric range for mass-produced plug-in hybrids is targeted to reach about forty miles before 2015.[8] But there are significant trade-offs between all-electric range and acceleration that have yet to be taken into account. Drivers, who accelerate rapidly to get into highway traffic or simply to enjoy the acceleration, may find the all-electric range of their vehicles significantly reduced. Whether and when alternative methods to boost power for short periods of acceleration, likely through the use of capacitors linked to regenerative braking, will achieve all-electric ranges at a cost that will appeal to buyers is uncertain.

Incremental capital costs of plug-in hybrids with an all-electric range of forty miles are targeted to fall to between $6,000 and $10,000 per vehicle by 2015. This estimated cost is predicated on the industrial scale manufacture of batteries and components. Whether that goal will be achieved is highly uncertain. Even at that low end of the estimated differential cost, major manufacturers are not expected to be able to charge enough to profit from manufacturing plug-in hybrids. It is widely assumed that profitable mass production of plug-in hybrids will require lower incremental costs.

Plug-in vehicles are likely to face the challenge of the new. Innovative technologies take a considerable time to proliferate. The adoption of conventional hybrid vehicles followed the disruptive technology adoption pattern of low initial sales followed by accelerating sales. It took a decade for cumulative U.S. hybrid sales to reach the 1 million mark. It is expected that widespread adoption will take about two decades. Whether plug-in hybrids will follow a similar path or benefit from consumer acceptance of conventional hybrids and be adopted more rapidly is uncertain. Since there are technological challenges still to overcome, the critical path to widespread plug-in adoption could be longer.

Current hybrid and plug-in hybrid sales estimates are premised on continued high gas prices that are expected to result from high oil prices or carbon taxes or both or cap and trade costs. Since the beginning of 2006, increased hybrid sales have closely tracked increased gasoline prices.[9]

As mentioned, only about 1 million hybrid vehicles were sold in the United States from 1997 to 2007, which represents only four-tenths of 1 percent of the current fleet.[10] Expected hybrid sales for 2008 are in the 400,000 range, about 2.7 percent of forecasted light-vehicle sales.[11] Sales recently have been limited by capacity constraints in the manufacture of these vehicles combined with a drawdown of inventories. Current sales rates are not satisfying demand and, as a result, dealers are charging premiums, and customers are waiting months in some cases to receive their hybrid vehicles. Hybrid sales are forecast by Morgan Stanley to grow at a 14 percent compound rate from 400,000 in 2008 to 2 million a year by 2020, which is about 13 percent of forecasted 2020 light-vehicle sales.[12]

Plug-in hybrids have yet to enter the market in subcommercial quantities.[13] The expectation is that they may begin to be present in subcommercial quantities in 2010 or 2011.[14] Given current expectations regarding technology, costs, and incentives, U.S. sales of plug-in hybrids are not expected to reach commercial levels in the United States until 2015.[15] From 2015 to 2020, Morgan Stanley forecasts plug-in hybrid sales growing from 250,000 vehicles per annum to 1 million, requiring a very aggressive 32 percent compound annual growth rate.[16]

Morgan Stanley's estimate, which is aggressive, calls for cumulative hybrid sales by 2020 of 15 million vehicles, of which 3.7 million are estimated to be plug-ins. The estimated plug-in share of the U.S. light-vehicle fleet is about 1.2 percent. Those fifteen million hybrid vehicles would be less than 5 percent of the fleet.[17]

Given the known technological challenges and supply chain limitations, there is no reason to believe that Morgan Stanley's forecast of 2020 sales is far off the mark. Perhaps their forecast will not be realized and perhaps an even higher share of sales and the light-vehicle fleet can be achieved by 2020, but we do not now have a basis for raising expectations.

The Post-2020 Forecast

The key parameters to estimate intermediate-term and long-term market penetration and impact of the plug-in hybrid involve at least the following: the total mileage that plug-in hybrids will be driven and the proportion of total mileage powered by electricity; the efficiency gains by the internal combustion engine and the hybrid vehicles and the amount of efficiency gain allocated to increased mileage, size, and performance; and the rate at which plug-in hybrids will enter the light-vehicle fleet. To develop a credible estimate of the potential contribution of plug-in hybrids, we need to evaluate each of these parameters and their interactions.

Parameter: the total mileage that plug-in hybrids will be driven and the proportion of total mileage powered by electricity

Overview

Widespread adaptation of plug-in hybrids is posited on the availability of batteries with cost-effective all-electric ranges. Here, there is reason for optimism. While such batteries are not yet available, they are widely expected to be available in the next several years.[18] The all-electric range of plug-in hybrids is expected to be a key driver of purchase decisions.

A great deal of the analysis of the practicality of the plug-in hybrid has focused on trips to work. Trip-to-work distances are important, but if most plug-ins are to be charged at home during off-peak hours, trip-to-work distances are an inadequate measure. Instead, vehicle miles traveled per day for all purposes is the appropriate measure to assess the proportion of travel that can be undertaken using the expected all-electric range and for estimating the savings available from the electricity-fueled operation of the plug-in hybrid.

TABLE 5-1. **Vehicle Miles of Travel (VMT) per Day for All Purposes**

Travel	Percentage of VMT	Cumulative percentage
Weekday vehicle miles of travel per day		
Less than or equal to 5	10	10
Greater than 5 and less than or equal to 10	12	23
Greater than 10 and less than or equal to 20	21	44
Greater than 20 and less than or equal to 30	16	60
Greater than 30 and less than or equal to 40	11	71
Greater than 40 and less than or equal to 50	8	79
Greater than 50 and less than or equal to 60	5	84
Greater than 60	16	100
Weekend vehicle miles of travel per day		
Less than or equal to 5	22	22
Greater than 5 and less than or equal to 10	21	42
Greater than 10 and less than or equal to 20	27	69
Greater than 20 and less than or equal to 30	7	77
Greater than 30 and less than or equal to 40	6	82
Greater than 40 and less than or equal to 50	4	86
Greater than 50 and less than or equal to 60	6	89
Greater than 60	11	100

Source: Bureau of Transportation Statistics, National Household Travel Survey 2001 and 2004, specifically the "2001 National Household Travel Survey User's Guide," version 3 (Washington: U.S. Department of Transportation, January 2004). See also 2001 National Household Travel Survey database, specifically the files DAYPUB, VEHPUB, HHPUB, LDTPUB, and PERPUB.

Analysis

The U.S. Department of Transportation has collected extensive data on commuting and other travel by private vehicles.[19] Table 5-1 provides the vehicle miles of travel per day for all purposes and the percentage of vehicles in each of eight distance categories, with a distinction made between weekday and weekend travel.

According to the Department of Transportation studies, 71 percent of vehicles travel forty miles or less per weekday for all purposes, and 82 percent travel forty miles or less per weekend day. Over three-fifths of all light-vehicle miles traveled could be fueled by overnight charging if the vehicle fleet was composed entirely of plug-in hybrids that had a forty-mile all-electric range. The all-electric travel percentage would be somewhat lower if the plug-in vehicles had a variety of all-electric ranges that averaged 40 miles. If and when battery ranges increase, assuming costs are held constant, the economics and appeal of plug-in hybrids will be enhanced.

By comparison, it is interesting that the proportion of miles traveled by the entire fleet within the forty-mile vehicle range is greater on weekdays than on weekend days. On weekdays 64.8 percent of the miles traveled by the entire fleet is within a posited forty-mile all-electric range. On weekends the proportion within a posited forty-mile all-electric range declines to 59.1 percent.[20] Nonetheless, assuming a forty-mile all-electric range and a solution to the range degradation that now results from rapid acceleration, the majority of plug-ins should be able to operate entirely on electricity on most days and to do so with a single overnight battery recharge. They would operate over 60 percent of the time within their all-electric range; however, this does not necessarily mean that they could always operate within their all-electric range without requiring supplementary power to recharge the batteries or to augment the electric motor.

If currently proposed all-electric ranges for plug-in hybrids can be attained in actual driving conditions, and if proposed battery costs and capacities can be realized, plug-ins are likely to be especially appealing to residents of suburbia.[21] They will be able to recharge at home and to fuel the majority of their travel with electricity with increased convenience and at a fraction of the cost of gasoline or diesel. Residents of cities, apartments, and dormitories are likely to find recharging plug-in vehicles more challenging since they rarely have garages or driveways with available power outlets. Therefore, they are less likely to buy plug-ins unless and until the problem of recharging can be overcome by the development of widely available recharging facilities.

Parameter: efficiency gains and the proportion allocated to increased mileage, size, and performance

Overview

In the absence of government regulations, reductions in oil consumption and greenhouse gas emissions will depend primarily on how manufacturers and consumers choose to allocate efficiency gains. To the extent that fuel prices exceed historical levels, consumers are likely to favor an increased allocation of efficiency gains to increases in miles traveled per gallon of fuel. Auto manufacturers are currently planning new vehicles on the assumption that high fuel prices will continue and that they will lead consumers to select more fuel-efficient vehicles in the future. Whether the industry focus on fuel efficiency will continue if fuel prices decline or stabilize at or near the $4-a-gallon level remains to be determined. The extent to which consumers will be willing to trade size and performance for fuel efficiency is uncertain, as are future fuel prices.[22]

Over the past three decades, the light-vehicle market has witnessed remarkable improvements in internal combustion engine technology. Anup P. Bandivadekar of MIT has produced important research that quantifies efficiency improvements made from 1970 to 2005. His work assesses the allocation of those gains between improving fuel economy and increasing size and performance. He also discusses the efficiency gains likely to be realized through continued improvement of internal combustion engines.[23]

Facts and Analysis

Bandivadekar notes that if the light-vehicle fleet had the same weight distribution and performance characteristics in 2003 as it had in 1980, fuel economy would have improved by one-third.[24]

According to the U.S. Environmental Protection Agency, fuel efficiency improved 54 percent for cars and 74 percent for light trucks between 1975 and 2007, measured as per ton of vehicle.[25]

In the United States, much of the efficiency gained has been used to enhance performance and to increase vehicle size. Average horsepower increased from just over 100 in the early 1980s to over 220 in 2007.[26] Acceleration from zero to sixty miles per hour improved from 14.1 seconds on average in 1975 to 9.6 seconds in 2007.[27] Average vehicle weight increased from about 3,200 pounds in the early 1980s to over 4,100 pounds in 2007.[28]

Corporate Average Fuel Economy (CAFE) standards led automakers to allocate efficiency gains to increased mileage as long as they were required to do so. Since the mid-1980s, when efficiency gains exceeded required mileage improvements, efficiency gains were largely allocated to enhanced size and performance rather than to reduced fuel consumption.[29]

One cause of optimism is that purchasers of hybrids and plug-in hybrids are likely to focus on fuel economy and greenhouse gas emissions more than purchasers of internal combustion–powered vehicles. As a result, the allocation of the efficiency gains of hybrids and plug-in hybrids are likely to be directed far more to fuel economy and emissions reduction. To the extent that efficiency gains of hybrids are allocated more to fuel economy than is the case with internal combustion engine–powered vehicles, hybrids can be expected to make larger contributions to reducing oil consumption and greenhouse gas emissions per unit of efficiency gain.

To the extent that regulatory requirements allow for efficiency gains to be allocated to anything other than increased mileage, efficiency gains are likely to continue to be allocated to enhanced size and performance. Fuel prices and climate change concerns may have to increase significantly to alter consumer preferences.

Parameter: the estimated rate at which plug-in hybrids will enter the light-vehicle fleet

Key Variables

The key variables that will determine the rate at which plug-in hybrids will enter the light-vehicle fleet include gasoline and alternative internal combustion fuel prices, which will be determined by oil costs and by taxes; battery costs, which represent the vast majority of the incremental costs of plug-in hybrids; available all-electric driving distances with vehicle performance acceptable to a large number of drivers; the difference in operating costs between internal combustion–powered and electricity-powered operation per vehicle mile traveled; the difference in initial purchase or lease costs; constraints of manufacturing capacity and supply chain for key components and for assembly of plug-ins; and the availability and attractiveness of alternative-vehicle technologies and fuels.

Since future prices, technological advances, and policies, particularly policies regarding incentives for consumers and manufacturers, cannot be known in advance, the best estimate of post-2020 fleet composition can be little more than an informed guess. Empirically informed scenario analysis can help us understand historical relationships such as that between capital and operating costs and the role of payback periods in vehicle choice. But such analyses may tell us little about future choices, especially if gasoline prices reach or exceed and maintain levels not previously seen.

Similarly, historical penetration rates of new vehicle configurations such as SUVs can inform us of the rates of acceptance reached by new vehicle types. The extent that adoption rates of plug-in hybrids will resemble those historical patterns is necessarily uncertain. Nonetheless, it is noteworthy that the growth of SUVs was a predictable outcome of regulatory double standards that defined SUVs as trucks and that imposed stricter mileage standards on cars than on trucks. The manufacture of SUVs allowed manufacturers to meet CAFE standards and to maintain the high profit margins that they realized on large vehicles. Although there was no mandate to develop SUVs, the CAFE regulations as implemented provided very strong incentives to do so.

An assessment of battery technologies can tell us what engineers know can be accomplished today and what they expect to accomplish in the near future, but it cannot provide much guidance as to what will be possible and at what cost a decade or more in the future. The result is that forecasts of market penetration of plug-in hybrids, incremental costs, cost-effectiveness, and performance vary widely.

The optimum trade-off between all-electric range and battery prices is unknown. It is possible that plug-in hybrids eventually will be offered with battery options in the same way that internal combustion–powered vehicles are offered with multiple engine options. Customers would choose the battery according to their typical travel distances and driving styles.

Battery costs are falling rapidly from very high levels. Batteries with a forty-mile all-electric range had estimated costs of more than $17,000 in 2006.[30] A forty-mile all-electric range has been widely targeted since many in the auto industry thought that it likely would make plug-in hybrids attractive to a large number of buyers. As discussed earlier, a forty-mile all-electric range would mean that travel for most people on most days could be powered entirely by electricity. It would also mean that plug-in hybrids were likely to be powered by electricity for a majority of all miles traveled.[31] If technological breakthroughs lead to significant all-electric range extension and price reduction in the next several years, plug-in hybrid economics would be significantly enhanced as would expectations of annual sales and fleet share late in the next decade and beyond.

For owners of a plug-in hybrid, the fuel costs per mile traveled powered by electricity is estimated to be a quarter to a third of the cost per mile traveled using gasoline alone.[32] This appears to provide significant savings, but even a 75 percent reduction in fuel costs for all electric miles would represent only a modest share of annual vehicle ownership costs.[33] In the example illustrated in the footnote, ownership costs are estimated at $7,600 per annum, including $1,600 for 400 gallons of gasoline, with fuel cost savings of $900 per annum available from a plug-in equivalent.

Estimates of the purchase premium that buyers would be willing to pay to realize savings in fuel costs of this magnitude vary widely.

Manufacturing capacity is likely to be constrained for key plug-in hybrid components for a decade or more. Of course, the extent to which that constraint is binding will depend on demand.

But a strict economic analysis may miss the point by being too narrow. Convenience measured by avoided trips to the gas station could be an additional motive for plug-in purchases. The obvious motive of environmental stewardship may trump the strict application of cost-benefit economics, provided that the costs for environmental stewardship are not viewed as excessive. If the claim that greenhouses gases lead to climate change is widely embraced, many may seek environmentally efficient vehicles, even if the economics are somewhat disadvantageous. But if the economics are disadvantageous, plug-ins can be expected to take longer to gain significant market and fleet share.

Facts

The character of the existing light-vehicle fleet and its evolution is an important starting point for any estimate of the character of the future fleet. The number of light vehicles in service in the United States is estimated at about 250 million in 2008, growing at about 1.75 percent a year, an average annual rate of fleet growth now of more than 4.3 million vehicles.[34]

New vehicle sales are estimated at 15 million to 16 million vehicles per annum, so only 11 to 12 million vehicles replace vehicles that are being scrapped or exported.[35] Annual sales of new vehicles are profoundly affected by demographics, consumer sentiment, and improved vehicle durability.[36] Whether increased vehicle durability will result in declines in sales or greater numbers of automobiles per household, or both, is uncertain.

On average, new vehicles are driven more miles than older vehicles are. With rising gas prices, especially at levels above $4 a gallon, more fuel-efficient vehicles are likely to get greater use when consumers have a choice. Thus fuel-efficient additions to the fleet can be expected to have an impact on fuel consumption beyond their proportion of the fleet.

A possibly useful comparison is with the rate of increase in sales of SUVs. SUV sales were 1.8 percent of sales in 1975 and reached 6.3 percent in 1988 and 28.9 percent in 2007.[37] No other vehicle type has increased its share of sales at anything close to that rate of increase for SUVs, which averaged 9 percent per annum for the thirty-two-year period and 8 percent for the period since 1988.[38] We do not have data on the increases in vehicles sold, but the percentage increase in SUVs sold would be somewhat higher since the total number of vehicles sold per annum grew during this period.

A mandate or significant incentives could lead to a higher rate of market share and sales increases for plug-in hybrids than was experienced by SUVs. A mandate could be technology specific or could specify required outcomes.[39] But it is important to keep in mind that the compound sales share growth rate of 9 percent per annum for SUVs was the result of an unprecedented and highly effective regulatory push that provided incentives to manufacturers to shift from producing cars to producing SUVs.

Forecast

Detailed sales forecasts of hybrids and plug-in hybrids are useful since they require explicit assumptions about future rates of sales growth.

We started from Morgan Stanley's forecast of plug-in hybrid sales discussed in the previous section, which we considered both reasonable and evidence based. We assumed an aggressive 15 percent compound annual growth rate for plug-in sales for the 2020 to 2030 decade. The result is 27 million plug-in vehicles in the United States in 2030, or 7.3 percent of the light-vehicle fleet.[40] We estimate plug-in hybrid sales in 2030 at just over 4 million, which would be about 25 percent of sales.

Two divergent forecasts for 2030 by highly qualified organizations reveal the extent of the uncertainty in the estimates of plug-in hybrid sales and share of the light-vehicle fleet. We did not see these estimates until after we had completed our forecast. For 2030 our annual sales share forecast for plug-in hybrids of 25 percent is close to the midpoint of the estimate from the study by Jon Creyts and others of McKinsey & Company and the Electric Power Research Institute (EPRI) aggressive case estimate.[41] Creyts and colleagues estimated that plug-ins might grow to 6 percent of new light-vehicle sales by 2030, which is a quarter of our estimate.[42] EPRI has analyzed the consequences of what it identifies as aggressive penetration of plug-ins, also in 2030, which is based on a 40 percent share of the on-road light-vehicle fleet and a 50 percent share of light-vehicle sales in 2030.[43] EPRI's estimated 2030 sales share is more than eight times that of Creyts and colleagues and twice our estimate.[44]

Extending our estimate to 2036 at the 15 percent compound growth rate increases the estimate of plug-in share of sales to more than 50 percent.[45] The estimated fleet share increases to more than 16 percent as well.[46] On the basis of our assumption that miles traveled by plug-ins would be fueled more than 60 percent by electricity, this would result in a 10 percent reduction in the use of liquid fuel. Presumably greenhouse gas emissions would also be reduced, with the reduction dependent on the miles fueled with electricity and the emissions content of that electricity. The 10 percent liquid fuel reduction is what we established at the beginning of this article as our "significant impact" threshold.

At this time, estimating future sales and fleet share of plug-in hybrids can be informed by history and technological and economic assessments, but knowledge is extremely limited. Future technological evolution and related costs are vitally important to future market acceptance yet highly uncertain. Equally uncertain is how public attitudes to greenhouse gases and climate change and environmental stewardship will alter the perceptions and demands of auto purchasers. As a result, future plug-in hybrid sales and fleet share are necessarily highly uncertain. Confidence in any estimate is unwarranted.

Conclusion: Meeting the Global Emissions Challenge

Our conclusion is in the form of a cautionary note. As yet, there is no decision to reduce oil dependence to a degree that would significantly enhance U.S. national security. As yet there is no agreement to reduce global greenhouse gas emissions to reduce global warming risk. Until there is a sense of urgency regarding the time frame to accomplish these goals, progress is likely to be fitful.

Stabilizing global greenhouse gas emissions in the next two decades will be extremely difficult. Reducing them will be far harder. Substantial emissions that will flow from increased electricity demand and increased light-vehicle fleets in China and India and from exploitation of nonconventional sources of petroleum, such as Canada's oil sands and Venezuela's Orinoco heavy oil belt, will add to the magnitude of the global emissions challenge. With emissions challenges of this magnitude, "silver bullet" solutions are unlikely to be available.

Presumably, time is of the essence, but the deadline is uncertain. As far as global warming is concerned, we do not know whether we are already too late or whether we have decades or more to reverse course.

This is the context in which we have been asked to assess the role of plug-in hybrids. In the intermediate term, plug-in hybrids can contribute significantly to a reduction in oil use and greenhouse gas emissions in the United States and globally. In the long term, plug-ins may come to dominate light-vehicle technology. But it would be a mistake to think of plug-in hybrids as the solution to ending oil dependence or decreasing greenhouse gas emissions in the light-vehicle sector during the next decade or two.

For now, plug-in hybrids represent one of a number of promising technologies. The economic production of large volumes of plug-in hybrids will require significant breakthroughs in technology, supply chain logistics, and manufacturing capacity. None of these elements are likely to present insuperable barriers, but all of them will require considerable financial and technological resources and time to resolve.

Similar challenges are present for other measures that are proposed to contribute to reducing global fossil fuel use and greenhouse gas emissions. Whether the proposed solution involves electricity production technologies, such as nuclear, solar, wind, and wave power; new fuels, such as cellulosic ethanol; or end-use conservation, such as low-energy lighting and building insulation, the time lines are long and the resource requirements substantial.

While the challenge is great, there are many promising paths to progress. If we are to curtail our fossil fuel use and greenhouse gas emissions, we will have to wage the battle broadly. Plug-in hybrids can make a significant contribution, but it is important to realize that they can do so only gradually. It is important that we do not assume a solution that cannot be achieved.

Notes

1. The *dominant technology* can be defined as that which has the largest share of new light-vehicle sales or that which has the largest share of the light-vehicle fleet. Sales share dominance precedes fleet share dominance.

2. Ten percent of U.S. light-vehicle fuel consumption now represents just over 4 percent of U.S. daily oil consumption and about 1 percent of world oil consumption. To realize a 10 percent reduction in fuel consumption by the fleet of light vehicles and

related greenhouse gas emissions, it is estimated that plug-in hybrids will need to reach at least a 15 percent share of the light-vehicle fleet.

3. Alan L. Madian, Lisa A. Walsh, Kim D. Simpkins, and Rebecca S. Gordon, "U.S. Plug-in Hybrid and U.S. Light Vehicle Data Book," hereafter PHEV Data Book (Washington: LECG), tab 2. Prepared for the conference Plug-in Electric Vehicles 2008: What Role for Washington? sponsored by Brookings and Google.org, Washington, June 11–12, 2008.

4. Lynette Cheah and others, "Factor of Two: Halving the Fuel Consumption of New U.S. Automobiles by 2035" (MIT Laboratory for Energy and Environment, October 2007).

5. Previously estimated at 5 to 6 percent per annum.

6. PHEV Data Book, tab 2.

7. If fuel costs rise well above $4.00 per gallon, hybrids and plug-in hybrids are likely to be increasingly competitive and to gain market acceptance sooner, but rising fuel costs will also lead to increased technological innovation and fuel economy for new internal combustion–powered vehicles.

8. For example, General Motors has targeted a late 2010 launch and a forty-mile all-electric range for the Chevy Volt that they propose to sell for between $30,000 and $40,000. Mass production is expected in 2015. GM forecasts that it will have to provide significant subsidies for a number of years to sell Volts at the proposed price. For details regarding the development of plug-in hybrids, see PHEV Data Book, tab 1.

9. PHEV Data Book, tab 5, figure 5.2, "Hybrid Sales and Real Monthly Gas Price (2006–2008)."

10. Jonathan Steinmetz and Ravi Shanker, "Plug-in Hybrids: The Next Automotive revolution," hereafter Morgan Stanley Report (New York: Morgan Stanley Research North America, March 11, 2008), p. 13, exhibit 8.

11. Morgan Stanley Report, p. 13, exhibit 8.

12. Morgan Stanley Report, p. 13, exhibit 8.

13. Morgan Stanley forecasts total plug-in-hybrid sales in 2012 of 100,000, up from 5,000 forecast for 2010.

14. Morgan Stanley Report, p. 13, exhibit 12.

15. PHEV Data Book, tab 1, overview. Commercial levels are defined as 250,000 units per annum, which is less than 1.6 percent of estimated annual sales of all light vehicles. The 2015 U.S. plug-in sales estimate is from Morgan Stanley, which we found to be the only credible near-term forecast. See Morgan Stanley Report, p. 13, exhibit 12.

16. LECG calculation from data in the Morgan Stanley Report, p. 13, exhibit 12.

17. LECG calculation from data in the Morgan Stanley Report, p. 13, exhibit 8.

18. See PHEV Data Book, tab 2, overview.

19. Bureau of Transportation Statistics, National Household Travel Survey 2001 and 2004, specifically the "2001 National Household Travel Survey User's Guide," version 3 (Washington: U.S. Department of Transportation, January 2004). See also 2001 National Household Travel Survey database, specifically the files DAYPUB, VEHPUB, HHPUB, LDTPUB, and PERPUB.

20. See PHEV Data Book, tab 2, overview.

21. Current proposals call for an all-electric range of forty miles or more by 2010. See PHEV Data Book, tab 1. For proposed battery costs and capacities, see PHEV Data Book, tab 2.

22. This chapter was written when gas cost more than $4 per gallon. As this volume was going to press, gas at the pump was running around $1.89 per gallon. Nonetheless, manufacturers appear to remain committed to developing fuel-efficient automobiles, and customers say that fuel efficiency will be an important consideration when they purchase a new vehicle. Whether manufacturers and consumers hold those positions if the price of gas does not increase markedly is uncertain. Industry, however, may be more likely to maintain its commitment in order to sustain government support.

23. Anup P. Bandivadekar, "Evaluating the Impact of Advanced Vehicle and Fuel Technologies in U.S. Light-Duty Vehicle Fleet," Ph.D. dissertation, Massachusetts Institute of Technology, January 2008.

24. Bandivadekar (2008), pp. 17, 61–64.

25. PHEV Data Book, tab 6, figure 6.7.

26. PHEV Data Book, tab 6, figure 6.9.

27. PHEV Data Book, tab 6, figure 6.9.

28. PHEV Data Book, tab 6, figure 6.9.

29. PHEV Data Book, tab 6, figures 6.8, 6.9.

30. The American Council for an Energy Efficient Economy (ACEEE) estimated a cost for a forty-mile battery at $17,500 in 2006, as cited in the presentation of John German, American Honda Motor Company, at the 8th International Advanced Automotive Battery and Ultra Capacitors Conference, Tampa, Florida, May 2008.

31. Travel patterns are discussed later in the text.

32. See, for example, Morgan Stanley Report, p. 6.

33. For example, a $30,000 vehicle owned for five years and sold for $10,000 has an average depreciation of $4,000 per annum. Insurance costs vary widely but are likely to be in the $1,000 range per annum for adult drivers. Maintenance, including replacement of tires and wear parts; license fees; and personal property taxes also vary widely and could add another $1,000 per annum. If gasoline is assumed to cost $4.00 per gallon and the vehicle or an equivalent nonhybrid averages 35 miles per gallon (mpg) on gasoline (the 2020 CAFE standard) and travels 14,000 miles per annum, total gasoline consumption while operating entirely on gasoline would be 400 gallons (14,000 miles/ 35 mpg), and total cost would be $1,600 ($4.00 per gallon × 400 gallons). If three-quarters of the mileage was electric powered at $1.00 per gallon equivalent, the all-electric fuel cost would be $300 [(10,500 miles/35 mpg) × $1.00 per gallon equivalent]. The gasoline cost for the remaining 3,500 miles would be $400 [(3,500 miles/35 mpg) × $4.00 per gallon], and the annual fuel costs would be $700 ($300 + $400) with savings of $900 ($1,600 – $700).

34. PHEV Data Book, tab 4, figures 4.2, 4.3.

35. PHEV Data Book, tab 6, figure 6.8 for the period 2000–07.

36. The latest estimate for average vehicle longevity is about 16 years: 16.9 years for cars and 15.5 years for trucks. See Bandivadekar (2008), p. 45.

37. PHEV Data Book, tab 4, figure 4.1.

38. LECG calculation.

39. Like mandates, incentives can increase sales significantly when compared with business as usual. Providing incentives for technologies that are not yet fully developed and tested presents a number of additional risks. Whether incentive programs that deal effectively with those risks can be developed is uncertain. Mandating adoption of technologies that are not fully developed, tested, cost-effective, and covered by warranties would be viewed by many as likely to be economically wasteful and as an irresponsible imposition of political power.

40. LECG calculation.

41. Jon Creyts and others, *Reducing U.S. Greenhouse Gas Emissions: How Much at What Cost?* (New York: McKinsey & Company and The Conference Board, December 2007), p. 46; EPRI, "Plug-In Hybrids on the Horizon: Building a Business Case," *EPRI Journal* (Spring 2008): p. 9.

42. Creyts and others (2007), p. 46.

43. EPRI, "Plug-In Hybrids on the Horizon," p. 9.

44. The EPRI estimate would require that plug-in sales reach 50 percent well before 2030 to achieve a 40 percent light-vehicle fleet share by 2030, but such sales forecasts are not provided.

45. LECG calculation.

46. LECG calculation.

CHAPTER SIX

Look Before You Leap:

Exploring the Implications of Advanced Vehicles for Import Dependence and Passenger Safety

IRVING MINTZER

The sleek lines of the black Tesla Roadster glistened as it slid gracefully into a high-speed curve along California's picturesque Pacific Coast Highway one evening in the summer of 2009. The whoosh of its tires was the only sound above a whisper, as its battery-powered electric motor and racing suspension propelled it rapidly along the precipice above the ocean's edge. In the oncoming lane, the muscular outlines of a prototype Chevy Volt suggested that the thrills of the pony-car days might be returning to America's roads.

The emergence of this new generation of vehicles—powered by electric drivetrains with energy from electric storage batteries—tantalizes the car-loving American consumer. These vehicles—including hybrid electric vehicles (HEVs), plug-in hybrid electric vehicles (PHEVs), and all-electric vehicles (AEVs)—promise to deliver a smooth driving experience with abundant acceleration, little vibration, and many creature comforts, while lowering oil consumption in transportation and reducing emissions of carbon dioxide as well as other air pollutants.

But a rapid transition to HEVs, PHEVs, and AEVs is not without risks. All current designs for these vehicles incorporate significant amounts of heavy metals and rare earth elements into critical drivetrain components. In many cases, today's world markets for these materials are quite tight.[1] Acquiring additional supplies may require relying on national governments that are unstable or overtly hostile to U.S. interests. In addition, some of the exotic materials used in these vehicles carry significant risks in the event of accidents or major malfunctions.[2] None of the risks, however, need be a "show-stopper" that keeps these promising new vehicles from entering the market. Nevertheless, avoiding the most dangerous risks will require careful attention to the available alternatives and may argue for development of an option that is neither cheapest in the short term nor closest to commercial readiness today. This chapter highlights some of the potential risks and identifies less risky alternatives.

Materials Requirements for Electric Drivetrains

What makes HEVs, PHEVs, and AEVs distinctive are their electric drivetrains (including electric motors, regenerative braking systems, and electric storage batteries). These components create unique design and manufacturing challenges for automakers and battery manufacturers.

Electric Motors and Related Subsystems

Electric motors generate torque to accelerate advanced vehicles; motors of several different designs can be used. The 2009 Tesla Roadster AEV, for example, incorporates a brushless, three-phase, four-pole induction motor that accelerates the vehicle from zero to 60 miles per hour (100 kilometers per hour) in about four seconds. The Toyota Prius and Honda Civic sedans, which dominate today's HEV market, use permanent magnet motors.[3] The motors in the Toyota and Honda hybrids generate far less torque than the Tesla, but they are powerful enough to reach highway speeds easily and safely.

Most current designs for HEVs, PHEVs, and AEVs use electric motors incorporating "hard magnets" that are fabricated from neodymium-iron-boron (Nd-Fe-B) alloys. They use similar hard magnets in their electric generators, power-assisted steering, and regenerative braking subsystems. This type of magnet was developed simultaneously in 1984 by General Motors (United States) and by Sumitomo Special Metals (Japan).[4] Raskin and Shah[5] and Chavasse[6] estimate that each current Toyota Prius employs, on average, 1 to 2 kilograms of neodymium (Nd) in these components, as well as nearly 0.075 kilograms of cobalt (Co) in its electric motors, brakes, and steering subsystems.

Electric Storage Batteries

Batteries based on nickel-metal-hydride (NiMH) chemistry meet the power, energy, and weight requirements of today's hybrids. They are employed in more than 95 percent of today's HEVs, including the 2008 models of the Toyota, Honda, Ford, and Lexus brands. NiMH batteries typically contain 4 to 6 percent cobalt by weight. In today's Toyota Prius, for example, the batteries weigh about 28 kilograms, including approximately 1.4 kilograms of cobalt.[7] Current hybrids also contain small amounts of samarium and lanthanum, additional rare earth elements.

Most analysts believe that tomorrow's HEVs, PHEVs and AEVs will require a new generation of stronger batteries. Batteries for these advanced vehicles must provide higher levels of *energy density* and *power density,* and they must sustain a larger number of charging and discharging cycles than the NIMH batteries in today's hybrids.[8] Several alternative battery chemistries are being developed to address these requirements, but none meets all of the U.S. Department of Energy's long-term goals for PHEV performance and cost effectiveness. The alternatives closest to achieving those long-term goals employ variations of conventional lithium-ion (Li-ion) chemistries. Material requirements, performance capabilities, and cost characteristics differ significantly among the possible alternatives.[9]

Figure 6-1 compares the current status of NiMH batteries with that of some Li-ion batteries currently under development. The dotted line illustrates the Department of Energy (DOE) long-term PHEV goals for energy density (labeled *specific energy* in the figure), power density (labeled *specific power* in the figure), and cost (measured in dollars per kilowatt-hour stored in the battery). The figure indicates that Li-ion batteries already have up to twice the energy density of NiMH batteries of similar size but still fall short of DOE's long-term goal for energy density. The power density achieved by the best Li-ion batteries, which can be as much as 2.5 times the power density of NiMH devices, could meet the long-term power density goal.[10] Neither conventional NiMH batteries nor current Li-ion batteries are anywhere close to achieving DOE's long-term goal for cost effectiveness.

First-Generation Li-ion Batteries. The Li-ion batteries that are closest to commercial readiness are "traditional" Li-ion batteries, which employ a cobalt-oxide cathode. This type of battery (called an LCO cell) was first

FIGURE 6-1. Battery Capabilities versus Long-Term PHEV Goals

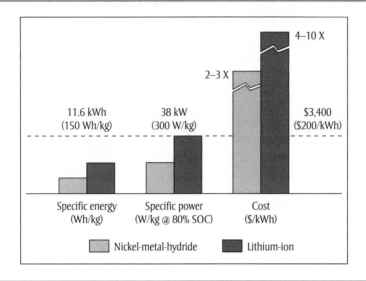

Source: Don Hillebrand, testimony before the U.S. House of Representatives Subcommittee on Energy and Water Development, *Overview Hearing on Gas Prices and Vehicle Technology*, 110 Cong., 2nd. sess., February 14, 2008.

introduced by Sony Corporation of Japan in 1991.[11] LCO cells account for about 70 percent of today's $7 billion market for small, rechargeable batteries,[12] and more than 1.3 billion LCO cells were manufactured globally in 2007.[13] Most current laptop computers and cell phones use this type of battery. Figure 6-2 presents a schematic illustration of an LCO cell. Some believe that this traditional LCO cell will be the first type employed in PHEVs and AEVs. Recent announcements support that belief: the all-electric Tesla Roadster as well as several low-cost PHEVs announced by Chinese auto companies are expected to use batteries containing LCO cells.[14] Part of the attraction of LCO cells for manufacturers is that they are inexpensive and widely available as a commodity in the international market.

Advanced Li-ion Batteries. In efforts to address safety concerns and other issues with LCO cells, a number of U.S. and international companies are working aggressively to develop advanced batteries using alternative chemistries.[15] Figure 6-3, which illustrates the evolution of battery technology, displays the range of new Li-ion chemistries currently under de-

FIGURE 6-2. Lithium-Ion Battery with Cobalt-Oxide Cathode

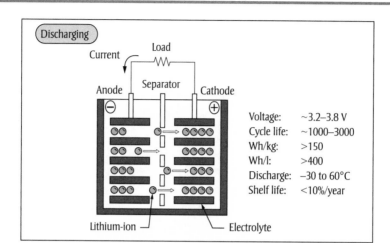

Source: Ahmad Pesaran, "Battery Choices and Potential Requirements for Plug-in Hybrids," National Renewable Energy Laboratory, February 13, 2007 (www.nrel.gov/vehiclesandfuels/energystorage/pdfs/41328.pdf [December 31, 2008]).

velopment. Some advanced Li-ion chemistries employ new composites and nano-materials. They require much smaller quantities of cobalt than do LCO cells and show significant potential for meeting DOE's long-term goals for PHEVs and AEVs. The most promising chemistries include

—lithium with nickel-cobalt-manganese and graphite electrodes (called NCM cells)

—lithium with nickel-cobalt-aluminum and graphite electrodes (called NCA cells)

—lithium-manganese-spinel with lithium-titanate (called LMS cells)

—lithium-manganese-oxide with lithium-titanate (called LTO cells)

—lithium-iron-phosphate with graphite electrodes (called LFP cells).[16]

Advanced HEVs, PHEVs, and AEVs using these new battery materials would likely contain from zero to 5 kilograms of cobalt, along with 0.1 to 0.5 kilograms of cobalt in other vehicle subsystems (today's Prius has about 1.5 kilograms of cobalt).[17] Table 6-1 compares batteries based on the new Li-ion chemistries with LCO cells.

FIGURE 6-3. Battery Chemistries over the Years

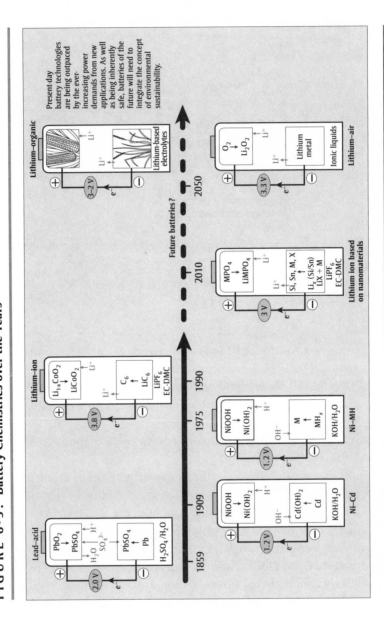

Source: Michel Armand and J-M. Tarascon, "Building Better Batteries," *Nature* 451 (February 7, 2008): 653. Reprinted by permission.

TABLE 6-1. Characteristics of Leading Advanced Li-ion Chemistries

Chemistry	Electrodes Positive (Negative)	Strengths	Limitations	State of development
Lithium cobalt oxide (LCO)	$LiCoO_2$ (Graphite)	Good power; good energy density	Safety and cost issues	In widespread use in consumer rechargeable goods; planned for use in Tesla Roadster
Lithium nickel cobalt manganese (NCM)	$Li(Ni_{1/3}Co_{1/3}Mn_{1/3})O_2$ (Graphite)	Potentially high energy density	Performance lower than that of NCA and LFP	In testing stage with several companies
Lithium nickel cobalt aluminum (NCA)	$Li(Ni_{0.85}Co_{0.1}Al_{0.05})O_2$ (Graphite)	Good power density, energy density, and lifetime	Safety and cost issues	In testing stage with several companies
Lithium manganese spinel (LMS)	$LiMnO_2$ or $LiMn_2O_4$ ($Li_4Ti_5O_{12}$)	Potentially excellent safety and lifetime and moderate cost	Moderate power and poor energy density	In intermediate development stage with several companies
Lithium titanium	$LiMnO_2$ ($LiTiO_2$)	Potentially good safety and lifetime	Poor to moderate power, poor energy, and high cost	In development stage with several companies
Lithium iron phosphate (LFP)	$LiFePO_4$ (Graphite)	Good power, moderate energy, moderate safety, and potentially good cost	Possibly significant limits on energy density	In advanced testing stage with several companies

Source: Alan Madian and others, *U.S. Plug-in Hybrid and U.S. Light-Duty Vehicle Data Book* (Washington: LECG Inc., 2008).

The Market for HEVs, PHEVs, and AEVs

More than 620 million light-duty vehicles are on the road today,[18] of
which about 235 million are registered in the United States.[19] In 2007
approximately 70 million new light-duty vehicles were sold worldwide,[20]
about 16 million of them in the United States.[21] Estimates of the future
size of the global light-duty vehicle fleet vary, depending on assumptions
about global economic conditions, future oil prices, new car sales, and the
future retirement rate for used vehicles. The International Energy Agency
estimated that the global fleet of cars and light trucks would reach 1.3 billion in 2030.[22] In 2007 Exxon estimated that the world's light-duty vehicle fleet would reach about 1.1 billion units in 2030.[23] *The Economist*
estimated that the global light-duty vehicle fleet could reach 1.25 billion
by 2025, growing to more than 2 billion vehicles by 2050.[24]

In 1997 Toyota sold the first hybrid Prius in Japan. Worldwide sales of
hybrid cars exceeded 500,000 units in 2007, with more than half sold in
the United States. By the end of 2007, the U.S. hybrid fleet exceeded
600,000 units (see figure 6-4).[25] In May 2008, Toyota's cumulative hybrid
sales topped 1.5 million units worldwide.[26] Analysts Raskin and Shah
and Hillebrand argue that hybrid sales will continue to grow in the
United States and in other developed countries because hybrids offer purchasers a host of desirable attributes.[27] In 2008 Hillebrand projected U.S.
hybrid sales to grow at an average annual rate of 30 percent through
2012, suggesting sales of more than 1,200,000 vehicles.[28] Chavasse projects that global sales of advanced vehicles will reach 4 to 6 million units
in 2015.[29]

Projections of the aggregate size of the global hybrid vehicle fleet have
increased in recent years. The International Energy Agency (IEA) estimated that by 2030 advanced vehicles (including hybrids and fuel cell
vehicles) would represent about 0.7 percent of light-duty vehicles worldwide and 15 percent of light-duty vehicles in North America.[30] The DOE
Energy Information Administration estimated that hybrids would grow
from 0.5 percent of the U.S. light-duty vehicle fleet in 2004 to about
30 percent in 2030.[31] Raskin and Shah projected that hybrids would represent 30 percent of the global light-duty fleet by 2020 (approximately
300 million vehicles) and reach 72 percent in 2030 (more than 900 million vehicles).[32]

Figure 6-4. Cumulative U.S. Sales of Hybrid Gas-Electric Vehicles

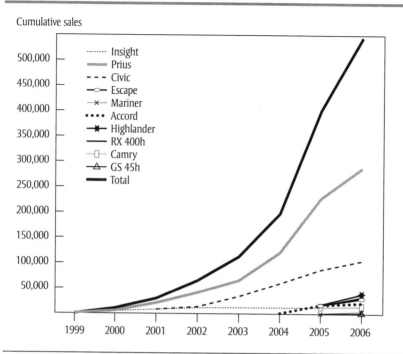

Cumulative sales

Source: Don Hillebrand, testimony before the U.S. House of Representatives Subcommittee on Energy and Water Development, *Overview Hearing on Gas Prices and Vehicle Technology*, 110 Cong., 2nd. sess., February 14, 2008.

Implications for U.S. Import Dependence

Growing concern about continued U.S. dependence on imported oil has created a sense of urgency about accelerating the commercialization of HEVs, PHEVs, and AEVs.[33] Shifting the U.S. light-duty vehicle fleet away from conventional gasoline vehicles toward advanced vehicles offers an important opportunity for reducing oil import dependence and simultaneously reducing U.S. greenhouse gas emissions from the transportation sector.

Although shifting to HEVs, PHEVs, and AEVs will reduce U.S. demand for gasoline (and thus oil imports), it will *not* necessarily reduce U.S. import dependence. The strategic materials and rare earth elements critical to current designs for advanced vehicles are neither mined nor refined in the United States today; they too will have to be imported, in increasing

TABLE 6-2. **Estimated 2030 Requirements for Cobalt and Neodymium in Successful Commercialization Scenarios for HEVs, PHEVs, and AEVs**[a]

Estimated sales (2030)	Global vehicle fleet (per year)	U.S. vehicle fleet (per year)
Total light-duty vehicles	72 million vehicles	15 million vehicles
HEVs, PHEVs, and AEVs	24 million vehicles	5 million vehicles
High-demand scenario (2030)		
Cobalt (5 kilograms per vehicle)	120,000 MT	25,000 MT
Neodymium (2 kilograms per vehicle)	48,000 MT	10,000 MT
Low-demand scenario (2030)		
Cobalt (0.5 kilogram per vehicle)	12,000 MT	2,500 MT
Neodymium (1 kilogram per vehicle)	24,000 MT	5,000 MT

a. Figures shown in this table are based on author's estimates that annual global sales of light-duty vehicles will increase from 70 million vehicles per year during the period April 2007–March 2008 to 72 million vehicles per year in 2030. Estimate for 2007–08 is based on data from Johnson Matthey (www.johnson-matthey.com/AR08/etd.html). Annual U.S. sales of light-duty vehicles are conservatively estimated by the author to decline and then level off at around 15 million light-duty vehicles per year in 2030. This is well below the DOE 2030 reference case projection of 20 million new domestic sales of light-duty vehicles presented in Department of Energy, Energy Information Administration, Annual Energy Outlook 2007 with Projections to 2030 (http://tonto.eia.doe.gov/ftproot/forecasting/0383(2007).pdf [December 31, 2008]). The author assumes that advanced vehicles will capture one-third of all new light-duty vehicle sales, both global and U.S., by 2030.
MT = metric tons.

volumes. Depending on which battery chemistries and power train configurations achieve substantial market penetration, this new import dependence may be quite extreme. In the case of certain materials—for example, cobalt and neodymium—rapid penetration of the U.S. light-duty vehicle market by HEVs, PHEVs, and AEVs could lead to extensive reliance on supplier countries whose governments are fragile and unstable or overtly hostile to the United States.

To investigate this issue, let us examine the materials requirements in two possible scenarios for successful commercialization of advanced vehicles. In both scenarios, the U.S. and world economies avoid major economic dislocations during the next two decades, despite continued high oil prices. Under those conditions, annual worldwide light-duty vehicle sales are conservatively estimated to reach 72 million vehicles in 2030, with U.S. sales of 15 million. Advanced vehicles are assumed to capture one-third of all new light-duty vehicle sales worldwide in 2030. Table 6-2 outlines a high-demand scenario and a low-demand scenario, illustrating in each scenario the author's estimates of U.S. and global requirements for cobalt and neodymium for advanced vehicle applications. In both of the scenarios, future demand for cobalt and neodymium depends strongly on the technologies chosen for batteries, electric motors, and other subsystems used in the vehicles. These two scenarios are used in the following sections to explore the implications of advanced vehicle deployment for future U.S. import dependence.

Sources and Availability of Cobalt

Cobalt is a strategic mineral and a heavy metal. It occurs naturally in low concentrations in the Earth's crust and is produced commercially as a by-product of extraction of other minerals, primarily nickel, copper, and arsenic. Global production of *raw* cobalt is dominated by copper mining operations in the Democratic Republic of Congo (DRC) and Zambia. Other large sources include nickel mining operations in Russia, China, Canada, Cuba, and Australia.[34] In 2007 worldwide production of raw cobalt was approximately 62,000 metric tons,[35] reflecting a decline of about 900 metric tons (MT) from 2005 to 2006 and a further decline of 5,000 MT from 2006 to 2007.[36] Part of the reason for the recent decline in world production was the deterioration of mining infrastructure in the DRC due to a violent civil war in the Shaba region, a conflict that has been under way since 1997. New deposits and potentially large sources of cobalt production have been identified in Cameroon, Australia, and Canada, but it may take many years for new mines to reach full-scale production in those locations.

The United States did not mine or refine cobalt in 2007.[37] Approximately 80 percent of U.S. cobalt consumption was derived from imports of *refined* cobalt, with the remainder coming from recycled scrap and sales from the government's strategic stockpiles. China is the world's largest refiner of cobalt ores. U.S. imports of refined cobalt and cobalt-containing products from China have increased steadily since 2003.[38] In 2007 the principal sources of refined cobalt imports to the United States were Norway (21 percent), Russia (19 percent), Finland (10 percent), and China (9 percent).[39] Table 6-3 shows where cobalt is mined or refined today and whether refinery capacities are increasing, decreasing, or likely to remain unchanged.

As market conditions evolved, the average world spot price for refined cobalt increased from nearly $11 per pound in 2003 to slightly more than $30 per pound in early 2007.[40] By December 2007, the spot price for refined cobalt had increased to about $40 per pound.[41] Recently, the world

TABLE 6-3. Countries Where Cobalt is Mined or Refined or Both and 2007 Estimated Production

Country	Mined	Refined	Approximate quantity (refined metric tons)[a]
Australia	✓	✓	3,400 ↑
Belgium		✓	2,850 ↓
Botswana	✓		
Brazil	✓	✓	900 ↓
Canada	✓	✓	5,000 ↑
China	✓	✓	12,700 →
Cuba	✓		
Finland		✓	8,600 ↑
France		✓	250 →
India		✓	1,200 →
Japan		✓	900 ↑
Morocco	✓	✓	1,400 ↓
New Caledonia	✓		
Norway		✓	5,000 →
Russia	✓	✓	4,700 →
Democratic Republic of Congo	✓	✓	600 ↓
Republic of South Africa	✓	✓	250 →
Uganda		✓	700 ↑
Zambia	✓	✓	5,000 ↓
Estimated total			53,450

Source: Cobalt Development Institute, "Cobalt Supply and Demand 2006," in *Cobalt Facts 2007* (Washington: Cobalt Development Institute, 2007).

a. Direction of arrows indicates whether production is estimated to increase (up), decrease (down), or remain the same (right).

market for cobalt has been as tight as the world oil market, despite rising metal prices. Although demand increased, availability of refined cobalt was slightly lower in 2007 (~53,500 MT) than in 2006 (~53,900 MT).[42]

How, then, might all this play out? In the high-demand scenario illustrated in table 6-2, successful commercialization of advanced vehicles leads to their capturing one-third of new light-duty vehicle sales. This scenario assumes that each advanced vehicle incorporates technology requiring 5 kilograms of cobalt; thus, incremental global demand for refined cobalt in HEVs, PHEVs, and AEVs reaches approximately 120,000 MT a year by 2030. This scenario suggests incremental U.S. demand for refined cobalt for advanced vehicles of approximately 25,000 MT in 2030. By contrast, the low-demand scenario assumes each advanced vehicle requires only 0.5 kilogram of cobalt. Thus, in the low-demand scenario, the implied global cobalt demand in 2030 for advanced vehicles is approximately 12,000 MT and the incremental U.S. demand for cobalt for these vehicles is 2,500 MT.

Global production of refined cobalt was approximately 53,000 MT in 2007. If we assume that all other cobalt demands remain unchanged, global cobalt production would have to more than triple by 2030 to meet incremental worldwide demand for cobalt for advanced vehicles in the high-demand scenario. Meeting just incremental U.S. cobalt demand in that scenario would require a nearly 50 percent increase above 2007 global cobalt production. The low-demand scenario—if all other demands for cobalt remain unchanged—would require expanding annual global cobalt production by about 23 percent of the 2007 level to meet world-wide demand for cobalt for advanced vehicles in 2030. In this scenario, meeting the needs for U.S. advanced vehicles alone would require less than a 5 percent increase above 2007 global cobalt production.

The cheapest Li-ion batteries and those closest to use in vehicle applications today incorporate LCO cells. Using LCO cells would lead to cobalt requirements similar to those illustrated in the high-demand scenario. However, some advanced lithium-ion chemistries currently under development for advanced vehicle applications would lead to much lower requirements.[43] Many of these alternative chemistries look extraordinarily promising and could reduce future U.S. cobalt imports.[44] Nonetheless, these alternative battery chemistries still face a number of engineering challenges related to battery lifetime, energy density, and ability to increase manufacturing output without raising production costs or reducing performance and reliability.[45]

The rate of growth in worldwide demand for refined cobalt has accelerated during the last few years and not only because of growing requirements for cobalt in rechargeable batteries. Other fast-growing applications include catalysts, anti-corrosion coatings, paint-drying additives, and super-alloys for turbine blades. The aggregate growth in cobalt demand is one explanation for the recent run-up in refined cobalt spot prices. If the future aggregate rate of growth in cobalt demand can be limited, then the projected price impacts and the possible implications for U.S. cobalt import dependence may be moderated.

Worldwide cobalt production can and will be increased. Nonetheless, it would be very difficult to meet the cobalt requirements of the high-demand scenario illustrated above. To meet global requirements in that scenario, much of the growth in cobalt mining and refining facilities would likely occur in countries where production could be expanded relatively quickly—China, Russia, Democratic Republic of Congo, Cuba, and Zambia. Needless to say, not all of these regimes are robust and thriving democracies, dedicated to the economic and environmental success of the United States. By contrast, in the low-demand scenario, expanded cobalt production from Canada, Australia, and Cameroon might be sufficient to meet incremental demand from advanced vehicles.

Sources and Availability of Neodymium

Current market conditions with respect to neodymium and other rare earth elements are similar to but perhaps more extreme than conditions in the cobalt market. The high-demand scenario illustrated in table 6-2 assumes that each advanced vehicle requires 2 kilograms of neodymium. In that scenario, incremental global demand for neodymium in HEVs, PHEVs, and AEVs reaches approximately 48,000 MT a year by 2030. In the same scenario, incremental U.S. neodymium demand for advanced vehicles reaches approximately 10,000 MT. By contrast, the low-demand scenario assumes that each vehicle requires 1 kilogram of neodymium. Thus, in the low-demand scenario, incremental global demand for neodymium in 2030 for HEVs, PHEVs, and AEVs is approximately 24,000 MT. Incremental U.S. neodymium demand reaches 5,000 MT.

Global neodymium production was approximately 7,300 MT in 2006.[46] If we assume that all other demands for neodymium remain unchanged, global production would have to increase more than five-fold in the high-demand scenario to meet incremental worldwide demand from advanced vehicles by 2030. Meeting just incremental U.S. neodymium demand in the high-demand scenario would require a 150 percent increase in annual global production. In the low-demand scenario—if all other demands remain unchanged—annual global neodymium production would have to more than triple the 2006 level by 2030 to meet worldwide demand from advanced vehicles. In the low-demand scenario, meeting the needs of U.S. advanced light-duty vehicles alone would require additional production equivalent to more than two-thirds of global output of neodymium in 2006.

Although such increases in world production are technically feasible, several factors suggest that they would be difficult to achieve in the near- to mid-term. Most global production of neodymium and other rare earth elements results from extraction of rare earth oxides (REOs). Extraction of REOs, unlike that of cobalt, is very concentrated geographically. Until the 1950s, most of the world's REO production occurred in India and Brazil.[47] Following the discovery of REO-rich monazite in South Africa, production shifted to that country.[48] In the 1970s and 1980s, global production was dominated by REO output from the large open-pit mine at Mountain Pass, California, which closed in 1998 for environmental and economic reasons.[49] Molycorp Minerals LLC purchased the Mountain Pass mine in September 2008 and plans to resume production of didymium at the site as soon as possible, but that will not increase neodymium supplies in the near term.[50] Currently, more than 95 percent of global REO production takes place in one country, the People's Republic of China.[51] Most Chinese REOs are extracted from the bastnaesite ores of Inner Mongolia, which are especially rich in neodymium.[52]

Significant deposits of REO-containing minerals have been found in a number of other countries, including Canada and the United States. But to increase production of rare earth elements at the rate implied by the high-demand scenario for neodymium would seem to depend strongly on the willingness of the Chinese government to increase current levels of output and to expand exports significantly. Recent events suggest that that may be unlikely. In 2008 Beijing stopped issuing permits to export any rare earth elements after domestic Chinese demand equaled current output levels. The export ban was imposed despite a recent run-up in the world price for neodymium and other rare earth metals.[53]

Global demand for neodymium will be affected by factors other than the commercial production of advanced automobiles. For example, Nd-Fe-B magnets are attractive and cost effective in a variety of other applications due to their outstanding magnetic properties, ease of manufacture, and relatively low cost. Nd-Fe-B magnets have found widespread use in non-automotive applications, including "stepper" motors for computer hard disk drives, speaker "cones" for in-ear headphones used with Ipods and other MP3 players, and even electric bicycles. One may reasonably expect that future demand for hard magnets will be driven not only by the growth in demand for advanced vehicles but also by their increasing use in non-automotive applications. Global competition for neodymium supplies is likely to be complicated by the growing demand for neodymium in applications ranging from colored phosphors used in LCD screens, colorants used in enamel coatings, and the optical amplifiers required for lasers.

Alternative materials exist for all hard magnet applications (including vehicles), although the alternatives generally have somewhat higher cost and lower performance.[54] Magnets based on samarium-cobalt alloys probably are the most attractive alternatives for use in advanced vehicles. (Samarium also is a rare earth element.) However, substitution of samarium-cobalt magnets in these applications would probably increase the cost for electric motors, regenerative braking systems, and steering-assist devices in the vehicles. In addition, it would increase global cobalt demand.

Mineral deposits containing mixtures of REOs exist in Canada, Australia, and the United States. Several could be developed over the next five to ten years. At today's high prices, promising locations include California's old Mountain Pass mine; a remote site in Saskatchewan, Canada, where a large deposit has been found alongside Hoidas Lake; and at several sites in Australia.[55] It would be difficult at best to bring new production from these sites online fast enough to meet the growing demand for neodymium or samarium in either the high- or the low-demand scenarios described above. A recent U.S. Geological Survey analysis concludes that China will dominate global production of rare earth elements in the near- to mid-term due to the favorable number, size, and elemental composition of Chinese REO deposits; much lower Chinese labor and regulatory costs; China's access to the continually expanding Asian electronics and manufacturing sectors; and the ongoing environmental and regulatory problems at Mountain Pass.[56]

In a world of tight supplies and rising prices for cobalt, neodymium, and other rare earth elements, the technologies developed for electric storage batteries, electric motors, regenerative braking systems, and other critical components of advanced vehicles could have big impacts on strategic competition among the United States, China, Japan, Russia, Korea, India, and the European Union. Making smart choices among the technology options available today or just over the horizon may help to reduce tomorrow's risk of dangerous geopolitical competition for scarce resources.

Hidden Dangers: Health and Safety Issues

Traditional LCO batteries are likely to be the first to market in advanced HEVs, PHEVs, and AEVs.[57] The structure of LCO batteries makes them very vulnerable to internal electrical short circuits, which can occur when a cell's separator membrane is squeezed or the battery case is punctured. Ignition or explosion also can occur, under some conditions, in the event of too-rapid discharge or overcharging during battery recharge.

Fire. One of the principal concerns about LCO batteries in vehicles is their potential to ignite or explode in a collision.[58] If battery cells experience a short circuit following a collision, a highly exothermic chemical reaction can be initiated within the cells, causing cell temperature to increase rapidly. If the process is not interrupted quickly, the cell can undergo what is called "thermal runaway," ultimately bursting into flames and often exploding. This type of failure sequence destroyed many laptop computer batteries and caused Sony Corporation to recall 3.5 million batteries in 2007.[59]

Injury. Fires resulting from thermal runaway in LCO cells are especially dangerous if they occur in a closed vehicle carrying fuel and passengers. Because combustion is fed with oxygen generated from the chemical reaction within the cell, the flames can be difficult to extinguish. In addition, once the failure sequence has started, inadvertent heating of adjacent cells in the battery pack can reinitiate thermal runaway, even after the fire in the first failed cell has been put out.

Exposure. The unusual characteristics of LCO battery fires may create special hazards and therefore require special training for first responders, who would be called upon to extinguish fires resulting from collisions involving advanced vehicles containing LCO batteries. The same characteristics will drive development of new standards for special fire-extinguishing compounds to be carried on fire engines or other rescue vehicles. They should lead to new protocols on when to use self-contained breathing apparatus during a vehicle rescue operation so as to avoid first responders' exposure to aerosols of fine metal particles emitted from burning batteries.

Risk Reduction

Several manufacturers have recently claimed that their proprietary Li-ion battery technology has addressed the problem of thermal runaway and eliminated the risk of fires from hybrid-vehicle batteries. Tesla Motors, which probably will be the first to bring a new AEV to market,[60] employs an active, highly redundant, battery management system coupled to the 6000+ LCO cells employed in the Tesla Roadster. Tesla claims that its system makes a fire due to battery failure extremely unlikely. The Massachusetts-based company A123, which will provide batteries for the Chevrolet Volt PHEV, argues that its nanophosphate LFP battery is inherently safe with respect to thermal runaway. A123 claims that LFP chemistry eliminates any buildup of excess lithium at the cell's graphite cathode, making it unlikely that lithium plating will occur during any overcharging episode and thus reducing the probability of an internal short circuit that could lead to thermal runaway. Other manufacturers, including 3M and Johnson Controls-SAFT, make similar claims for their NMC and NCA battery chemistries.

The Federal Role in Development of HEVs, PHEVs, and AEVs

The choice of battery and electric motor technologies for advanced HEVs, PHEVs, and AEVs can strongly affect the cost and resulting market penetration rates for these vehicles. Furthermore, technology choices have important implications for U.S. import dependence and will affect the character of the health and safety risks associated with advanced vehicles.

The federal government should work with vehicle manufacturers and battery producers to achieve the best long-term solution for U.S. environmental interests and national security. Its role is especially important if federal policies provide subsidies or other incentives to accelerate market uptake. The federal government must balance the desire to accelerate commercialization of HEVs, PHEVs, and AEVs with the necessity to encourage automakers and battery manufacturers to make smart choices among technology alternatives—choices that will advance U.S. environmental and security interests. Subsidizing development of the cheapest options—or the first alternatives to reach the commercial market—is not necessarily the best long-term solution for the nation.

The Environmental Protection Agency, Department of Energy, Department of Transportation, Federal Highway Safety Administration, and Federal Transportation Safety Board should develop consistent testing procedures and coordinate their efforts to set standards for battery safety and performance as well as standards for electric motors, regenerative braking systems, and steering-assist units. To the extent practical, government policies should discourage increased dependence on exotic or strategic materials for which the United States must rely excessively or exclusively on imports. The associated standards should encourage recapture, reuse, and recycling of all exotic materials in order to maximize their value to the U.S. economy.

Many governments—including those of Japan, Korea, and China—have designated production of advanced batteries as a strategic industry. They seek to establish global dominance in the advanced battery industry and are willing to subsidize its domestic development; they therefore will go to great lengths to ensure access to critical inputs for their companies. Understanding the global trajectory of industry development will require increased federal attention to smuggling and to global trade in illegal materials. In addition, particular attention should be paid to efforts by the Chinese government and Chinese industrial groups to corner the market in strategic minerals in Africa.

Lisa Margonelli has suggested that federal policy could encourage U.S. automakers or electric utilities to become the permanent owners of the batteries used in advanced vehicles. She argues that federal policy should require the companies to recycle or reuse the batteries when they are no longer fit for use in vehicles. Doing so, she observes, could completely change the economics of the battery business, making it worthwhile for U.S. battery manufacturers to develop a cradle-to-cradle design philosophy, investing in more expensive—but easily recyclable—designs that pose lower risks to the economy and the environment. Such an approach could improve U.S. battery manufacturers' competitive position with respect to their Japanese, Korean, and Chinese counterparts, even though their foreign competitors are directly subsidized by their governments and may treat vehicle batteries as "throwaway" commodities.[61]

Conclusions: Look before You Leap

This preliminary assessment regarding advanced vehicles leads to several principal conclusions:

—HEVs, PHEVs, and AEVs can play a significant role in addressing U.S. oil import dependence, but some vehicle development paths may lead to important vehicle safety issues and create new forms of import dependence.

—It would be extraordinarily prudent now, during the earliest stages of commercial development of advanced vehicles, to examine those risks systematically and from a systemic perspective. Such an analysis could stimulate the design of thoughtful and flexible policies that have the lowest likelihood of creating dangerous future safety and import-dependence problems.

—To the extent possible, concurrent initiatives to provide subsidies or other incentives for accelerating commercialization of advanced vehicles should avoid promoting technologies that would exacerbate potential future problems.

—Efforts made now to establish adequate federal standards for performance and recycling of HEV, PHEV, and AEV batteries as well as other power train components could reduce future risk of import dependence and avoid negative environmental impacts from the widespread deployment of advanced vehicles.

If efforts to "look before you leap" are not undertaken now, the United States could replace its dangerous current dependence on foreign oil with a new dependence on unstable or hostile foreign governments to supply strategic materials and rare earth elements to the U.S. transportation sector. Furthermore, dependence on first-generation lithium-ion batteries could increase the probability of a few spectacular and fatal collisions that might significantly dampen consumer acceptance of the broader family of advanced vehicle technologies that might be developed down the road. To best facilitate commercialization of advanced HEVs, PHEVs, and AEVs, the federal government must set strong standards to ensure the safety of advanced vehicles and to encourage the development of vehicle technologies that will advance the energy and security interests of the United States.

None of these potential safety and import dependence risks need be a "show stopper" for advanced vehicle development. Federal agencies can work together to fashion adequate policies and standards, thereby avoiding the worst outcomes. But if we fail to address those risks now, giving them the careful attention that they require, then we collectively "roll the dice," having done nothing more than hope that everything works out for the best.

Notes

1. Roland Chavasse, "Developments in Hybrid Vehicles and Their Potential Influence on Minor Metals," paper presented at Minor Metal Trade Association Conference, Lisbon, Portugal, 2005 (www.evworld.com/library/hybrids_minormetals.pdf [December 17, 2008]).

2. See, for example, A. Hammami, N. Raymond, and Michel Armand, "Lithium-Ion Batteries: Runaway Risk of Forming Toxic Compounds," *Nature* 424 (August 7, 2003): 635–36.

3. Amy Raskin and Saurin Shah, "The Emergence of Hybrid Vehicles: Ending Oil's Stranglehold on Transportation and the Economy," Alliance Bernstein, June 2006 (www.calcars.org and www.alliancebernstein.com).

4. University of Birmingham, *Magnetic Materials: Hard Magnets* (2008) (www.magnets.bham.ac.uk/magnetic_materials/hard_magnets.htm).

5. Raskin and Shah, "The Emergence of Hybrid Vehicles."

6. Chavasse, "Developments in Hybrid Vehicles and Their Potential Influence on Minor Metals."

7. Ibid.

8. The energy density of a battery is a measure of the storage capacity of the device per unit weight; it is usually reported in watt-hours per kilogram (Wh/kg). The power density of a battery measures how much power the device can deliver per unit weight; it is usually reported in watts per kilogram (W/kg).

9. Don Hillebrand, testimony before the U.S. House of Representatives Subcommittee on Energy and Water Development, *Overview Hearing on Gas Prices and Vehicle Technology*, 110 Cong., 2 sess., February 14, 2008.

10. Ibid.

11. Ibid.

12. "In Search of the Perfect Battery," *The Economist*, March 6, 2008 (www.economist.com/PrinterFriendly.cfm?story_id=10789409).

13. "In 2007, China Surpassed Japan for the First Time in Li-Ion Battery Production," SmartBrief, July 25, 2008 (www.smartbrief.com/news/aaaa/industryBW-detail.jsp?id=AF93B80E-02D6-4EA0-9198-15EB4C1FBBAC).

14. Don Cox, "How I Fell in Love with the Tesla Roadster," November 15, 2006 (www.teslamotors.com/blog5/?p=37).

15. Michel Armand and J-M. Tarascon, "Building Better Batteries," *Nature* 451 (February 7, 2008): 653.

16. Alan Madian and others, *U.S. Plug-in Hybrid and U.S. Light-Duty Vehicle Data Book* (Washington: LECG Inc., 2008).

17. Chavasse, "Developments in Hybrid Vehicles and Their Potential Influence on Minor Metals."

18. Michael Renner, "Vehicle Production Rises, but Few Cars Are 'Green,'" Worldwatch Institute, May 21, 2008 (www.worldwatch.org/node/5461).

19. A. P. Bandivadekar, "Evaluating the Impact of Advanced Vehicle and Fuel Technologies in U.S. Light-Duty Vehicle," Ph.D. dissertation, Massachusetts Institute of Technology, February 2008.

20. Ibid.

21. Green Car Congress, "GM Dedicates $400m Global Powertrain Engineering Development Center," July 25, 2008 (www.greencarcongress.com/vehicle_manufacturers/index.html).

22. International Energy Agency, *World Energy Outlook* (Paris: 2004); see also L. Fulton and G. Eads, "IEA Model Documentation and Reference Case Projection," IEA, July 2004.

23. Sherman J. Glass Jr., "Sharing Perspectives on the Global Petrochemical Industry," presentation to the CMAI World Petrochemical Conference, March 21, 2007; and Jason Hammer, "The Outlook for Energy: A View to 2030," presentation to the Texas Energy Council, March 6, 2008.

24. "A Survey of Cars in Emerging Markets," *The Economist*, November 13, 2008 (www.economist.com/specialreports/displaystory.cfm?story_id=12544947).

25. Hillebrand, testimony before the U.S. House of Representatives Subcommittee on Energy and Water Development.

26. Edmunds Inside Line, "Toyota's Ambitious Green Initiative Includes Plug-in Hybrid Vehicle for U.S. by 2010"(www.edmunds.com/insideline/do/News/articleId=126966).

27. Raskin and Shah, "The Emergence of Hybrid Vehicles"; Hillebrand, testimony before the U.S. House of Representatives Subcommittee on Energy and Water Development.

28. Hillebrand, testimony before the U.S. House of Representatives Subcommittee on Energy and Water Development.

29. Chavasse, "Developments in Hybrid Vehicles and Their Potential Influence on Minor Metals."

30. IEA, *World Energy Outlook*, as cited in Raskin and Shah, "The Emergence of Hybrid Vehicles."

31. Energy Information Administration, "Annual Energy Outlook Analyses: Advanced Technologies for Light-Duty Vehicles," 2006 (www.eia.doe.gov/oiaf/aeo/otheranalysis/aeo_2006analysispapers/atldv.html).

32. Raskin and Shah, "The Emergence of Hybrid Vehicles."

33. See, for example, G. Luft, testimony before the U.S. Senate Foreign Relations Committee on Near Eastern and South Asian Affairs, "America's Oil Dependence and Its Implications for U.S. Middle East Policy," October 20, 2005; R. James Woolsey and Anne Korin, *Turning Oil into Salt*, National Review Online, September 25, 2007 (http://article.nationalreview.com/?q=OTlmMjFjYWRjOWI3ZGI0MzUxZDJjYTBlMmUzOTc2Mzc=).

34. Idaho Cobalt Project, "Cobalt Uses," based on information compiled from the 2005 International Conference Proceedings on the Cobalt Industry and from "Cobalt Facts Update" (Cobalt Development Institute) (www.idahocobalt.com/s/CobaltUses.asp [December 17, 2008]).

35. U.S. Geological Survey, *Mineral Commodity Summaries: Cobalt*, January 2008.

36. Cobalt Development Institute, "Cobalt Supply and Demand 2006," in *Cobalt Facts 2007* (Washington: Cobalt Development Institute, 2007).

37. U.S. Geological Survey, *Mineral Commodity Summaries: Cobalt,* January 2008.

38. Ibid.

39. Ibid.

40. Cobalt Development Institute, "Cobalt Supply and Demand 2006."

41. U.S. Geological Survey, *Mineral Commodity Summaries: Cobalt*, January 2008.

42. Geovic Mining Corporation, *Cobalt Mining and Cobalt Demand* (www.geovic.net/about_cobalt.php).

43 Madian and others, *U.S. Plug-in Hybrid and U.S. Light-Duty Vehicle Data Book*.

44. Ibid.

45. J. Axsen, A. Burke, and K. Kurani, "Batteries for Plug-in Hybrid Electric Vehicles (PHEVs): Goals and the State of Technology" UCD-ITS-RR-08-14, May 2008 (pubs.its.ucdavis.edu/download_pdf.php?id=1169).

46. P. Campbell, "Supply and Demand, Part 1: Neodymium," *Magnetics Business and Technology*, December 2007–January 2008 (www.magnetweb.com/Col04.htm).

47. E. R. Rose, "Rare Earths of the Grenville Sub-Province Ontario and Quebec," GSC Report 59_10 (Ottawa: Geological Survey of Canada, Department of Mines and Technical Surveys, 1960).

48. Ibid.

49. S. Kohler, "California's Non-Fuel Mineral Production: 2001" (Sacramento: California Geological Survey, 2002).

50. Antara News, "Molycorp Closes on Purchase of Mountain Pass Rare Earth Mining Ops," October 16, 2008 (www.antara.co.id/en/arc/2008/10/16/molycorp-closes-on-purchase-of-mountain-pass-rare-earth-mining-ops/ [December 17, 2008]).

51. D. Lague, "China Corners Market in High-Tech Necessity," *International Herald Tribune*, January 22, 2006 (www.iht.com/articles/2006/01/22/business/rare.php?page=1).

52. G. Haxel, J. Hedrick , and J. Orris, "Rare Earth Elements Critical Resources for High Technology," USGS Fact Sheet: 087_02 (Reston, Va.: U.S. Geological Survey, 2006).

53. Campbell, "Supply and Demand, Part 1."

54. Cost comparison available online at Total Magnetic Solutions, "Samarium Cobalt" (www.magnetsales.com/SMCO/Smco1.htm#comparisonndfeb).

55. Great Western Minerals Corporation, "Where Are Rare Earth Elements Found?" (www.gwmg.ca/rare-earths/faq).

56. Haxel, Hedrick , and Orris, "Rare Earth Elements Critical Resources for High Technology."

57. Tesla Motors, "Now in Production: The Tesla Roadster" (www.teslamotors.com). See also Rick Popely, "2008 Shaping Up to Be the Year of the Plug-In," *Chicago Tribune*, February 16, 2008, for discussion of the AFS Trinity hybrid (www.venturacountystar.com/news/2008/feb/16/2008-shaping-up-to-be-the-year-of-the-plug-in/).

58. Kevin Bullis, "Are Lithium-Ion Electric Cars Safe?" in *Technology Review*, August 3, 2006 (www.technologyreview.com/read_article.aspx?id=17250).

59. For a short YouTube video clip illustrating thermal runaway, see "Notebook Battery Fire at PC Pitstop.com" (www.justlaptopbattery.com/news/notebook-battery-fire-at-pc-pitstop/).

60. Tesla Motors, "Now in Production." See also Andrew Chu, "Nanophosphate Lithium-Ion Technology for Transportation Applications," Twenty-Third Electric Vehicle Symposium, Anaheim, California, December 2007.

61. Private communication in 2008 from Lisa Margonelli, an Irvine Fellow at the New America Foundation.

PART **III**

Policies

Current Federal Authorized Programs on Plug-In Hybrids, Battery Electric Vehicles, and Related Efforts

DEAN TAYLOR

Plug-in electric vehicles have emerged as a major policy focus in Congress and in the 2008 presidential election. This chapter traces the emergence of plug-in vehicle programs and recent legislative activity to establish a comprehensive guide to federal policy on plug-in transportation. The chapter details more than forty existing provisions, including tax breaks and other consumer and fleet purchase incentives; manufacturing incentives; authorizations for research, development, and demonstrations; and programs for other types of electric vehicles and electric transportation issues (buses, trains, forklifts and electrification of truck stops and shipping ports). The chapter also details recent regulations, executive orders, and appropriations; identifies several provisions that did not make it through the conference committee into the Energy Independence and Security Act of 2007; and lists several federal electric vehicle (EV) incentives from the 1990s that have expired.

Plug-in hybrid electric vehicle (PHEV) and battery electric vehicle (BEV) provisions in existing law date back to the 1992 Energy Policy Act (EPAct), but the bulk of new law on plug-in vehicle technology did not emerge until the 2005 Energy Policy Act (EPAct 2005), the 2007 Energy Independence and Security Act (EISA), and the 2008 Emergency Economic Stabilization Act (EESA).[1]

EPAct 2005

While there were many provisions for electric drive transportation in the House- and Senate-passed versions of the 2005 energy bill, tax credits for BEVs and electric vehicle infrastructure as well as several authorizations were rejected in the conference committee and not included in EPAct 2005. PHEVs were mentioned for the first time in three sections of EPAct 2005 (sections 911, 706, and 915). The first specific mention of PHEVs in an energy bill's authorization for research and development was in section 911.[2] Section 706 authorizes a demonstration program for flexible-fuel PHEVs, and section 915 authorizes a program on secondary use of EV and PHEV batteries. Plug-in vehicles first appeared in the tax code in the credit for qualified battery electric vehicles in 1992 and as part of the alternative fuel vehicle infrastructure tax deduction. Those tax breaks expired at the end of 2006, and new tax breaks for PHEVs and BEVs were established in EESA in 2008.

EPAct 2005 did establish tax credits for hybrid vehicles. Section 1341 creates a tax credit that includes all types of hybrid EVs, including light-, medium-, and heavy-duty PHEVs, although they are not explicitly mentioned. However, it is unlikely that PHEVs will be commercially available before the credit expires in 2009. Hybrid vehicles or conventional vehicles converted with an after-market kit do not qualify for the credit. In addition, the tax credit sliding scale (based on fuel economy benefits) is designed to give the most reward to the best traditional hybrid EVs (no-plug design). Thus PHEVs receive no extra benefit for their all-electric miles and concomitant additional societal benefits.

Senator Orrin Hatch (R-Utah) was the author of a stand-alone bill creating hybrid credits (the CLEAR ACT) and a leading proponent of EPAct 2005, section 1341. He worked extensively with the Electric Drive Transportation Association (EDTA), other alternative fuel groups, and environmental groups on this provision. Because BEVs are not included and PHEVs are not appropriately recognized in EPAct 2005 tax credits, Senator Hatch continued the effort in subsequent Congresses, along with EDTA and others, to establish follow-on legislation, with Senator Maria Cantwell (D- Wash.) and Senator Barack Obama (D-Ill.), that addresses those omissions.[3] That effort ultimately succeeded with the signing of EESA in October 2008.

While electric drive vehicles had gained significant attention from the utility industry by 2005, they had not yet gained the attention of the president, automakers, or Congress. The omission of substantial support for emerging electric vehicle technologies contributed to the interest in revisiting energy policy in later sessions of Congress. Many technology and policy factors led to the passage of the Energy Independence and Security Act in December 2007. Constituent pressure due to concerns over high oil prices and climate change was a major factor. Typically a decade or more can pass before a new omnibus energy bill is passed, but EISA 2007 was signed only twenty-eight months after EPAct 2005.

The change in congressional leadership after the 2006 midterm elections also had a favorable impact on the advanced technology agenda. Electric drive was not a partisan issue, however; President Bush gave more than twenty speeches in 2006 and 2007 calling for PHEV programs and incentives. In that same time frame, automobile and battery manufacturers began announcing production goals and showing increased interest in new policies to accelerate technology development. A significant milestone in automobile manufacturers' public commitment to plug-in development came with GM's announcement of plans for its extended-range BEV (the Chevy Volt) and its plug-in hybrid (Saturn Vue) in January 2007.

Many bills were introduced in 2006, 2007, and 2008 to encourage use of electric drive vehicles, and many interest groups supported those efforts. This chapter goes into detail on the sponsors and major supporters of each provision. The Electric Drive Transportation Association is the major advocacy group supporting electric drive legislation at the national level.[4] In the end, the sponsors of the DRIVE Act (Dependence Reduction through Innovation in Vehicles and Energy Act), who worked to add their electric provisions in at least seven committee votes and one Senate floor vote, were the most successful in securing provisions in EISA. The DRIVE Act, which had more than twenty sponsors in the Senate—including senators Evan Bayh (D-Ind.), Joseph Lieberman (I-Conn.), Sam Brownback (R-Kan.), Norm Coleman (R-Minn.), and Ken Salazar (D-Colo.) as the leadership team—was introduced in the 110th Congress as S. 339; it was introduced as HR 670 in the House, with more than sixty bipartisan sponsors led by representatives Eliot Engel (D-N.Y.) and Jack Kingston (R-Ga.).[5] The Set America Free coalition worked closely with the DRIVE Act sponsors on the entire bill,

while the ad hoc PHEV and BEV coalition worked closely with the sponsors on the plug-in vehicle and other electric transportation sections of
the bill.[6] The ad hoc PHEV and BEV coalition, led by Southern California Edison, eventually included more than forty firms and associations,
including utilities, business groups such as the Edison Electric Institute
and Silicon Valley Leadership Group, and others.[7]

2007 Energy Independence and Security Act

EISA includes more than $500 million in authorizations for PHEVs,
BEVs, and related electric transportation programs as well as six new
manufacturing incentives and a substantial increase in the federal fuel
economy standards. A summary of EISA's major provisions follows.

Section 641 authorizes six research and development programs on
energy storage competitiveness, including energy storage R&D on electric
drive vehicles (light-, medium-, and heavy-duty and non-road), stationary
applications, and electricity transmission and distribution.

—basic research: $50 million a year for ten years
—applied research: $80 million a year for ten years
—energy storage centers: $100 million a year for ten years to translate
basic research into applications in electric drive vehicles, stationary applications, and electricity transmission and distribution
—stationary energy storage systems demonstrations: $30 million a
year for ten years
—vehicle energy storage systems demonstrations: $30 million a year
for ten years
—secondary applications and disposal: $5 million a year for ten years.

Section 131(b) authorizes $90 million a year for five years for a plug-
in electric drive vehicle demonstration program, including grants for
light-, medium-, and heavy-duty demonstrations of plug-in hybrid electric
vehicles and battery electric vehicles.

Section 109 extends until 2019 a special bonus credit under the federal
fuel economy laws—commonly known as CAFE (corporate average fuel
economy) laws—for dual-fuel vehicles such as PHEVs. Under current regulations, a PHEV with a ten-mile all-electric range receives the same
bonus CAFE credit as a PHEV with a sixty-mile all-electric range.

Section 132 creates a domestic manufacturing conversion program for
grants to automakers and suppliers and manufacturers of hybrid vehicle

components to encourage domestic production of BEVs, PHEVs, hybrid electric vehicles (HEVs), and advanced diesel vehicles.

Section 136 creates an advanced technology vehicle manufacturing incentive program that authorizes loans of up to $25 billion, and a grant program for engineering integration, equipment investment, or part of the cost of creating advanced vehicle and associated component manufacturing facilities. BEVs and PHEVs qualify.

Section 134 authorizes loan guarantees for manufacturers of fuel-efficient automobiles and parts, including BEVs and PHEVs.

Section 135 authorizes loan guarantees for construction of facilities to manufacture advanced vehicle batteries and battery systems that are developed and produced in the United States, including lithium-ion batteries, hybrid electrical systems, component manufacturing, and software design.

Overview of Existing Incentives for Consumers and Fleets

Section 131(b) of EISA authorizes a competitive grant program for projects to encourage the use of PHEVs and BEVs (light-, medium-, and heavy-duty) and other emerging electric vehicle technologies. Specifically, it authorizes $90 million a year for the years 2008 through 2012, with not less than one-third of that amount to be available to local and municipal governments. The program establishes other grant-making priorities, reporting requirements, and cost-sharing requirements. Senator Salazar and Representative Engel led the DRIVE Act team that introduced the amendments for this section in committee. Interest groups behind this section included the ad hoc PHEV and BEV coalition and EDTA.

Section 131(c) requires the Department of Energy (DOE), in consultation with the Environmental Protection Agency (EPA) and the Department of Transportation (DOT), to establish a near-term program of grants for "qualified electric transportation projects" (non-road projects covering goods and services such as electric forklifts, truck stop electrification, port electrification, electric material- and cargo-handling equipment, electric truck refrigeration units, electric or dual-mode electric rail, and various types of related infrastructure). Priority is given to large-scale projects and aggregators. Specifically, section 131(c) authorizes $95 million a year from 2008 to 2013. This provision derived from the efforts of the ad hoc PHEV and BEV coalition and EDTA. It was sponsored by Senator Salazar (of the

DRIVE Act team) in committee and on the floor and by Representative Engel in committee.

Fleet Mandate Reforms

EPAct 1992 established requirements for federal government, state government, and alternative fuel provider fleets to purchase a certain percentage of alternative fuel vehicles for their light-duty fleets in most areas.[8] Alternative fuel provider fleets typically include those of electric and natural gas utilities. EPAct 1992 also allows DOE to require privately owned fleets and local government fleets to purchase alternative fuel vehicles, but DOE has opted not to do so several times. Use of battery electric vehicles to comply with fleet requirements has been allowed since 1992; however, the reforms detailed below also allow use of other types of electric drive vehicles such as PHEVs and hybrid EVs to comply. One shortcoming of the EPAct 1992 requirements was that they applied solely to the acquisition of the vehicles, not to their actual use, except for alternative fuel provider fleets. In practice, most flex-fuel vehicles were run on gasoline because E-85 was not generally available. Subsequent reform efforts have attempted to incorporate a performance element to such mandates.

EPAct 1992 requires federal fleets to ensure that 75 percent of the new vehicles that they acquire are alternative fuel vehicles. In addition, Executive Order 13149 (1999) states that they also had to develop and implement a strategy to reduce their petroleum use by 20 percent of FY 1999 levels by FY 2005.[9] Specific requirements include use of alternative fuel in alternative fuel vehicles the majority of the time that the vehicles are in operation and an increase in the average combined fuel economy of newly acquired light-duty vehicles of at least 1 mile per gallon by FY 2002 and 3 miles per gallon by FY 2005. In addition, Executive Order 13031 provides additional credit (two credits to one vehicle) for each zero-emission vehicle in federal fleets. During the Bush administration, an executive order issued on January 24, 2007, includes requirements for federal agencies to reduce their greenhouse gas consumption by 3 percent annually, reduce their fleet's petroleum consumption by 2 percent annually, increase their fleet's use of nonpetroleum fuel by 10 percent annually, and purchase PHEVs when they become commercially available.[10]

Section 703 of EPAct 2005 gives state government fleets and alternative fuel provider fleets a new option for compliance based on the option's ability to reduce petroleum use.[11] A fleet may use that option for all or part of its EPAct requirements. Examples of eligible technologies under section 703 are the dedicated alternative fuel technologies used in the historical EPAct fleet mandates as well as many other petroleum-reducing technologies, such as traditional hybrid electric vehicles, vehicle downsizing, PHEVs, and vehicles with cylinder deactivation. Infrastructure is not eligible, and non-road alternative fuel technologies are not eligible in most cases. Other environmental considerations are not part of this compliance option, which is separate from the traditional EPAct credits under the original EPAct 1992 as modified by EISA section 133. It also is separate from the special credit program for biodiesel.[12] The origins of this provision date back to about 2001 and the efforts of Senate staff to respond to industry concerns. A different provision presented by Senator Ron Wyden (D-Ore.) and supported by EDTA was rejected in conference committee.

Currently under EPAct, 90 percent of new light-duty vehicles purchased by a utility must be alternative fuel vehicles and must use the alternative fuel if available.[13] Penalties for noncompliance are civil penalties of $5,000 per violation, criminal fines of $10,000 per willful violation, and a criminal fine of $50,000 for willful and repeated violations. The Department of Energy currently is working on additional enforcement efforts for other fleets that are subject to EPAct compliance requirements. Substantial changes in the EPAct fleet requirements as well as new requirements were established in EISA and EPAct 2005, including the following:

—Section 133 of EISA adds PHEVs, hybrid EVs, and other types of electric drive vehicles to existing fleet mandates in EPAct 1992.

—Section 703 of EPAct 2005 adds a compliance alternative to the existing fleet mandates in EPAct 1992 that benefits electric drive as well as other options.

—Sections 141 and 142 of EISA amend existing mandates on federal government fleets.

Section 133 of EISA revises fleet requirements under section 508 of EPAct 2005 to explicitly include the following investments as eligible for EPAct credits: purchase of non-road electric vehicles, investment in alternative fuel infrastructure, purchase of traditional hybrid electric vehicles (light-, medium-, and heavy-duty), purchase of PHEVs (light-, medium-, and heavy-duty), purchase of neighborhood EVs (which are low-speed vehicles), and purchase of fuel cell EVs. DOE is directed to allocate credits for acquisition of these vehicles and investments by 2009. In addition,

DOE can grant between one and five credits for investment in emerging vehicle technologies that reduce petroleum demand and emissions; various sizes of PHEVs, BEVs, HEVs, and fuel cell EVs are expected to benefit from these credits. Section 133 authorizes such sums as are necessary for 2008 through 2013. No rulemaking has been announced. The ad hoc PHEV and BEV coalition and EDTA were the main advocates for this provision. Senator Salazar introduced the floor amendment that created section 133; in the House, Representative Tammy Baldwin (D-Wis.) introduced this section in subcommittee.

Section 141 of EISA amends section 303 of EPAct 1992 to require that all federal agency vehicle purchases of light- or medium-duty vehicles be "low greenhouse gas–emitting vehicles," as determined by EPA. Exceptions are made when the agency certifies that no such vehicle that meets the agency's needs is available and when the agency has taken more cost-effective alternative measures to reduce petroleum consumption that will result in equal or greater reductions in greenhouse gas emissions.

Section 142 of EISA directs that federal fleet regulations be issued to require federal fleets, beginning in 2010, to reduce petroleum consumption and increase alternative fuel consumption enough so that by 2015 and every year afterward each agency achieves a 20 percent reduction in petroleum consumption and a 10 percent increase in alternative fuel consumption, using 2005 levels as the baseline. Plug-in electric vehicles are one of many options. This provision is similar to an amendment introduced by Senator Ted Stevens (R-Alaska) and adopted on the floor.[14]

Additional Fleet Programs

Section 706 of EPAct 2005 creates a grant program to commercialize traditional HEVs and PHEVs that also are flex-fuel vehicles.[15] Preference is given to proposals that achieve the greatest reduction in petroleum consumption, achieve not less than 250 miles per gallon, and have the greatest potential for commercialization within five years. Senator Obama sponsored this section in committee. This section authorizes a total of $40 million from 2006 through 2009, but no funds have ever been appropriated for the program.

Section 721 of EPAct 2005 authorizes $200 million a year for an advanced fleet vehicle pilot program administered under Clean Cities that many technologies qualify for. Many types of BEVs and PHEVs, including non-road EVs and electric bikes, Segways, and scooters qualify. Representative Boehlert (now retired) sponsored this section, which EDTA and other alternative fuel groups advocated.

Section 741 of EPAct 2005 authorizes grants for a clean school bus program; section 742 authorizes grants for a diesel truck fleet modernization program; and sections 791 through 797 authorize a diesel emission reduction grant and loan program for fleet vehicles. BEVs and PHEVs are examples of qualified technology in all three programs.

There are a number of federal efforts, including grants for the use of alternative fuel vehicles at the airport and in airline-owned fleets.[16] EDTA has long advocated for such programs.

Overview of Existing Incentives for Manufacturers

The Energy Independence and Security Act of 2007 contains a number of programs intended to help manufacturers meet new regulatory requirements and to establish domestic capacity in advanced technology vehicles and components.

Section 109 allows PHEVs and other dual-fuel vehicles to qualify for an additional compliance credit under CAFE laws until 2019.[17] Prior to EISA, this credit for dual-fuel vehicles was set to expire in 2008. The credit in effect gives alternative fuel vehicles, including electric vehicles and plug-in hybrid vehicles, a much higher mile-per-gallon (mpg) rating than they would have otherwise.[18] For example, an electric vehicle can receive a 300+ mpg credit, based on a formula under which electric miles from off-board sources are given a special petroleum equivalency factor of 82,049 watt hours per gallon rather than 33,400 watt hours per gallon, which is used in many other formulas, such as that used in the Society of Automotive Engineers fuel economy test (J1711).[19] However, an automaker's total fleet average benefit is limited to 1.2 miles per gallon for all of its automobiles in that compliance year.[20]

Flex-fuel and dual-fuel vehicles also can receive this bonus credit until 2019, but they do not receive as much credit as a dedicated alternative fuel vehicle. CAFE legislation and associated regulations currently treat PHEVs as dual-fuel vehicles as long as they have at least 7.5 miles of all-electric range in the city and 10.2 miles on the highway, according to EPA driving tests (see the 1998 DOT ruling).[21] CAFE regulations apply a formula to estimate how many miles are driven on off-board electricity by assuming that the vehicle operates on electricity 50 percent of the time. Additional all-electric range above 10.2 miles is not recognized or rewarded under CAFE regulations, and new types of PHEVs (such as blended mode) are not recognized.

This type of regulatory credit goes to manufacturers. The intent is to promote production of alternative fuel, flex-fuel, or dual-fuel vehicles that can boost fleets' average fuel economy. Section 109 first appeared in a conference committee draft and is understood to be part of a broader compromise on increasing fuel economy standards.

Section 132 amends the EPAct 2005 section 712 program (still not funded) to encourage domestic production and sales of efficient hybrid and advanced diesel vehicles and components. Section 132 authorizes grants to automakers and suppliers and hybrid component manufacturers to encourage domestic production of PHEVs, BEVs, traditional hybrids, and advanced diesel vehicles. It gives priority to retooling or refurbishing recently (or soon to be) closed facilities and authorizes the necessary funds.

Section 134 further modifies section 712 (still not funded) of EPAct 2005 to include "loan guarantees under Section 1703," the EPAct 2005 loan guarantee program for innovative technologies, whose list of eligible projects is amended to include production facilities for fuel-efficient vehicles and parts, including electric drive and advanced diesel vehicles. Interest groups such as EDTA and the ad hoc PHEV and BEV coalition supported its inclusion as a new financing method for startup and incumbent manufacturers making large capital investments in facilities.

Section 135 provides loan guarantees for construction of facilities to manufacture advanced vehicle batteries and battery systems that are developed and produced in the United States, including lithium-ion batteries, hybrid electrical systems, component manufacturing, and software design. Loan guarantees may be provided if the applicant is otherwise unable to secure credit on reasonable terms or under conditions sufficient to finance construction of the facility; if there is reasonable assurance of repayment; and if the loan bears a reasonable interest rate. Preference is given to proposals that meet state and federal permitting requirements, that are most likely to be successful, and that are located in local markets that have the greatest need for the facility. The loan guarantee authority is provided for ten years from enactment of EISA; such sums as are necessary are authorized for the program. Interest groups such as EDTA and the ad hoc PHEV and BEV coalition supported the concept of the provision.

Section 136 creates an incentive program for manufacturing advanced technology vehicles that provides both grants and loans for vehicle and component manufacturers. Subsection b provides grants for up to 30 percent of the cost of re-equipping or establishing advanced vehicle and component manufacturing facilities, for equipment investment (including investment in development of manufacturing processes), and for engineering integration. Advanced vehicles are vehicles that meet Tier 2 Bin 5 standards or any Clean Air Act standard for fine particulate matter and that achieve at least 125 percent of the average base year combined fuel economy for vehicles with similar attributes. The facilities or equipment must be placed in service before December 30, 2020; engineering integration costs must be incurred after enactment but before the same date.

Subsection d directs the secretary of the Department of Energy, within a year, to carry out a program that provides "not more than" a total of $25 billion in direct loans to eligible individuals and entities for advanced vehicles and parts manufacturing and engineering integration. In fall 2008 funding for the $25 billion loan program was appropriated. The loan applicant must provide written assurance of payment of prevailing wages to workers. Eligible projects must be financially viable without the federal funding; the investment must be expended efficiently and effectively; and other criteria, as determined by the secretary, must be met. Section 136 is authorized from 2008 through 2012 at such sums as are necessary.

Overview of Existing Programs for Research, Development, and Education

Section 641 of EISA establishes a research, development, and demonstration program to support U.S. competitiveness in energy storage for electric drive vehicles, stationary applications, and electricity transmission and distribution. Section 641 also establishes an advisory council, made up of representatives from the U.S. energy storage industry, to develop a five-year plan for integrating basic and applied research in order to maintain U.S. competitiveness in energy storage for electric drive vehicles, stationary applications, and electricity transmission and distribution. EDTA and the ad hoc PHEV and BEV coalition were the major advocates of this lengthy section, which includes large parts of a previous Senate bill introduced by senators Jeff Bingaman (D-N.M.) and Pete Domenici (R-N.M.)[22] and large parts of the House Science Committee's HR 3776. Section 641 authorizes six different programs:

Basic research. $50 million a year is authorized for 2009 through 2018 for basic research on energy storage systems, including materials design, electrode-active materials, and thermal behavior and life degradation mechanisms. Nanoscience centers also are included. Funds are to be awarded to national labs and a range of public, private, and academic stakeholders.

Applied research. $80 million a year is authorized for 2009 through 2018 for an applied research program that benefits electric drive vehicles, stationary applications, and electricity transmission and distribution technologies. Specifically mentioned is applied research on ultracapacitors, batteries, flywheels, compressed air energy systems, power conditioning electronics, thermal management systems, manufacturing technologies for energy storage systems, and hydrogen storage as an energy storage medium. Funds are to be awarded to national labs and a range of public, private, and academic stakeholders.

Energy storage centers. $100 million a year is authorized for 2009 through 2018 for creation of not less than four energy storage centers, to be managed by the DOE Office of Science, to promote the goals of the energy storage advisory council and to translate basic research into applications in electric drive vehicles, stationary applications, and electricity transmission and distribution. Participants can be from the national labs as well as industry. Patent and licensing protections are detailed.

Stationary energy storage system demonstrations. $30 million a year is authorized for 2009 through 2018 for demonstrations of stationary energy storage systems that are regionally diversified and that expand on existing DOE demonstrations. Stakeholders include rural electric co-ops, municipal and investor-owned utilities (IOUs), energy storage system and electric drive vehicle manufacturers, renewable energy producers, the fuel cell industry, and others. Objectives include energy storage to improve microgrids or islanding[23]; integration of an energy storage system with a self-healing grid and with renewable energy production; use of energy storage to improve emergency response infrastructure and emergency backup power; advancement of power conversion systems; and use of energy storage devices for load management or during non-peak generation periods.

Vehicle energy storage system demonstrations. $30 million a year is authorized for 2009 through 2018 for vehicle energy storage demonstrations conducted through consortia, which may include energy storage system and electric drive vehicle manufacturers, rural electric co-ops, municipal utilities and IOUs, state and local governments, institutions of higher learning, and others. Objectives include novel, high-capacity energy storage; onboard management; integration into electric drive vehicle platforms and the grid; and new technologies and processes that reduce manufacturing costs.

Secondary applications. $5 million a year is authorized for 2009 through 2018 for research, development, and demonstration of secondary applications of electric drive vehicle energy storage devices and technologies and processes for recycling and disposal of the devices.

Section 131(d) of EISA establishes a national electric drive transportation technology education program through the Department of Energy. In this area, section 131(d) creates the Dr. Andrew Frank Plug-in Electric Vehicle Competition for colleges and universities, authorizes financial assistance to support engineering degree programs, and authorizes the development of secondary school teaching materials and higher education program assistance relating to electric drive systems and component engineering. It authorizes such sums as are necessary. This effort derived from the ad hoc PHEV coalition and EDTA efforts referenced above. Representative Engel introduced this section in the Energy and Commerce Committee, and Senator Salazar added this section by floor amendment.

Overview of Tax Breaks in the 2008 Emergency Economic Stabilization Act

Consumer tax credits for plug-in electric drive vehicles were not included in the 2007 EISA because the bill contains no tax title. Versions of plug-in electric drive credits passed the Senate and House and were agreed to by a conference committee. However, partisan disagreement over offsetting the tax title provoked a filibuster in the Senate that proponents could not overcome. Sixty votes were necessary to break the filibuster; fifty-nine votes were cast in favor. Specifically, opponents objected not to tax credits for plug-in electric drive vehicles but to paying for the tax credits by removing EPAct 2005 tax incentives to oil companies. Once the entire tax credit section was removed, the Senate passed EISA by more than eighty votes in December 2007.

In 2008 EDTA and other advocates continued to work on tax credits for plug-in electric drive vehicles and their infrastructure. EDTA worked extensively to support S. 1617, sponsored by Senators Cantwell, Obama, and Hatch, and the language in S. 1617 is close to the final language in EESA sections 205 and 207. The lead author of the House version of tax credits for plug-in electric drive vehicles was Representative Lloyd Doggett (D-Tex.). EDTA and other advocates preferred the Senate version because it was larger and applied to both light- and heavy-duty vehicles. In 2008 both the House and Senate passed different versions of tax breaks several times, but a final bill did not seem to be possible because of the same offset issue that derailed efforts in 2007. With the September 2008 economic crisis, however, the dynamics changed. Several tax breaks were added by the Senate to the Emergency Economic Stabilization Act (commonly known as the bailout bill), and President Bush signed it.

Section 205 of EESA establishes a new tax credit for plug-in electric drive vehicles, which are defined to include BEVs, PHEVs, extended-range EVs, and plug-in hybrid fuel cell EVs. The credit applies to plug-in electric drive vehicles with batteries of at least 4 kilowatt-hours, which qualifies the vehicles for a $2,500 tax credit. An additional $417 is provided for each additional kilowatt-hour, up to $7,500 for vehicles weighing up to 10,000 pounds; up to $10,000 for vehicles weighing between 10,001 and 14,000 pounds; up to $12,500 for vehicles weighing between 14,001 and 26,000 pounds; and up to $15,000 for vehicles weighing more than 26,001 pounds. Battery kilowatt-hours are based on the total size of the battery as opposed to the usable size. Taxpayers may claim the full amount of the allowable credit up to the end of the first calendar quarter after the quarter in which the total number of qualified plug-in electric drive vehicles sold in the U.S. exceeds 250,000. After that time the tax credit is reduced in size in a one-year phase-out period. Similar to the EPAct 2005 tax credits, this tax credit is available to non–tax-paying entities. In that case, the person who sold the vehicle is treated as the taxpayer, but only if that person clearly discloses the amount of the credit allowable. In addition, the credit is available against the alternative minimum tax.

Section 206 of EESA establishes an exemption from the heavy-vehicle excise tax for the cost of idling reduction units, such as diesel auxiliary power units (APUs) or truck stop electrification systems, which are designed to eliminate the need for truck engine idling (for example, to provide heating, air conditioning, or electricity) at vehicle rest stops or other temporary parking locations. Section 206 also provides an exemption for the installation of advanced insulation, which can reduce the need for energy consumption by transportation vehicles carrying refrigerated cargo. Both exemptions are intended to favor technologies that reduce carbon emissions in the transportation sector.

Section 207 of EESA extends an existing EPAct 2005 tax credit to electric drive vehicle infrastructure. Specifically, it extends the 30 percent credit for alternative refueling property, such as natural gas or E-85 pumps, through 2010, and adds electric vehicle recharging property to the types of property eligible for the credit. Details on what types of electric vehicle recharging property qualify (chargers, panel upgrades, trenching, and so forth) are unclear; they will be determined through the Internal Revenue Service rulemaking process.

Section 306 of EESA provides accelerated depreciation for smart electric meters and smart electric grid equipment. Under current law, taxpayers generally are able to recover the cost of such property over a twenty-year period. Section 306 allows taxpayers to recover the cost over a ten-year period, unless the property already qualifies under a shorter recovery schedule. Smart meters are expected to be used by many electric utilities for BEVs and PHEVs.

Overview of Other Authorized Programs

The Clean Air Act Amendment of 1990 has several programs that can benefit electric transportation.[24] While the law has programs to promote alternative fuels, federal regulators pursued that goal through others, such as the alternative fuels program, within the EPAct 1992. The Clean Air Act has resulted in new national ambient air quality standards for several pollutants and the setting of new nonattainment areas, increasing the interest in both non-road and on-road electric transportation technologies.[25] The Clean Air Act also has programs geared to national parks, which account for many electric transportation projects.

The U.S. Department of Transportation has several programs that can benefit electric transportation. The surface transportation reauthorization legislation (passed in 1991, 1998, and 2005) has grant and loan funds for alternative fuel buses, electric light rail, and various special R&D projects as well as a large grant program, the congestion mitigation air quality (CMAQ) program, which has benefited many alternative fuel vehicle projects in the past.[26]

The Department of Energy's Clean Cities Program was created in EPAct 1992 and funded every year in order to promote the use of alternative fuels in fleets. In section 503 of EPAct 1992, DOE is required to estimate alternative fuel use and alternative fuel vehicle use in the United States and to calculate the geographic distribution of those uses and of greenhouse gas emissions. Section 1605 of EPAct 1992 requires DOE to establish a system and procedures for voluntary reporting of greenhouse gas emissions. DOE also provides funding to individual states through its state energy program, which has benefited EVs in the past.

Low-speed electric vehicles were allowed on U.S. roads for the first time in 1998 by the National Highway Transportation Safety Administration. These vehicles are limited to a maximum speed of 20 to 25 miles per hour and are required to be equipped with headlights, stop lights, turn signals, tail lights, reflex reflectors, parking brakes, rearview mirrors, windshields, seat belts, and vehicle identification numbers.[27] EDTA was active in advocating for legalization of these vehicles.

Access to carpool lanes by single-occupant BEVs is allowed by language in the 1998 surface transportation reauthorization bill, and access by single-occupant HEVs and PHEVs and other "inherently low-emission vehicles" is allowed by language in the 2005 surface transportation reauthorization law. Individual states, however, must adopt their own laws as well. EDTA and other alternative fuel coalitions were active in advocating for these laws.

Section 752 of EPAct 2005 authorizes the Environmental Protection Agency to conduct a study of the potential use of mobile source emission reduction credits by stationary source emission sources to meet emission offset requirements within a nonattainment area. The Natural Gas Vehicle Coalition advocated for this study.

Section 756 of EPAct 2005 authorizes the Environmental Protection Agency to create a program to reduce idling from trucks and to conduct several truck-related studies. Both truck stop electrification and electric truck refrigeration units are eligible.

Title XVI (Climate Change Strategies) and EPAct Title XVII (Incentives for Innovative Technologies) of EPAct 2005 create several programs that can benefit electric transportation technologies.

An executive order issued on May 14, 2007, directs federal agencies to cooperate in protecting the environment with respect to greenhouse gas emissions from motor vehicles, non-road vehicles, and non-road engines.[28] Electric transportation should benefit.

Title 1, Subtitle A (Ten-in-Ten Fuel Economy Act) of EISA raises the fuel economy standards for automobiles as well as work trucks and commercial medium-duty and heavy-duty on-highway vehicles. Electric vehicles and plug-in hybrid vehicles are examples of two of many technologies that auto and truck makers can use to comply with these new standards.

Section 131(a), section 133, and section 641 of EISA create new definitions in federal law that affect electric transportation. EDTA and the ad hoc PHEV coalition were key advocates of these changes. Section 131(a) defines "non-road vehicle" (electric is included), "electric transportation technology," and "qualified electric transportation project." Section 133 defines "medium- or heavy-duty electric vehicle," "neighborhood electric vehicle," and "plug-in electric drive vehicle." Section 641 defines "electric drive vehicle," "islanding," "flywheel," "microgrid," "self-healing grid," "spinning reserve services," and "ultracapacitor." In addition, many key terms relating to truck stop electrification are in section 756 of EPAct 2005.

Section 206 of EISA authorizes a study by the Environmental Protection Agency of the feasibility of adding battery electric vehicles powered by electricity from renewable sources to the renewable fuel standard, section 211(o) of the Clean Air Act. PHEVs are effectively excluded from this study because they do not meet this section's definition of electric vehicles. The study also will identify the source of electricity to power BEVs. This study was requested by Senator Reid's office.

Sections 1301 through 1309 of EISA refer to new smart grid programs, many of which relate to PHEVs, BEVs, and other types of electric transportation and to both new and used advanced energy batteries used in conjunction with the smart grid. Of particular interest is section 1304(a), on smart grid technology research and development (authorized at such sums as are necessary), which specifically mentions promoting the use of underutilized electricity generation capacity to substitute for liquid transportation fuels and of electricity stored in vehicles to meet peak loads. Section 1304(b) authorizes $100 million a year for a demonstration program related to section 1304(a).

Several Department of Defense programs focus on the National Automotive Command. Electric vehicles are of interest because they have no heat signature, they are quiet, and they can be linked on the battlefield to provide an "island grid." In addition, they are of interest in home base applications and provide many benefits there too.

Overview of Appropriations

It is always very difficult to separate PHEV-specific funding within the vehicle technologies budget at the Department of Energy because the research program activities are significantly integrated. A rough estimate is that appropriations for PHEVs only (not counting shared programs with traditional HEVs or fuel cell EVs) rose from $1 million in FY 2005 to about $7 million in FY 2006 to $14 million in FY 2007 and about $35 million in FY 2008. Distinguishing battery EV funding creates the same difficulty, but increases in the funding for the energy storage program provide a general indication of the trend and the level of federal interest.

On June 25, 2008, the House Appropriations Committee approved its FY 2009 energy and water development appropriations bill. The bill if adopted would appropriate

—$30 million for advanced technology vehicle manufacturing grants authorized in section 136(b) of EISA

—$150 million in budget authority to cover the cost of $1 billion in EISA section 136 direct loans to advanced vehicle manufacturers

—an increase to $305 million for DOE's vehicle technology program, which is about $84 million more than the administration requested. That includes $77 million for energy storage as authorized in EISA section 641 (about $27 million more than the administration requested), and $173 million for hybrid electric systems ($70 million more than the administration requested).

—$47 million for energy storage programs at the DOE Office of Science

—$20 million to establish the plug-in vehicle demonstrations authorized in section 131 of EISA

—$25 million for the DOE Clean Cities Program, more than double the original funding.

Again, it is hard to estimate how much this appropriations bill provides for electric transportation. It is much less than the more than $500 million authorized by EISA but substantially more than the rough estimate of $35 million for PHEVs and other forms of electric transportation in FY 2008. The Senate Appropriations Committee passed its bill on July 10, 2008. It directs $100 million to energy storage, including half to applied research under EISA section 641(g).[29] However, no floor action is expected on either the House or Senate bill, because the congressional leadership has said that it plans to use a long-term continuing resolution to push FY09 funding decisions past the election into next year. However, these numbers will serve as important benchmarks in negotiating final numbers in the future. Both EDTA and the ad hoc PHEV and BEV coalition have been active in requesting increases in appropriations. Dozens of senators and representatives signed bipartisan letters in 2007 and 2008 calling for large increases in appropriations in various programs for PHEVs, BEVs, and other types of electric transportation.

Outside the Department of Energy, electric transportation funding is even more difficult to track. Electric transportation–related appropriations are not the subject of line item appropriations at other agencies, such as the Department of Defense, the Environmental Protection Agency, and the Department of Transportation, but each does work on electric drive transportation: EPA does work on vehicle emissions and efficiency tracking, DOT on electric drive transit applications, and DOD on defense logistics programs.

Overview of Draft Provisions Dropped from EISA 2007

Several draft provisions were dropped in the conference committee (during House and Senate's final negotiations).

—Limits on research, development, and demonstration funds to national labs[30]

—A program to assess the electric transportation market, electricity use, and barriers to commercial production of electric vehicles[31]

—A study of the feasibility of a new class of electric vehicles called city cars, similar to those in other countries, which are not just low-speed electric vehicles but full-function, freeway-capable electric vehicles[32]

—A program in which key stakeholders work with federal agencies on electric drive vehicle testing protocols and benefits assessment for a variety of types of on-road and non-road electric transportation, and a program that works with utilities on grants and other efforts relating to off-peak use of electricity[33]

—A program to transition EPA regulations on control of mobile source emissions to a fuel and technology–neutral program over ten years so that electric transportation can count toward compliance with regulations[34]
—Manufacturing tax credits for electric drive transportation[35]
—Tax credit for conversion of HEVs into PHEVs[36]
—Definition of the term "plug-in hybrid electric vehicle"
—The low-carbon fuel standard.[37]

Overview of Expired Incentives

Many electric vehicle programs authorized under the 1992 EPAct were never funded. In addition, BEVs and PHEVs can no longer receive the following three tax credits:

—a 10 percent tax credit under EPAct 1992 to the consumer for purchase of battery EVs and hybrids that were fueled primarily by electricity (up to a cap of $4,000). The credit was extended a few times but expired in 2006. Some PHEVs probably could have met the test of "primarily fueled by electricity," but that was never put to the test by a manufacturer's request.

—a tax deduction of up to $100,000 under EPAct 1992 for businesses that install electric vehicle infrastructure. That too was extended a few times but expired in 2006.

—Finally, under Public Law 101-508, title XI, EVs were granted a higher limit on a federal luxury tax.[38] Specifically, vehicles that cost more than $30,000 were taxed with an additional tax called the luxury tax, but electric vehicles were not subject to the luxury tax unless they were priced at 150 percent or more of $30,000. However, the luxury tax expired in 2002.

Notes

1. P.L. 109-58, P.L. 110-140, and P.L. 110-343, respectively.
2. This section authorizes an average of $866 million for research, development, demonstration, and commercial application to increase the energy efficiency of vehicles (including PHEVs), buildings, and industrial processes.
3. See S. 1617 (sponsored by senators Cantwell, Obama, and Hatch) in the 110th Congress. BEV and PHEV tax credits similar to those in S. 1617 passed the House and Senate and were in the conference committee version of EISA but did not make it into the final version. At the sponsors' request, EDTA developed most of the vehicle and manufacturing tax credit structure of S. 1617.

4. See www.electricdrive.org. The EDTA Policy Committee includes about 100 members from the utility, automotive, and component supplier industries.

5. In the 109th Congress, the DRIVE Act was known as the Vehicle and Fuel Choices for America Act, with essentially the same Senate and House sponsors. See S. 2025 and HR 4409 in the 109th Congress.

6. Set America Free, "The Coalition" (www.setamericafree.org/coalition.html) brings together prominent individuals and nonprofit organizations concerned about the security and economic implications of America's growing dependence on foreign oil. See www.setamericafree.org/who.htm.

7. The ad hoc PHEV and BEV coalition is an informal alliance of electric utilities, truck and component manufacturers, trade associations, and others supporting provisions on electric transportation within HR 6, HR 3221, HR 3776, and the DRIVE Acts (S. 339, HR 670, S. 2025, and HR 4409) as well as appropriations for electric transportation programs. Past assistance in the coalition has come from Southern California Edison, Austin Energy, Set America Free, Southern Company, Sacramento Municipal Utility District, Public Service New Mexico, Public Service Enterprise Group (New Jersey), FirstEnergy, Edison Electric Institute, American Public Power Association, National Rural Electric Co-op Association, Seattle City Light, Silicon Valley Leadership Group, PacifiCorp, Rocky Mountain Power, Plug-in America, Cascadia, American Electric Power, Progress, Navistar, Eaton, Hawaiian Electric Company, Sempra, Pacific Gas and Electric, Centerpoint, New York Power Authority, Duke, AES, Energy and Environmental Study Institute, Detroit Edison, Southern California Public Power Authority, Mid-American Power, and South Carolina Electric and Gas.

8. U.S. Code 42, sections 13212, 13257(o), and 13251.

9. Executive Order 13149, April 21, 2000 (www1.eere.energy.gov/vehiclesand fuels/epact/pdfs/executive_order_13149.pdf).

10. Executive Order: Strengthening Federal Environment, Energy, and Transportation Management, January 24, 2007 (www.whitehouse.gov/news/releases/2007/01/20070124-2.html). Sections of interest include "Sec. 2. Goals for Agencies. In implementing the policy set forth in section 1 of this order, the head of each agency shall: improve energy efficiency and reduce greenhouse gas emissions of the agency, through reduction of energy intensity by (i) 3 percent annually through the end of fiscal year 2015, or (ii) 30 percent by the end of fiscal year 2015, relative to the baseline of the agency's energy use in fiscal year 2003; . . . (g) ensure that, if the agency operates a fleet of at least 20 motor vehicles, the agency, relative to agency baselines for fiscal year 2005, (i) reduces the fleet's total consumption of petroleum products by 2 percent annually through the end of fiscal year 2015, (ii) increases the total fuel consumption that is non-petroleum-based by 10 percent annually, and (iii) uses plug-in hybrid (PIH) vehicles when PIH vehicles are commercially available at a cost reasonably comparable, on the basis of life-cycle cost, to non-PIH vehicles."

11. The rules and guidelines for implementing section 703 can be found at Vehicle Technologies Program, Energy Policy Act (EPAct) (www1.eere.energy.gov/vehicle sandfuels/epact/state/state_resources.html).

12. Ibid.

13. DOE, *A Guidebook to the U.S. Department of Energy Alternative Fuel Transportation Program for State and Alternative Fuel Provider Fleets* (2001).

14. Details on the fleet mandates can be found at www1.eere.energy.gov/vehicle sandfuels/epact/about/index.html; www1.eere.energy.gov/vehiclesandfuels/epact/state/ index.html; www1.eere.energy.gov/femp/about/fleet_requirements.html; and www1. eere.energy.gov/vehiclesandfuels/epact/private/index.html.

15. Flex-fuel vehicles have only one fuel tank and can switch between different grades of biofuel and gasoline blends (for example, E-10 and E-85). HEVs are single-fuel vehicles using only gasoline. PHEVs are dual-fuel vehicles; that is, they have two fuel systems—gasoline and electricity—and two "tanks" for storing them. Section 706 is for PHEVs that also are flex-fuel capable (for example, a PHEV that uses E-85 or E-10 blends with gasoline).

16. Alternative Fuels and Advanced Vehicles Data Center, Airport Publications (www.eere.energy.gov/afdc/fleets/airports_publications.html).

17. U.S. Code 42, sections 32901 through 32919.

18. The law behind this special incentive is the Alternative Motor Fuels Act (AMFA) of 1998, which included a section on manufacturing incentives for automobiles. That section modified CAFE laws and the 1992 EPAct, which added electricity to the definition of alternative fuels.

19. HEV Working Group, "Comparing the Benefits and Impacts of Hybrid Electric Vehicle Options," EPRI report 1000349, June 2001, pp. 6–9.

20. Through 2014, when the 1.2 mpg rule will be decreased and phased out by 2019 (see section 109 of EISA).

21. *Code of Federal Regulations* 49, part 538 (1998).

22. Section 244 of the Senate's HR 6 was amended three times on the Senate floor: Senator Salazar's amendment 1528, Senator Steven's amendment, and Senator Bingaman's own amendment.

23. The term *islanding* refers to the powering of a location by a distributed generator or energy storage device in the absence of electric power from the primary source (EISA Section 641a).

24. Text of the act and "The EPA Plain English Guide to the Clean Air Act" can be accessed at EPA, Air and Radiation, Clean Air Act (www.epa.gov/oar/caa/).

25. Nonattainment areas are regions that the Environmental Protection Agency has determined do not meet the National Ambient Air Quality Standards for one or more air pollutants.

26. See Federal Highway Administration, TEA-21 (www.fhwa.dot.gov/tea21/ index.htm); SAFETEA-LU (www.fhwa.dot.gov/safetealu/legis.htm); and Congestion Mitigation and Air Quality (CMAQ) Improvement Program (www.fhwa.dot.gov/ environment/cmaqpgs/).

27 Federal Motor Vehicle Safety Standard No. 500 (49 CFR 571.500) (www.nhtsa. dot.gov/cars/rules/rulings/lsv/lsv.html).

28. Executive Order: Cooperation among Agencies in Protecting the Environment with Respect to Greenhouse Gas Emissions from Motor Vehicles, Nonroad Vehicles, and Nonroad Engines (www.whitehouse.gov/news/releases/2007/05/20070514-1. html).

29. The House recommended $76 million; the administration had requested $50 million.

30. HR 6 section 245(g)(3) as passed by the Senate in 2007.

31. Almost identical sections in HR 6, section 245(c) and section 245(d), as passed by the Senate, and in HR 3221, section 9407(b), as passed by the House in 2007.

32. HR 3221, section 9408, as passed by the House in 2007.

33. HR 6, section 245(f)(2), as passed by the Senate in 2007.

34. See HR 670, section 401(g) and a similar program in S. 339.

35. These credits were considered in the Senate Finance Committee (see S. 1617) and House Ways and Means Committee but did not make it to the HR 6 conference committee.

36. HR 6, section 842, as passed by the Senate in 2007.

37. This provision was not under consideration in the HR 6 conference committee. However, several different low-carbon fuel standards were introduced in the 110th Congress in both the House and Senate. The most prominent were the Boucher proposal and the Alexander amendment to S. 2191, which passed the Senate Environment and Public Works Committee. The Alexander amendment is in many ways similar to the proposed California low-carbon fuel standard.

38. Cornell University Law School, Legal Information Institute, "U.S. Code Collection" (www4.law.cornell.edu/uscode/uscode26/usc_sec_26_00004001----000-.html).

Tax Credits for Electric Cars:
Stimulating Demand through the Tax Code

BENJAMIN H. HARRIS

Tax policy and energy policy have long been interrelated, and the connection has grown stronger with the emergence of energy policy as one of the nation's most pressing issues. This chapter reviews one specific aspect of energy tax policy—tax credits for the purchase of energy-efficient vehicles—and comments on recently passed legislation creating a tax credit for plug-in cars. The chapter concludes by recommending guidelines for future changes to the tax credit for electric vehicles.

Congress has a long tradition of using the tax code to further various energy policies, including such examples as tax incentives for oil and gas production, tax subsidies for production of alternative fuels (including tax credits for the production of ethanol and biodiesel), and tax credits for the purchase of energy efficient vehicles.[1] The Joint Committee on Taxation (JCT), in its annual publication of tax expenditures, estimates that there were twenty-two separate energy-related tax expenditures in 2007, with these tax expenditures totaling $9.3 billion in 2007 and projected to total $32.2 billion over the next five years.[2] Generally, energy-related tax provisions fall into one of three broad categories: tax provisions that encourage increased production of conventional energy

The author thanks Eric Toder and Bill Gale for helpful comments and Chris Geissler and Ruth Levine for research assistance.

sources, provisions that encourage decreased consumption of conventional energy sources through improved energy efficiency, or provisions that encourage the substitution of alternative energy sources. Many of the energy-related tax provisions in the tax code seem to have opposing goals, such as preferential tax treatment for the purchase of both sport utility vehicles and energy-efficient hybrids, leading to a conflicting set of incentives for energy producers and consumers alike.

Although the bulk of the energy-related tax provisions are directed toward encouraging certain behavior from corporations and businesses involved in the production of energy, recent tax law has also focused on generating higher consumer demand for products utilizing energy-efficient technologies. The Energy Policy Act of 2005 (EPAct), the first major piece of energy legislation in over a decade, included several incentives aimed at decreasing the after-tax price of energy-efficient products.[3] For example, EPAct provided individuals with a tax credit for the purchase of energy-efficient doors, windows, insulation, and other home improvement products. EPAct also provided a credit of up to $2,000 for taxpayers who installed solar water heating equipment in their homes; however, these provisions expired in 2008.

EPAct also included several provisions aimed at stimulating demand for energy-efficient cars.[4] These provisions were aimed at vehicles utilizing four different technologies for power: fuel cell, "lean-burn" diesel, hybrid, and alternative fuel. There are no vehicles in production that meet the criteria for the "lean burn" diesel credit, making that provision largely irrelevant. For the remaining three provisions, the formula used to determine the value of the credit is complicated and is based primarily on the weight of the vehicle and some measure of the vehicle's energy efficiency. The combined revenue loss (or "cost") from these provisions is relatively small. JCT estimates that these provisions combined will cost the Treasury just $800 million over 10 years, equal to about 6 percent of the tax cuts contained in EPAct.[5] As a percentage of the energy-related tax expenditures, tax credits for alternative vehicles make up about 3 percent of the total expenditure in 2007.

The total tax credit for hybrid cars is the sum of two components: a tax credit for fuel economy and a tax credit for conservation. The tax credit for fuel economy increases on a sliding scale from $400 to $2,400 according to the efficiency of the hybrid relative to a comparable nonhybrid model's 2002 standards. A hybrid that achieves between 125 percent and

150 percent of 2002 fuel economy standards (for the nonhybrid model) would be eligible for a $400 tax credit, while a hybrid that achieves an excess of 250 percent of 2002 standards would be eligible for a $2,400 credit. Similarly, the conservation credit is based on the total number of gallons conserved by the hybrid over the life of the vehicle, relative to a comparable model's nonhybrid 2002 standards. A hybrid that conserves between 1,200 and 1,800 gallons would receive a tax credit worth $400, while a hybrid that conserves in excess of 3,000 gallons would receive a conservation credit worth $1,000. In total, taxpayers could potentially receive a tax credit of up to $3,400 for the purchase of a hybrid.[6] The net result of this tax provision is that some of the least energy-efficient hybrids receive some of the largest tax credits because the value of the credit is based on the model's efficiency relative to its nonhybrid model, rather than on its fuel efficiency relative to other hybrids. For example, in 2008 the tax credit for a Nissan Altima hybrid was $650 less than the tax credit for the two-wheel drive Ford Escape hybrid, even though the Altima has better fuel efficiency than the Escape.[7]

The total value of the hybrid tax credit is further complicated by a phase-out for models produced by manufacturers that have sold in excess of 60,000 eligible vehicles, a provision designed to help U.S. carmakers who trail Toyota and Honda in hybrid technology.[8] Once a manufacturer has sold its 60,000th hybrid vehicle (for all models combined), the ability of taxpayers to claim the tax credit phases out over the course of a year. Toyota sold its 60,000th hybrid in June 2006, and therefore, its models are no longer eligible for a tax credit. In August 2007, Honda sold its 60,000th hybrid, meaning that taxpayers would have just over a year to claim the credit for hybrids and that the value of the credit would diminish rapidly. Taxpayers who purchased a Honda hybrid could claim a full credit if it was purchased before the end of 2007, half-credit if purchased between January 1 and June 30, 2008, one-quarter credit if purchased between July 1 and December 31, 2008, and no credit if purchased after that time.

Despite this complexity and limited duration, tax credits for plug-in vehicles appear to have been popular tax breaks, and they likely were a significant factor in the increased demand for hybrid vehicles in the United States.[9] A recent study found that the existence of a state income tax incentive for purchase of a hybrid vehicle increased the demand for hybrids by 13 percent, while a state sales tax incentive increased demand by 28 percent.[10] Another study of hybrid tax incentives found that consumers (rather than dealers or manufacturers) were the primary beneficiaries of hybrid tax incentives, further suggesting that federal tax incentives may be an effective mechanism for stimulating consumer demand.[11]

The success of the hybrid tax credit set the stage for Congress to adopt a tax credit for plug-in electric vehicles (PEVs).[12] EPAct provided tax incentives for consumers of nearly every type of alternative-fuel vehicles except those powered by electricity, which, due to their energy efficiency and potential for mass production, are arguably the one type of vehicle most suited to receive a tax benefit. Ironically, a tax credit for electric vehicles was in place from 1993 through 2006, when the prospect of widespread production of plug-in vehicles was dim. Originally inserted into the Energy Policy Act of 1992 and briefly extended through the Working Families Tax Relief Act of 2004, the credit equaled 10 percent of the purchase price of a vehicle, with a maximum benefit of $4,000.[13]

Indeed, the continued upward pressure on fuel prices, adverse economic effects of oil importation, and sustained concern about the detrimental effects of greenhouse gas emissions made the (re)implementation of a tax incentive for electric vehicles inevitable. In October 2008, tax writers added more than $100 billion in tax cuts to the Emergency Economic Stabilization Act of 2008, a bill providing the Treasury with the authority to use up to $700 billion to purchase troubled assets from banks and other financial institutions. Included in these additional tax breaks was a provision that provides purchasers of electric cars with a tax credit of up to $7,500.

The newly implemented PEV tax credit grants taxpayers a credit of $2,500 for the purchase of a qualified electric-powered vehicle, plus $417 for each additional kilowatt-hour of battery power in excess of 4 kilowatt-hours. The tax credit caps the value of the credit at $7,500 for vehicles with gross vehicle weights under 10,000 pounds; larger vehicles qualify for a larger maximum credit. The Chevy Volt, with 16 kilowatt-hours of battery capacity, will qualify for the maximum credit of $7,500.

The phase-out of the PEV tax credit is based on the total number of qualifying vehicles sold in the United States. Starting the count in 2009, after 250,000 PEVs have been sold in the United States, the availability of the credit gradually phases out over the course of approximately fifteen months. After the quarter year in which the 250,000 vehicle threshold is reached, the full credit will be available for one quarter year. Then, the value of the credit will decline by 50 percent for another half year, after which it will decline to 25 percent of its value for another half year. After this time the value of the credit is phased out completely.

The ultimate efficacy of the PEV tax credit will be determined by the credit's ability to help establish PEVs as a viable mainstream option for American automobile consumers. A secondary practical consideration is the fiscal cost (or lost tax revenue) resulting from the tax incentive; an effective tax credit is one that achieves its objective while minimizing the reduction in tax revenue. Given these objectives and constraints, the following seven guiding principles can be used to evaluate Congress's recent action and to guide Congress in future efforts to refine and extend existing policy.

The tax credit should be large enough to make PEVs competitive with traditional cars.

The most important aspect of a PEV tax credit is that it be large enough to make PEVs competitive with conventionally powered vehicles. A tax credit that is too small to induce significant changes in consumer behavior has little value. Naturally, the determination of the cost difference between a conventionally powered car and a PEV depends on the ability of the automotive and, in particular, the battery industry to produce batteries in a cost-effective manner.

Initial estimates indicate that the cost of producing a PEV relative to producing a conventional vehicle is approximately an additional $8,000; this difference is likely to converge as battery technology progresses and the production of PEVs increases.[14] Also, consumers will likely account for fuel savings over the life of the vehicle, which will depend not only on gasoline prices but also on the price of electricity. Last, the estimated life of the battery (and replacement value) should also factor into the price differential between conventional vehicles and PEVs; the greater the frequency with which batteries need to be replaced, the larger a PEV credit needs to be to make the cost of owning a PEV comparable to owning a conventional vehicle.

Given current technology and expected costs of batteries given mass production, the newly implemented tax credit worth $2,500 to $7,500 seems appropriate. Scoring by the Joint Committee on Taxation of the Emergency Economic Stabilization Act indicates that this credit would not be particularly expensive relative to other tax provisions, costing $314 million over five years and $758 million over ten years.[15] Such a public investment appears reasonable given the benefits of reduced oil consumption and greenhouse gas emissions.

The tax credit should be simple.

Simplicity is an important aspect of any effective tax cut. Taxpayers are less likely to take advantage of a tax cut if they do not understand it. Even when compared with complicated tax provisions, the hybrid tax credit is relatively complex. For taxpayers to calculate the value of their benefit, they need to account for factors such as their total tax liability, whether or not they would be subject to the alternative minimum tax (AMT) in the current tax year, the total number of hybrid models sold by a particular manufacturer, the date the vehicle would be "placed into service," the total number of gallons conserved over the lifetime of the vehicle, and the efficiency of the vehicle relative to 2002 standards. Fortunately, the IRS incorporated information from the latter two factors into a single credit amount specific to each vehicle model, although this still required taxpayers to account for a wide variance in credit amount between models.

In contrast, the new PEV tax credit is simpler than the hybrid tax credit. The most important difference is the change in structure of the phase-out. Basing the phase-out of the PEV tax credit on the aggregate number of cars sold, rather than on the number of cars sold by a particular manufacturer, means that consumers will not have to account for multiple phase-outs when comparing models. The relatively high number of vehicles needed to trigger the phase-out—250,000 cars—means that the full PEV credit will likely be in place for several years. It is unlikely that consumers will have to consider the phase-out before 2013 at the earliest. Like the hybrid tax credit, Congress based the value of the PEV credit on the efficiency of the vehicle. Using such criteria adds to the credit's complexity, since it requires the IRS to calculate different tax credit values for each model. However, the gains from inducing consumers to demand (and manufacturers to produce) more-efficient batteries is likely worth the trade-off loss in simplicity.

Further simplicity can be achieved by adopting other broad recommendations outlined in this chapter. For example, making the credit refundable and allowing it to count against the AMT would be an important first step in reducing complexity.

The tax credit should be indexed to inflation, refundable, and a true tax credit (rather than a deduction).

These three conditions—being indexed, being refundable, and being structured as a tax credit—are generally sound principles when designing a tax provision. Indexation ensures that inflation does not erode the value of the credit over time, as a lack of indexation can have a significant impact on the value of a tax credit. For example, a $7,500 tax credit enacted in 2008 would be worth about $1,000 less, in real terms, in 2012.

Structuring the tax credit as a *refundable* tax credit ensures that the value of the tax credit is shared equally among taxpayers. Refundability means that tax payers with low or no income tax will still be able to receive the full value of the tax credit. If the tax credit were worth $8,000, for example, only 19.1 percent of taxpayers (25.9 million) in 2008 would be able to claim the full credit if it were nonrefundable. The full value of a refundable tax credit, conversely, would be available to every American filing a tax return. Not only would a refundable tax credit be more effective because of its larger size, but it would also reduce the complexity of the tax credit as taxpayers would not have to calculate their income taxes to determine the value of the tax credit.

The most important of these three conditions is that any tax provision for electric cars has to be structured as a tax credit, rather than as an income tax deduction. Tax credits reduce tax liability on a dollar for dollar basis, while deductions reduce taxable income; the value of a deduction varies by taxpayers and is based on the taxpayer's marginal tax rate. Therefore, deductions are worth more to high-income taxpayers and are generally worth nothing to those taxpayers that do not itemize (about two-thirds of all taxpayers).[16]

The PEV tax credit enacted by Congress meets just one of these criteria: being structured as a tax credit rather than as a deduction. Unfortunately, the PEV tax credit is not refundable and is not indexed to inflation. The omission of these characteristics from the credit's design will diminish its effectiveness.

The tax credit should have a broad phase-out range and a minimum expiration date.

The tax credits for hybrids include a provision that phases out the benefits for purchasers of a certain make of car (for example, Honda, Ford, or GMC) after the manufacturer sells 60,000 hybrid units in the United States. This provision serves to level the playing field for those automakers that have less advanced hybrid technology (essentially every major automaker other than Honda and Toyota) and also to limit the revenue cost of the tax provision. However, the narrow phase-out range also limits the extent to which the tax benefit is able to stimulate demand for hybrid cars. As noted earlier, both Toyota and Honda have sold over 60,000 hybrid cars in the

United States, and cars produced by these companies no longer qualify for a hybrid tax credit.[17] Since the Toyota Prius and Honda Civic are some of the most efficient hybrid cars on the market, the 60,000-unit phase-out provision for manufacturers has the negative side effect of making the most fuel efficient hybrids less attractive compared with similar models, effectively reversing the purpose of the tax credit.

Implementing a similarly narrow and complicated provision for electric cars would undermine the tax credit's effectiveness—consumers should not have to track auto sales to determine the potential value of their tax credit. Any phase-out range should not be manufacturer specific; instead it should be based on the total number of units sold by all manufacturers combined. Structuring the tax credit in this way has the added benefit of not punishing the most popular and effective manufactures of electric cars. Given the trajectory of hybrid sales during the past several years, it seems clear that the minimum aggregate number of electric cars produced before a phase-out of a credit is applied should be at least 500,000.[18] David Sandalow, in *Freedom from Oil*, recommends that a full tax incentive be offered to the purchasers of the first million PEVs and that a partial tax incentive be available to purchasers of the next million.[19] Such a wide phase-out range would ensure that the tax benefit would help to stimulate demand for electric cars until the technology was well-established in the American market.[20]

Last, any provision for a tax credit for PEVs should have a minimum period before the phase-out can begin, regardless of the number of units sold. For example, the tax credit could be structured to provide for a certain level of tax benefits for the first five years of enactment, regardless of the number of electric cars purchased by American consumers. Such a clause is more consistent with U.S. tax policy and would also serve to simplify the provision during its initial years of existence.

The recently implemented tax credit for PEVs has no minimum expiration date and, as described above, phases out after 250,000 models have been sold. In its scoring of the provision, JCT estimates that the credit will be fully phased out by 2015.[21] If the PEV industry is sufficiently established by 2015, the 250,000 phase-out trigger will be appropriate. However, if the industry has yet to become established after 250,000 units have been sold, Congress may opt to increase the phase-out threshold to allow the tax credit to further aid the development of the PEV industry.

The value of the tax credit should be based on the efficiency of the vehicle, not on the purchase price.

As noted earlier, the recently expired deduction for electric vehicles was based on the purchase price of a vehicle. Under the old law, a taxpayer who purchased a $20,000 electric car would receive a tax credit equal to 10 percent of the purchase price of the vehicle, or $2,000, while a taxpayer who purchased a vehicle that was twice as expensive ($40,000) would receive twice the tax benefit. Structuring the tax incentive in this fashion provides car manufactures less incentive to produce affordable cars.

By structuring the tax credit in a way that provides a greater benefit to purchasers of more expensive cars, Congress inadvertently subsidized the consumption of automobile components unrelated to energy production. Imagine two identical PEVs selling for $30,000, except that one car was outfitted with an extra $10,000 in car stereo equipment and subsequently sold for $40,000. The purchaser of the more expensive car would receive an additional $1,000 subsidy (based on the old formula of a 10 percent credit) for the purchase of the car; probably not the type of behavior Congress hoped to subsidize. Instead, the value of the credit should be based directly on the original reason for the subsidy: a car's ability to produce power in an energy-efficient manner.

Under current law, the value of the tax credit for hybrid cars is based exclusively on three factors: the weight of the vehicle, the efficiency of the vehicle, and the extent to which the vehicle conserves fuel. While this formula may be unduly complicated, it does have the added benefit of specifically rewarding taxpayers for purchasing the vehicle that maximizes the intended purpose of the credit: increased energy efficiency.

The new tax credit for electric cars incorporates this characteristic by tying the value of the credit to the energy capacity of the PEV's battery, measured in kilowatt-hours. The end result of structuring the tax credit in this fashion is an increased incentive for consumers to purchase vehicles that are the most energy efficient.[22] However, the structure of the PEV tax credit—with the value of the tax credit increasing for battery capacity between 4 kilowatt-hours and 16 kilowatt-hours—means that consumers receive no additional tax incentive for purchasing vehicles that provide battery capacity beyond 16 kilowatt-hours. Congress may opt to restructure the tax credit to provide manufacturers with the incentive to produce vehicles with battery capacity beyond 16 kilowatt-hours. In addition, battery capacity is not a perfect measure of energy efficiency. Some PEV advocates complain that basing the value of the tax credit on the battery capacity simply encourages larger battery packs and provides no incentive for carmakers to achieve better energy efficiency by designing more aerodynamic cars or using lighter materials in production.[23]

The implementation of the tax credit should be part of a larger revenue neutral tax reform aimed at improving the structure of energy policy.

In an era of persistent budget deficits, a tax cut's attractiveness increases if the tax cut is *revenue neutral*, that is, if the tax cut is coupled with revenue raisers that make the estimated net revenue effect of the legislation neutral. While the plug-in tax credit was created by legislation that was not revenue neutral—the net revenue effect of the legislation was to reduce expected tax receipts by $110 billion over 10 years—certain parts of the legislation were revenue neutral. Specifically, the part of the bill that created the PEV tax credit, the Energy Improvement and Extension Act of 2008, offset the collection of energy-related tax cuts with a series of tax increases, many of which had nothing to do with energy policy.[24]

Congress missed the opportunity to reevaluate some of the energy tax breaks present in the tax code and to pay for the new energy tax breaks with the repeal or modification of existing energy tax breaks. As discussed above, JCT estimated that the PEV tax credit would decrease revenues by $758 billion; there are several potential offsets to the tax code that would have raised at least this much revenue while furthering other beneficial energy policies.

The most attractive revenue-raising options are those that repeal tax incentives for companies that subsidize the production of environmentally damaging energy sources or those that encourage the purchase of energy-inefficient products. Although the purpose of this chapter is not to recommend broad changes to U.S. energy policy or the tax code, examples of potential reforms include extending the gas-guzzler tax to light trucks (raising $9.4 billion over five years), repealing special expensing provisions for oil and gas producing companies (raising $17.1 billion over five years), and increasing the excise tax on gasoline and diesel (the Congressional Budget Office estimates that a 12-cent increase would raise $85.5 billion over five years).[25] In addition, House-passed energy legislation in 2007 included $18 billion in rollbacks of tax incentives for oil and

gas companies.[26] Each of these examples would provide more than sufficient revenue to have made the PEV tax credit revenue neutral.

The tax credit should count against the alternative minimum tax.

Taxpayers should be able to claim the tax credit for PEVs regardless of
whether or not they are subject to the alternative minimum tax (AMT).
The AMT is a complex "parallel" tax system that was originally designed
to ensure that wealthy taxpayers could not take advantage of certain tax
loopholes to drastically reduce their tax liability.

Although many taxpayers do not have the tax filing characteristics that
require them to compute their AMT liability, technically all taxpayers
owe the higher value of their regular tax liability and their AMT liability.
If a taxpayer is "on the AMT," or owes more under the AMT than under
the regular tax, certain tax credits may be unavailable. For example, taxpayers with children can claim the child tax credit regardless of whether
their AMT liability is higher than their regular tax liability, but they can
claim the full tax credit for hybrid cars only if they are not subject to the
AMT. Also, some taxpayers may have the value of their tax credit limited
if the credit pushes their regular tax liability below their AMT liability.[27]
Such a situation is not uncommon: In 2007, 3.5 million taxpayers were
directly subject to the AMT, and another 0.4 million had the value of
their tax credits limited.[28]

The newly created tax credit for PEVs does not count against the
AMT. To make the PEV credit as simple and as effective as possible, Congress should allow those taxpayers who are subject to the AMT to claim
the credit. Doing so will allow an additional 4 million taxpayers to claim
the full value of the credit and will simplify the credit for those affected
by the AMT as well.

Conclusion

Tax credits for hybrid cars have been an effective mechanism for inducing taxpayers to purchase cleaner, more fuel-efficient vehicles. As the
introduction of mass-produced plug-in cars to the U.S. market approaches, the recent congressional action to implement a tax credit for
electric vehicles was a critical step in promoting the rapid development of
the electric car industry. The new tax credit is relatively simple, based on
the efficiency of the vehicle, and, most important, large enough to com-

pensate for the higher cost of plug-in cars relative to the cost of conventionally powered cars. Still, further action is needed. Congress should consider refining the credit so that it is refundable, indexed to inflation, and allowed to count against the AMT.

Consumer response to the tax credit over the next several years will determine if the PEV tax credit was successful in stimulating demand for plug-in vehicles. Such an accomplishment will help further the policy objectives of reducing greenhouse gas emissions and decreasing our dependence on foreign oil.

Notes

1. For a summary of the history of energy tax policy in the United States, see Salvatore Lazzari, "Energy Tax Policy: History and Current Issues," CRS Report for Congress RL33578, 110 Cong. 1 sess. (Washington: Congressional Research Service, November 7, 2007).

2. See Joint Committee on Taxation, "Estimates of Federal Tax Expenditures for Fiscal Years 2007–2011," JCS-3-07, 110 Cong. 1 sess. (Government Printing Office, September 24, 2007).

3. For a summary of EPAct, see Joint Committee on Taxation, *Description and Technical Explanation of the Conference Agreement of H.R. 6, Title XIII, the "Energy Tax Incentive Act of 2005,"* JCX-60-05, 109 Cong. 1 sess. (Government Printing Office, July 28, 2005).

4. Before EPAct, taxpayers could receive a deduction (as opposed to a credit) worth up to $2,000 for the purchase of a hybrid vehicle. This provision was significantly smaller than the one enacted under EPAct.

5. The tax provisions for hybrid and alternate fuel vehicles expire in 2010, while the tax credit for vehicles powered by fuel cells expires in 2015. The expiration dates, combined with a phase-out provision for hybrid vehicles, makes the cost of the bill decline rapidly over the ten-year budget window. In 2005, when tax credits were available to all purchasers of hybrid vehicles, the estimated revenue loss was $283 million.

6. In 2006 there were forty-four different vehicle models that were eligible for a credit, with the maximum credit being $3,150.

7. Martin Sullivan discusses this issue in detail and calculates the tax credit per gallon saved for popular models. See Martin A. Sullivan, "Time to Tune Up Tax Credits for Gas-Saving Cars," *Tax Notes* 120, no. 2 (July 14, 2008): 91–94.

8. See Justin Hyde, "Automakers Fight for Favor in New Congress," *Detroit Free Press,* December 17, 2006, p. BU7.

9. A number of articles in the popular press document the impact of tax credits on demand for hybrids. See, for example, Ken Thomas, Associated Press, "Toyota Seeks Extended Hybrid Tax Credits," *Washington Post,* November 29, 2006 (www.washingtonpost.com/wp-dyn/content/article/2006/11/29/AR2006112900992.html);

Chris Woodyard, "Toyota: Extend Hybrid Tax Credit," *USA Today*, January 16, 2007, p. B5.

10. See Kelly Sims Gallagher and Erich Muehlegger, "Giving Green to Get Green: Incentives and Consumer Adoption of Hybrid Vehicle Technology," Faculty Research Working Paper RWP08-009 (Harvard University, February 2008).

11. See James M. Sallee, "The Incidence of Tax Credits for Hybrid Vehicles" (University of Michigan, Department of Economics, 2008) (www-personal.umich.edu/~jsallee/jobmarket/sallee_job_market_paper.pdf).

12. There are several different types of automotive technologies that use electric power. Hybrids (hybrid electric vehicles or HEVs), such as a Toyota Prius, use an internal combustion engine supplemented by an electric motor. Plug-in hybrid electric vehicles (PHEVs), alternatively, have additional batteries and can derive electric energy by being "plugged-in" to a traditional wall socket. Electric vehicles (EVs) derive their energy solely from electricity and do not have an internal combustion engine. This chapter uses the term *plug-in electric vehicle* (PEV) to refer to both PHEVs and EVs that utilize plug-in technology.

13. The credit was phased down to a maximum value of $1,000 in 2006 and expired in 2007.

14. See, for example, Ben Hewitt, "The 110-Volt Solution," *Popular Mechanics*, May 2007, p. 64. The article notes that "according to an industry rule of thumb, every kilowatt-hour of capacity adds about $1,000 to the price of a battery."

15. See Joint Committee on Taxation, "Estimated Budget Effects of the Tax Provisions Contained in an Amendment in the Nature of a Substitute to H.R. 1424, Scheduled for Consideration on the Senate Floor on October 1, 2008," JCX-78-08, 110 Cong. 2 sess. (Government Printing Office, October 1, 2008).

16. A few select deductions are *above the line* deductions, meaning that they may be claimed by all taxpayers, regardless of whether the taxpayer elects to itemize deductions. It is true for all deductions, however, that the value of a deduction increases with a taxpayer's marginal tax rate.

17. Through the end of 2008, hybrid cars produced by Honda are eligible for a credit worth one-quarter of the credit's original value.

18. In 2006, 256,000 hybrids were sold in the United States. Estimates predict total hybrid sales will reach 350,430 in 2007 and 315,761 in 2008. See J.D. Power and Associates, "Seven New Hybrid Models to Enter Market in the Second Half of 2007," press release, August 2, 2007, and *Automotive News* (www.autonews.com/article/20090123/ANA05/901229967/1186).

19. David Sandalow, *Freedom from Oil: How the Next President Can End the United States' Oil Addiction* (New York: McGraw-Hill, 2007).

20. One might argue that there should be no phase-out of hybrid tax credits and that the provision should instead be permanent. Such a view would be consistent with the economic argument that a tax cut (effectively a subsidy) is necessary to correct for the market's failure to effectively incorporate the cost of the negative externalities associated with the operation of traditional engines (for example, air pollution). An alternative economic argument for the implementation of a PEV tax credit is that such a credit would be necessary to support the PEV industry in its initial years of existence, similar to the argument for import tariffs to protect infant industries. This chapter

acknowledges both economic arguments while conceding the political reality that implementing a permanent tax cut for PEVs is unlikely.

21. See Joint Committee on Taxation, "Estimated Budget Effects of the Tax Provisions Contained in an Amendment in the Nature of a Substitute to H.R. 1424."

22. An extension of this argument is to offer *all* car owners a tax credit that is based exclusively on the fuel efficiency of their vehicle, regardless of the technology utilized by the engine. Such a plan, perhaps, would be more consistent with economic theory concerning market failures and externalities, but is politically implausible.

23. See Jim Motavalli, "Hybrid Credit: Bigger is Better," *New York Times*, October 12, 2008, p. AU6.

24. The Energy Improvement and Extension Act of 2008 included approximately $17 billion in energy-related tax cuts. These tax cuts were offset by five revenue-raising provisions, including the extension of a surtax on employee wages for unemployment insurance and a change in the way the cost of securities are reported by financial firms.

25. This potential revenue estimate regarding repeal of special expensing provisions is higher in the short term than in the long run. After this provision is fully phased in, the annual revenue gain is approximately $1 billion. Craig Hanson and David Sandalow recommend several reforms to the existing energy tax policy. See Craig Hanson and David Sandalow, "Greening the Tax Code," *Tax Reform, Energy and the Environment Policy Brief* 1 (Brookings and World Resources Institute, April 2006). Eric Toder also provides a discussion of possible changes in incentives for energy use in the tax code. See Eric Toder, "Energy Taxation: Principles and Interests," *Energy—A Special Supplement to Tax Notes, State Tax Notes, and Tax Notes International* (November 27, 2006), p. 93.

26. The Energy Improvement and Extension Act of 2008 partially limited the domestic manufacturing deduction for oil and gas companies; this limitation raised revenues by an expected $4.9 billion over ten years.

27. As an example, consider a taxpayer in 2007 with a $6,000 regular tax liability and a $5,500 AMT liability who purchases a two-wheel-drive Ford Escape and is eligible for a $3,000 tax credit. This taxpayer could only claim $500 of the tax credit because the remainder of the credit is limited by the AMT.

28. In addition, about 100,000 taxpayers lost the value of deductions because of the AMT.

CHAPTER NINE

Cost-Effectiveness of Greenhouse Gas Emission Reductions from Plug-in Hybrid Electric Vehicles

DANIEL M. KAMMEN, SAMUEL M. ARONS,
DEREK M. LEMOINE, and HOLMES HUMMEL

Cars and light trucks in the United States consume about 8 million barrels of gasoline per day, which is more than the total amount of petroleum produced in the United States and accounts for 18 percent of national greenhouse gas (GHG) emissions. Consumption and emissions have been rising at about 1.5 percent per year.[1]

Plug-in hybrid electric vehicles could alter these trends. On a vehicle technology spectrum that stretches from fossil fuel–powered conventional vehicles (CVs) through hybrid electric vehicles (HEVs) to all-electric vehicles (AEVs), PHEVs fall between the latter two types: they can run either in gasoline-fueled hybrid electric mode (like an HEV) or in all-electric mode with grid-supplied energy (like an AEV).[2] PHEVs are intriguing because they combine the best aspects of CVs (long range and easy refueling) with the best aspects of AEVs (low tailpipe emissions and reduced use of petroleum) and hence promise to reduce transportation-related GHG emissions, improve urban air quality, reduce petroleum consumption, and

Research for this paper began as a course project at University of California–Berkeley undertaken by author Samuel M. Arons and James Wilcox, with the help of Richard J. Plevin. Timothy E. Lipman and Zack Subin (University of California–Berkeley), as well as John German (American Honda Motor Company), provided helpful comments on draft versions. We thank T. J. Glauthier and David Sandalow for highly insightful com-

expand competition in the transportation fuels sector. Several companies now offer to convert HEVs to PHEVs, and several automakers, notably General Motors, Daimler-Chrysler, and Toyota, have announced PHEV development projects.

Fueling these announcements is the growing popular consensus that HEVs provide significant reductions in petroleum use and GHG emissions at small costs and the corresponding hope that PHEVs (as well as AEVs and fuel cell vehicles) may offer even more of these benefits. At least one prior study, however, found that neither the fuel savings from HEVs' increased efficiency—nor the value to society of their lower emissions of air pollutants and GHGs—offset their increased capital costs.[3] However, fuel prices in recent years have been higher than those of the early 2000s used by that study—and at these higher prices, fuel savings contribute more toward offsetting increased capital cost. In any case, few consumers base their decisions about which vehicle to purchase primarily on the cost of fuel, and many are willing to pay a premium for the symbolic and environmental benefits of HEV ownership.[4] Like PHEVs, AEVs and fuel cell vehicles promise deeper reductions in emissions, but their higher capital costs make these reductions expensive.[5] One study, which compared the social costs of CVs and AEVs, concluded that the value of AEVs' reduced pollution only offsets the high cost of their batteries if the electricity is produced with very low air pollution; however, the CV emission rates in that study were up to an order of magnitude higher than the current standards in California.[6] Because capital costs similar to those for AEVs would be required to obtain the benefits of PHEVs' reduced GHG emissions, these findings suggest that we must be cautious before applying conventional wisdom about HEV cost-effectiveness to PHEVs.

Caution is warranted because PHEV batteries cost more than their HEV counterparts since they must store more energy. Until recently, only HEVs

ments on this paper. This research was made possible by support from the Class of 1935 of the University of California–Berkeley, the Energy Foundation, the Karsten Family Foundation (to Daniel M. Kammen), and the National Science Foundation's Graduate Research Fellowship Program (GRFP) (to Derek M. Lemoine).

We dedicate this paper to Dr. Alex Farrell, collaborator, colleague, and friend who passed away in April 2008, during work on an earlier version of this project.

had been analyzed according to the cost-effectiveness criterion; though now, at least one study has examined PHEVs along these lines as well.[7] In the PHEV study, the authors found that in the specific case of a compact car PHEV20 (that is, it can travel twenty miles using only grid-supplied electricity) under current market and policy conditions, the expected fuel savings from increased efficiency do not compensate consumers for the increased capital cost. Derek Lemoine reaches a similar conclusion despite using a real options approach to better value the fuel flexibility provided by PHEVs' batteries in a world of uncertain fuel prices.[8] Therefore, PHEVs could be consigned to an insignificant market share, unless their symbolic benefits relative to those of HEVs become sufficiently strong, market conditions become sufficiently favorable, battery technologies become sufficiently cheaper, or policies are implemented that sufficiently support these new vehicles.

A separate consideration, which the authors of the PHEV study leave open, is PHEVs' cost-effectiveness in reducing GHG emissions, measured in $/t-$CO_2$-eq (dollars per metric ton of carbon dioxide equivalent).[9] This question is important because PHEVs' reduced emissions of GHGs (as well as other pollutants) have real economic value to society, and hence governments, firms, or individuals might be willing to subsidize PHEV purchases to achieve these benefits—provided that the $/t-$CO_2$-eq cost is not too great. The purpose of this chapter is to address this question, comparing PHEVs with other options for mitigating GHGs (for example, reforestation or improving building insulation) on a cost curve such as that found in the report by Jon Creyts and others.[10] Note that while we focus on PHEVs' value as a strategy to abate GHGs, PHEVs also offer social benefits through reduced petroleum consumption and reduced urban air pollution that many other GHG abatement options will not. Any comparison of PHEVs with other abatement technologies on the basis of the metric $/t-$CO_2$-eq is therefore incomplete. However, we consider only GHGs and leave other air pollutants for future research. Though we conclude that PHEVs are not currently a cost-effective means of mitigating GHGs (see the section Break-Even Battery Costs), we find that they could become so under certain scenarios that we present below (see the section PHEV Cost-Effectiveness in Reducing GHGs, and Sensitivity Analyses). We conclude by discussing the commercial and policy implications of our results.

Methods and Results

We compare a CV, an HEV, and two PHEVs—one that can travel twenty miles using only grid-supplied electricity (called a PHEV20) and one that can travel sixty miles using only grid-supplied electricity (called a PHEV60)—in two models: compact car and full-size SUV, resulting in eight vehicle scenarios, following the assumptions made in prominent prior studies (see table 9-1).[11] Note from the table that while PHEVs are much more efficient at using gasoline than are CVs, they are only slightly more efficient than HEVs, and thus almost all of the benefits of converting from HEVs to PHEVs lie in PHEVs' ability to switch fuels, allowing a portion of PHEVs' miles to be driven on cheaper and cleaner electricity. Note also that while these prior studies model PHEVs' gasoline-mode fuel economy as higher than that of HEVs, the opposite may turn out to be true because of the extra weight of the PHEVs' batteries.

Following the Electric Power Research Institute, we assume that PHEVs operate as AEVs over some number of miles, drawing power only from their batteries until the batteries are depleted, before switching to operation as a hybrid vehicle and drawing power from the gasoline engine. Such PHEVs would need batteries possessing the characteristics of both "energy batteries" (a type of battery that can store and deliver large amounts of energy over longer timescales) and "power batteries" (which can deliver large amounts of energy quickly for the high-power portions of the driving cycle).

Fuel Prices and Vehicle Purchase Incentives

The conditions under which PHEV owners would have an economic incentive to use electricity rather than gasoline are determined by the relative fuel efficiencies of each operational mode and the prices of the two energy sources. Following the methodology of D. M. Lemoine, D. M. Kammen, and A. E. Farrell, table 9-1 shows the electricity rates whose cost per mile of PHEV operation is the same as that for various gasoline prices. Lower rates than the ones shown would encourage PHEV owners to drive in electric mode, while higher rates would favor the gasoline-fueled hybrid electric mode. For comparison, average U.S. residential electricity rates are about $0.083 per kWh, and U.S. gasoline prices averaged about $2.75 per gallon in 2006.[12]

On the one hand, the higher efficiency of PHEVs and their ability to switch to a generally cheaper fuel result in cost savings over the lifetime of the vehicles that have the potential to offset PHEVs' higher capital cost and to incentivize their purchase. But because of utility tariff and tax structures, PHEV owners may pay electricity rates that are higher than the average rates, which would erode the vehicles' cost savings (see Lemoine, Kammen, and Farrell for a discussion of tariff and tax considerations). On the other hand, a "grid optimal" nighttime charging arrangement could enhance PHEV cost savings and take advantage of possibly idle low-GHG generation capacity (though there are several caveats—see the section GHG Emission Reductions). We therefore make the simplifying assumption of a constant $0.10/kWh electricity price along with a constant $2/gal gasoline price for our base case scenario, described in the section PHEV Cost-Effectiveness in Reducing GHGs and Sensitivity Analyses.

Break-Even Battery Costs

Following the methodology of Lemoine, Kammen, and Farrell, we define the *marginal fuel savings* as the net present value (NPV) of a vehicle's fuel-savings cash flow relative to that of a comparison vehicle, and we divide these marginal fuel savings by the additional nominal battery capacity required by the first vehicle to obtain the *break-even battery cost* of the first vehicle relative to the second. The break-even battery cost is the price (in $/kWh) to which batteries must fall so that consumers can obtain an exact payback from the marginal fuel savings on their more expensive vehicle purchase (compared with having bought the cheaper—and less efficient—comparison vehicle). Rating the different vehicle types along a continuum of efficiency upgrades, we make comparisons between HEVs and CVs, PHEV20s and HEVs, and PHEV60s and PHEV20s. In the base case, we assume that consumers possess a 16 percent discount rate, that batteries represent the entire *marginal vehicle cost*, and that batteries last the entire twelve-year vehicle lifetime.[13] We also assume that the vehicles drive 11,000 miles (17,700 kilometers or km) annually and that PHEV20s drive 39 percent of their miles in all-electric mode while PHEV60s drive 74 percent of their miles in electric mode.[14]

Break-even battery costs for the purchase of HEVs and PHEVs at various gasoline prices are presented in table 9-1. For comparison, the U.S. Advanced Battery Coalition (USABC) has adopted a target of $150/kWh, and our calculated upper bound for battery prices is about $1,300/kWh (though we have seen an estimate of $500/kWh).[15] Using our estimated value, we find that consumers' break-even costs are lower than actual HEV or PHEV battery prices, implying that, under current battery prices, fuel savings alone would not offset the vehicles' increased capital cost and hence would not justify their purchase (this result is consistent with Lemoine, Kammen, and Farrell and with L. B. Lave and H. L. MacLean in the case of HEVs).[16]

GHG Emission Reductions

To determine the GHG emissions that are avoided by the use of HEVs and PHEVs, we use a well-to-wheels assessment of the transportation fuel sector called the Greenhouse Gases, Regulated Emissions, and Energy Use in Transportation (GREET) model.[17] Note that we do not include emissions from vehicle or battery manufacturing.[18] We update GREET with GHG emission data for the full fuel life cycles of a number of different power plant types.[19] Then we calculate the life cycle GHG emissions in units of g-CO_2-eq/mile of each vehicle type when operating in gasoline mode and, when applicable, in electric mode. We present our results in table 9-2.

The efficiency gains achievable by simply adopting a hybrid drivetrain are significant, as evidenced by the 23 percent lower GHG emissions for compact HEVs and 34 percent lower emissions for SUV HEVs compared with their CV counterparts. PHEVs essentially eliminate petroleum consumption per mile when operating in electric mode, but their GHG emission reductions depend critically on the type of electricity generation used to power the vehicles. We include the U.S. average and California average electricity grid mixes in the table for purposes of comparison, but because PHEVs represent new electricity demand and consume electricity produced by the marginal plant, in the short run it is incorrect to calculate the environmental impacts of PHEVs using average electricity emissions. In the long run, if PHEVs become numerous enough to lead to new investment in electricity generation, then an analysis using average emissions becomes more reasonable (in the absence of regulatory constraints on the GHG intensity of new power plants), but even under the most aggressive market penetration scenarios, this would not occur for five to ten years.[20]

The marginal power plant varies with time and location, but under the standard U.S. power system arrangement, it is often a thermal plant

TABLE 9-1. Efficiency, Battery, and Cost Characteristics of Modeled Vehicles[a]

	Fuel economy[b]		Grid electricity to travel AER (kWh)	Battery pack size[b] (kWh)	Equivalent electricity price[c] ($/kWh)			Break-even battery cost[c] ($/kWh at $0.10/kWh electricity)		
	(mi/gal)	(mi/kWh)			$2.00/gal gasoline	$3.00/gal gasoline	$4.00/gal gasoline	$2.00/gal gasoline	$3.00/gal gasoline	$4.00/gal gasoline
Compact car										
CV	37.7	--	--	--	--	--	--	--	--	--
HEV	49.4	--	--	2.2	--	--	--	$326	$490	$653
PHEV20	52.7	4.01	4.99	5.1	$0.152	$0.228	$0.304	$149	$320	$490
PHEV60	55.0	4.04	14.9	15.2	$0.147	$0.220	$0.294	$29	$68	$106
Sport utility vehicle (full-size SUV)										
CV	18.2	--	--	--	--	--	--	--	--	--
HEV	27.6	--	--	5.2	--	--	--	$412	$618	$825
PHEV20	29.5	2.31	8.66	8.9	$0.157	$0.235	$0.313	$220	$461	$702
PHEV60	30.2	2.43	24.7	25.3	$0.161	$0.241	$0.322	$37	$79	$121

Source: Authors' calculations.
AER = all-electric range (twenty miles for a plug-in hybrid electric vehicle or PHEV20, sixty miles for a PHEV60).
-- Not applicable.
a. See the discussions on battery types and sizes, fuel prices and sizes, fuel prices and vehicle purchase incentives, and break-even battery costs for details of assumptions and calculations.
b. EPRI (2001, 2002).
c. Expanded from the methodology of Lemoine, Kammen, and Farrell (2008).

TABLE 9-2. Per-Mile Petroleum Consumption and GHG Emissions of Modeled Vehicles[a]

	Petroleum use[b] (BTU/mi)		GHG emissions from gasoline use and from electricity use with different generation mixes[b] (g-CO_2-eq/mi)						
	Gasoline	NGCC electricity	Gasoline	U.S. avg	Calif. avg	NGCC	IGCC without CCS	IGCC with CCS	Wind
Compact car									
CV	3,260	--	294	--	--	--	--	--	--
HEV	2,490	--	225	--	--	--	--	--	--
PHEV20	2,330	10	211	199	116	135	282	38	1.4
PHEV60	2,240	10	203	198	115	134	280	37	1.4
Sport utility vehicle (full-size SUV)									
CV	6,750	--	605	--	--	--	--	--	--
HEV	4,450	--	401	--	--	--	--	--	--
PHEV20	4,170	18	375	346	202	234	490	65	2.4
PHEV60	4,070	17	367	329	192	222	466	62	2.3

Source: Authors' calculations.

BTU = British thermal units; CCS = carbon capture and sequestration; IGCC = integrated gasification combined cycle; GHG = greenhouse gas; NGCC = natural gas combined cycle; PHEV20 = plug-in hybrid electric vehicle that can travel twenty miles using only grid-supplied electricity; PHEV60 = can travel sixty miles on grid-supplied electricity; g/t-CO_2-eq = grams per metric ton of carbon dioxide equivalent.
-- Not applicable.
a. See the discussions on reductions in GHG emissions for details of assumptions and calculations.
b. Wang (2001); Pacca and Horvath (2006); Morgan, Apt, and Lave (2005).

burning natural gas because the output of such plants can be controlled, making them "dispatchable." In contrast, nuclear power plants (as well as many coal plants) attempt to operate at maximum capacity at all times, though they may end up operating below capacity at night when demand is low. Many renewable electricity generators (such as wind or photovoltaic arrays, but not solar thermal; large-scale hydroelectric; or geothermal) must generate using whatever resource level is available and so cannot be dispatched, and they are often given the highest priority in the electricity system's loading order.[21] Therefore, unless these renewable electricity generators would have needed to scale back their production in the absence of PHEVs—by, for instance, shedding wind during low-demand nighttime hours—they cannot be considered the marginal plants for PHEV charging, and it would be inappropriate to consider new PHEV demand as being supplied by them.[22] Under other theoretical power system arrangements involving more actively managed charging, it might be possible for wind turbines to charge PHEVs, but such arrangements would have many complexities and require further study.

If PHEVs are operated on coal electricity through integrated gasification combined cycle (IGCC) without carbon capture and sequestration (CCS), compact and SUV PHEVs reduce GHG emissions by 4 percent and 19 percent, respectively, relative to their CV counterparts. But these GHG reductions are actually *less* than those achieved by HEVs running on gasoline (23 percent and 34 percent, respectively). Thus, when the marginal plant is such a coal plant, it is better from a GHG perspective to drive either an HEV or (almost equivalently) a PHEV in gasoline-fueled hybrid electric mode rather than a PHEV in grid-supplied all-electric mode. In comparison with CVs running on gasoline, however, PHEVs charging from coal are the better option (though more so in the case of SUVs than compacts). These findings may have severe implications if electric utilities want to push PHEV charging into off-peak hours when coal-fired units may be the marginal plants in some U.S. regions.

If PHEVs are operated on electricity generated by less GHG-intensive power plants, GHG reductions are greater. When the electricity is generated from a natural gas combined cycle (NGCC) power plant, compact and SUV PHEVs reduce GHG emissions by 54 percent and 61 percent, respectively, relative to their CV counterparts. For very low-GHG plants, such as IGCC plants with CCS, wind turbines, or nuclear plants, PHEVs can reduce GHG emissions by as much as 85 percent relative to CVs under average driving conditions and could reduce GHG emissions by nearly 100 percent when driven only in electric mode.

PHEV Cost-Effectiveness in Reducing GHGs and Sensitivity Analyses

We define the size of the subsidy that is necessary to incentivize PHEV purchases as the marginal vehicle cost minus the marginal fuel savings, assuming that expected fuel costs determine which type of vehicle a buyer purchases (CV, HEV, or PHEV) within a broader class of vehicles (compacts or SUVs) (see the section Break-Even Battery Costs). If no subsidy is needed, we set the size of the subsidy at $0, precluding negative values for GHG abatement costs. As mentioned at the beginning of the chapter, consumers do not explicitly follow net present value calculations when they purchase vehicles, but the comparison between expected fuel savings and additional capital cost is an interesting one and may serve as a passable proxy for the general attractiveness of PHEVs. To measure the cost-effectiveness of GHG mitigation, we divide the subsidy size for each vehicle option by its GHG reductions to obtain the GHG mitigation cost ($/t-$CO_2$-eq). Note that while we discount future fuel savings, we do not similarly discount future GHG emission reductions. As we describe below, we conclude that neither HEVs nor PHEVs currently represent a cost-effective means of reducing GHG emissions, although under lower battery prices, less GHG-intensive electricity, or higher gasoline prices, certain types of PHEVs could become cost-effective.

In the base case, we perform these cost-effectiveness calculations using the GREET model for PHEVs charging from an NGCC plant at an electricity price of $0.10/kWh and with a gasoline price of $2 per gallon, a battery price of $1,000/kWh, a discount rate of 16 percent, no battery replacement over the twelve-year lifetime of the vehicle, and no carbon price.[23] The cost-effectiveness of PHEVs' GHG abatement is determined by the size of the subsidy needed to persuade cost-conscious vehicle buyers to purchase the vehicles (the numerator in the $/t-$CO_2$-eq cost expression) and by the GHG emission reductions achieved by the PHEV (the denominator in the $/t-$CO_2$-eq cost expression). Thus, if we wanted to increase the cost-effectiveness, we could take actions to decrease the numerator, increase the denominator, or both.

We also perform a number of sensitivity analyses and find that the parameters whose variation produces the greatest change in cost-effectiveness are battery price ($200/kWh in the sensitivity analysis as

KAMMEN, ARONS, LEMOINE, and HUMMEL

TABLE 9-3. Cost of GHG Emission Reductions Implied by Subsidizing Purchases of HEVs and PHEVs[a]

	Compact cars			Sports utility vehicles		
	$CV \rightarrow HEV \rightarrow PHEV20 \rightarrow PHEV60$			$CV \rightarrow HEV \rightarrow PHEV20 \rightarrow PHEV60$		
Base case[b]	$163	$429	$2,498	$113	$270	$1,994
Wind-generated electricity	$163	$196	$982	$113	$128	$904
$200/kWh batteries	$0	$26	$440	$0	$0	$338
Wind and $200/kWh batteries	$0	$12	$173	$0	$0	$153
$4-a-gal. gasoline	$84	$258	$2,298	$34	$103	$1,820
$100/t-CO$_2$-eq carbon tax	$120	$373	$2,441	$70	$215	$1,940

Source: Authors' calculations.

GHG = greenhouse gas; HEV = hybrid electric vehicle; PHEV = plug-in hybrid electric vehicle.

a. Costs of GHG emission reductions are in the valuation of dollars per metric ton of carbon dioxide equivalent ($/t-CO$_2$-eq).

b. The base case uses natural gas combined cycle (NGCC) generation for PHEVs' electricity, $1000/kWh batteries, $2-a-gal gasoline, no carbon tax, $0.10/kWh retail electricity prices, a discount rate of 16 percent for fuel savings, a twelve-year vehicle lifetime, and no anticipated battery replacement. The other five scenarios are deviations from the base case. Vehicles are valued only on the basis of their fuel consumption (by consumers) and their GHG emissions (by the government). Vehicle characteristics and emission rates are as in tables 9-1 and 9-2.

compared with $1,000/kWh in the base case), electricity GHG intensity (with very low-GHG for wind-generated instead of NGCC-generated electricity), and gasoline price ($4 per gallon compared with $2 per gallon). We additionally perform a carbon price sensitivity analysis (no price compared with a $100/t-CO$_2$-eq price) but find that it is not nearly as important as the other three parameters. We present these select results in table 9-3 and figure 9-1, which show how increasing subsidies encourage "transitions" to more efficient vehicles, which generally follow the CV-HEV-PHEV20-PHEV60 chain of increasingly efficient and increasingly expensive vehicles.

The battery price sensitivity analyses in table 9-3 and figure 9-1 illustrate the critical importance of low battery prices: without affordable batteries, the GHG emission reductions from PHEVs cost well over $100 per metric ton of carbon dioxide equivalent, which is expensive compared with a benchmark price of approximately $50/t-CO$_2$-eq.[24] The sensitivity analyses for low-GHG electricity and for the gasoline price illustrate the importance of these parameters as well.

According to the carbon price sensitivity analysis, a $100/t-CO$_2$-eq carbon price does not change GHG mitigation costs as significantly as do the other parameters. Additionally, because the effect of the carbon tax

FIGURE 9-1. GHG Abatement Cost Implied by Subsidizing Purchases of HEVs and PHEVs[a]

Cost of GHG emission reductions in dollars
($/t-CO$_2$-eq)

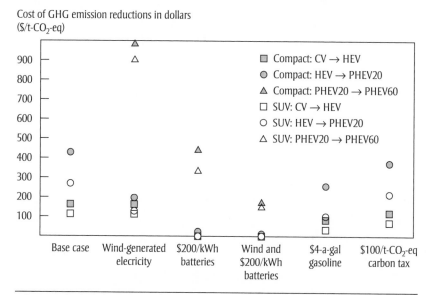

Source: Authors' calculations.

GHG = greenhouse gas; HEV = hybrid electric vehicle; PHEV = plug-in hybrid electric vehicle.

a. The GHG abatement cost implied by the subsidy needed to persuade cost-conscious buyers of compact cars and sport utility vehicles (SUVs) to forgo conventional vehicles (CVs) for hybrid electric vehicles (HEVs), HEVs for plug-in hybrid electric vehicles with a twenty-mile all-electric range (PHEV20s), and PHEV20s for plug-in hybrid electric vehicles with a sixty-mile all-electric range (PHEV60s). The base case uses natural gas combined cycle (NGCC) generation for PHEVs' electricity, $1,000/kWh batteries, $2/gal gasoline, no carbon tax, $0.10/kWh retail electricity prices, a discount rate of 16 percent for fuel savings, a twelve-year vehicle lifetime, and no anticipated battery replacement. The other five scenarios are deviations from the base case. Vehicles are valued only on the basis of their fuel consumption (by consumers) and their GHG emissions (by the government). Vehicle characteristics and emission rates are as in tables 9-1 and 9-2. Some values (see table 9-3) are greater than $1,000/t-CO$_2$-eq ($1,000 per metric ton of carbon dioxide equivalent).

scales linearly with the size of the tax, the effect of a $10/t-CO$_2$-eq tax would be 1/10 that of the $100/t-CO$_2$-eq tax presented here. Thus we conclude that a carbon tax or economy-wide GHG cap-and-trade system would not be particularly helpful in making PHEVs a cost-effective option for GHG mitigation.

Table 9-3 and figure 9-1 additionally show that vehicle class (CV, HEV) is also an important determinant of the cost-effectiveness of GHG mitigation: we find that because of the very low fuel efficiency of conventional (CV) SUVs, it is more cost-effective to replace them with HEV or PHEV varieties than to replace CV compact cars with more efficient versions. This is because the same percentage increase in fuel efficiency (for example, in miles per gallon) saves more fuel when the initial fuel efficiency is lower. An even better and more cost-effective way to reduce GHGs, of course, would be to replace CV SUVs with *compact* HEVs or PHEVs, but we take consumers' vehicle class preferences as given and thus do not consider cross-class efficiency upgrades. In any case, this result suggests that any automotive strategy for GHG mitigation should focus on reducing emissions from larger vehicles by shifting purchases toward smaller vehicles and by improving the efficiency of larger vehicles.

Additionally, we find that vehicle type (CV, HEV, and PHEV) is an important determinant of cost-effectiveness. Under most market conditions, replacing CVs with HEVs represents the least costly GHG mitigation step, although with cheap enough batteries, replacing HEVs with PHEV20s can be cost-effective in its own right, setting aside the GHG abatement benefits. For example, the cost-effectiveness of replacing SUV HEVs with PHEV20s does not depend on GHG valuation if batteries cost $200/kWh. However, replacing PHEV20s with PHEV60s represents a costly GHG abatement strategy, under base case conditions—where it can cost more than $2,000/t-$CO_2$-eq—and the same is true under other scenarios we consider. These findings suggest that automotive GHG reduction strategies should focus initially on vehicles with smaller and cheaper batteries, such as HEVs and PHEV20s, as opposed to vehicles with larger batteries, such as PHEV60s and AEVs. Nonetheless, vehicles with larger batteries may have more value in longer-term abatement strategies that look beyond the directly achievable GHG emission reductions.

Finally, we acknowledge that several of the assumptions outlined above probably make our direct abatement cost results a lower bound. Taking these considerations into account, then, would reduce PHEVs' cost-effectiveness further (that is, increase our calculated $/t-$CO_2$-eq values). However, the fact that PHEVs might turn out to be even less cost-effective than we have calculated here would not qualitatively change our conclusions because the break-even battery costs in table 9-1 are already rather ambitious in comparison with current battery prices. That is, whether battery prices need to decline to $500/kWh (as our results suggest) or to a still lower level, the best strategy in either situation would be to undertake a broad and sustained portfolio of battery research and development (R&D).

Discussion

Policymakers might pursue two separate goals with respect to PHEVs. The first is to make the vehicles more cost-effective from the consumer's point of view. To do so, legislators might enact policies encouraging or supporting a broad program of battery R&D, with the goal of increasing battery lifetimes, bringing down prices below $500/kWh (which is approximately the upper bound of the break-even battery costs presented in table 9-1), or both—as opposed to the ambitious $150/kWh target of the U.S. Advanced Battery Coalition (USABC).[25] Battery companies should aim for this target as well. Policymakers might also encourage PHEV adoption by reducing vehicle costs or increasing vehicle benefits. Such policies could include providing loans, rebates (whether stand-alone or as part of a feebate program), tax incentives, or nonmonetary incentives (such as preferred parking spaces or access to carpool lanes) to consumers who purchase PHEVs. Additionally, they could include making the price of gasoline disproportionately higher than the price of electricity, as might occur if energy security concerns become paramount.

The second goal policymakers might pursue is to increase the cost-effectiveness of PHEVs in mitigating GHGs. The above policies for consumer cost-effectiveness would help here as well, as would policies (such as a renewable portfolio standard) that lower the GHG intensity of the electricity grid and especially of marginal generators. It is important to note, however, that enacting a carbon tax or an economy-wide cap-and-trade system would not be directly useful for making PHEVs cost-effective in terms of fuel savings or direct GHG abatement.

Note, however, that incentivizing the adoption of PHEVs before costs become sufficiently low or battery lives become sufficiently long could negatively affect the public's perception of the vehicles and thus impede widespread adoption. As attractive as PHEV technology is today, policymakers must remain cognizant of such trade-offs when considering the adoption of these types of policies.

At least one of the policies outlined above, the renewable portfolio standard (RPS), has been enacted in a number of jurisdictions, and other regulations, such as green electricity marketing, have been enacted or are being considered as well. The existence of such policies could affect our analysis because concerns over double counting make it unclear whether

PHEVs would achieve the GHG abatement we have estimated. This is because renewable electricity production currently creates power as well as renewable energy credits (RECs), which are purchased by the utility to satisfy RPS requirements or by a particular customer to validate his or her purchase of renewable energy. If renewable or low-GHG power that is used to charge a PHEV creates a REC that is sold to some other party (such as the utility), then it may be deemed inappropriate to also assign the GHG emission reductions to the PHEV. Another possible solution is to create a third commodity for the PHEV, an emission reduction credit (ERC), but that too may be considered double counting. Similarly, PHEVs might be used to meet the recently adopted Low Carbon Fuel Standard for California, though again, how to do so without double counting or interfering with the operation of other policies is not yet clear.[26]

Actual and proposed plans to control GHG emissions from the electric power sector in general also complicate this analysis. For example, if GHG emissions from the electricity sector are capped, PHEV use brings a fraction of transportation emissions under a hard cap—and if that cap is binding, then use of electricity by PHEVs generates no new GHG emissions. In this case, we can say that PHEVs that replace CVs or HEVs avoid 100 percent of gasoline GHG emissions for miles driven in electric mode, irrespective of the marginal plant or vehicle efficiency. However, expanding the electricity sector's allowed GHG emissions to account for demand growth due to PHEV adoption would erode this effect.

In the long term, if pro-PHEV policies and technological advances prove successful and PHEVs become widely adopted, their increased electricity demand could have implications for the electric power sector, potentially changing the shape of the daily load curve and raising electricity prices. In Lemoine, Kammen, and Farrell's study of the impact of PHEV charging in northern California, the authors found that charging became important when PHEV adoption rates were very high, between 5 and 10 million PHEVs out of a fleet of some 17 million cars and light-duty trucks.[27] PHEVs could also have implications for the sector if their batteries were used to provide ancillary services to the grid because of the challenge of setting up and running such a service. Thus, managing the economic and environmental implications of PHEVs will be a major challenge that will require new technical, commercial, and regulatory interfaces. However, governments may be justified in undertaking a broad and sustained program of research, development, and demonstration of appropriate technologies, regulations, and policies because PHEVs have the potential to achieve such significant GHG reductions (even though they may prove rather costly without steep declines in battery prices and increases in low-GHG electricity generation). Advances in these areas could encourage the adoption of PHEVs in conjunction with the decarbonization of the electricity supply.

Promoting PHEVs by Amending the Federal Renewable Fuels Standard

The above policies can provide strong incentives for the use of PHEVs, although an ongoing concern is to make sure that credits for carbon abatement are only rewarded once within a single regulatory program (that is, generators and PHEV drivers should not both be able to claim credit for the same avoided emissions). Meanwhile, the United States has already enacted a Renewable Fuel Standard (RFS) policy that deserves reconsideration in light of unintended consequences arising from competition for resources common to the production of food, fuel, forests, and feedstocks. These environmental and economic impacts are expected to intensify as refiners deliver an increasing volume of biofuels to meet the RFS mandate, and credit for the use of fuel electricity in PHEVs may be able to offer a compelling solution.

If the volumetric RFS were converted to a qualitative Low Carbon Fuel Standard (LCFS), the new policy could be structured to reward forms of transit with the very lowest GHG per mile, which generally include mass transit, reductions in vehicle miles traveled, and the use of PHEV vehicles. Despite the fact that several key lawmakers support an LCFS, leaders of the 110th Congress that authorized the RFS through the Energy Independence and Security Act in 2007 have indicated little interest in revisiting that policy debate, which limits the extent of modifications that may be accomplished in the near term.

The federal RFS obligates refiners to deliver a certain quantity of biofuels to market each year as an alternative to gasoline. The policy distinguishes between four categories of renewable fuels that are differentiated according to environmental attributes—and avoided greenhouse gas emissions in particular. Among them, the RFS reserves the largest market quota for a category called "renewable biofuel," which is defined as a fuel with a greenhouse gas emissions profile that is 20 to 50 percent less than gasoline. Refiners are required to increase purchases of renewable biofuels each year, reaching 15 billion gallons in 2022. However, the law also waives the basic environmental performance criterion of a 20 percent reduction in greenhouse gas emission relative to gasoline for 13.5 billion gallons of corn ethanol production capacity that was preexisting or under construction at the time of passage. The RFS is then, in effect, a government mandate requiring refiners to buy all the corn ethanol production available from plants that were under construction in 2007, no matter how large the greenhouse gas footprint of the fuel cycle, and new studies indicate that the GHG impact of corn ethanol may be high enough to invalidate it as a renewable fuel under the RFS.

In an EPA study completed before the passage of the RFS, the only other transportation fuel source in the 20 to 50 percent GHG reduction range was electricity, which delivered a 46 percent reduction based on the national average carbon content of electricity. By allowing electricity to serve as a substitute to satisfy the renewable biofuel mandate in the RFS, the United States could accomplish the same energy security goals (reduced oil imports through reduced gasoline use) while improving its carbon footprint and also mitigating the detrimental impact that the RFS for corn ethanol is having on other markets as well as on the environment.

The key to this policy modification is the structure of compensation for major actors. Under the terms of the 2008 Farm Bill, the United States is obligated to pay fuel blenders $0.45 for each gallon of ethanol they buy to displace gasoline. In the congressional budgeting process, those funds have already been committed and "paid for" through 2022. As a result, the federal government is committed to paying $2,100 in subsidies for corn ethanol to displace 4,600 gallons of gasoline, approximately the same amount avoided by a 100-mpg PHEV over its life compared with a 30-mpg passenger car.[28]

If electricity used by PHEVs qualified as an RFS offset (namely a substitute) for the corn ethanol mandate, the blenders could claim a calculated credit of 4,600 gallons simply by reallocating money they would have spent on ethanol and instead paying automakers a fee. For example, the refiner could pay approximately $6,000 for every 100-mpg PHEV, avoiding $7,000 in ethanol purchases it otherwise would be mandated to make.[29] Furthermore, the federal government would be relieved from paying the equivalent of $2,100 for the avoided 4,600 gallons under the corn ethanol mandate, which could also be redirected to manufacturers of plug-in cars using fuel electricity. The total benefit to manufacturers of

PHEVs could be $8,100 a vehicle, which would accomplish the policy imperative to cover the (diminishing) cost premium for the production of next-generation battery technologies. To accomplish this goal, the RFS would be modified to require or encourage fuel producers to pay this fee on the basis of PHEV sales through individual blender–automotive company deals, or, more simply, an industry-wide payment scheme could be instituted to reflect PHEV sales to private individuals or fleets. The blenders would save because of a reduced need to purchase fuels, which are currently running at or above the cost of gasoline.

The policy would fit entirely within the budgetary framework of the existing RFS, with no net cost to the federal government. The net benefit to the blenders would be $1,000 per PHEV, which could be warranted as they drive the market for their core product out of the transportation sector altogether. Automobile manufacturers would receive a source of cash to drive down their costs, and even if none of the $7,000 payments from the blenders were passed onto consumers, the cost of conserved gasoline for PHEV drivers would still be less than half the present cost of gasoline. Finally, from a social benefit perspective, this addition of electricity as an alternative to ethanol in the RFS would be rewarding improvements in energy security, food security, and GHG emissions—all with one simple modification to an existing policy framework.

Conclusion

Plug-in hybrid electric vehicles could significantly reduce automotive greenhouse gas emissions and petroleum consumption, while improving energy security and urban air quality. However, their widespread adoption depends upon technological and economic advances in batteries because fuel savings do not fully or rapidly compensate consumers for the capital costs of batteries today. For PHEV purchases to become economical to consumers, battery prices must fall below $500/kWh, or U.S. gasoline prices must rise to, and remain at, roughly $5 per gallon—or the federal government must institute policy innovations with equivalent effects, such as policies to lower battery cost and increase battery lifetimes (for example, a broad and sustained program of battery R&D) or those to widen the difference between gasoline and electricity prices (for example, changes in energy taxes).

However, even if PHEVs do *not* become economical for consumers, their purchase might still be valuable to society if their significant GHG reductions can be achieved cost-effectively (using a benchmark price of about $50/t-$CO_2$-eq).[30] Using the GREET model, we determined that for PHEVs' reductions to become cost-effective, either their purchase must approach near-economical levels—requiring the same policy innovations described above—or very low-GHG electricity must be used to power them, which would require policies to decrease the GHG intensity of electricity, such as renewable portfolio standards (as well as technologies and regulations to integrate PHEVs into an electricity grid with a greater proportion of intermittent renewables). It is important to note that we determined that any carbon price would have to greatly exceed $100/t-$CO_2$-eq to render PHEVs' reductions cost-effective, and hence a carbon price represents an impractical means of achieving this goal.

We additionally determined that given current technologies and prices, replacing full-sized conventional SUVs with hybrid (HEV) SUVs is actually a *more* cost-effective GHG abatement strategy than is subsidizing the adoption of compact car PHEVs. That is because conventional SUVs have such comparatively low fuel efficiency that the same percentage efficiency increase saves more fuel for SUVs than it does for compact cars. In the near term, then, policymakers could reduce the most GHG emissions by pursuing policies to encourage SUV hybridization (or efficiency increases in general). In the longer term, however, PHEVs could enable much greater GHG abatement, and hence the policy innovations described above—to lower battery cost and increase battery lifetimes, to widen the difference between gasoline and electricity prices, and to decrease the GHG intensity of electricity—appear justified.

Furthermore, to immediately accelerate financial support for PHEV development and deployment, Congress could make a modest change to the new Renewable Fuel Standard, offering flexibility to refiners that are obligated to buy billions of gallons of ethanol to displace gasoline. Because the national average carbon content of electricity has a much smaller carbon footprint than corn ethanol does, refiners could make a payment to PHEV manufacturers instead of ethanol producers, receiving RFS credits equal to the gallons of gasoline the PHEV would displace with electricity.

Notes

1. See U.S. Environmental Protection Agency, *Inventory of U.S. Greenhouse Gas Emissions and Sinks: 1990–2002* (Washington: EPA, Office of Policy, Planning, and Evaluation, April 15, 2004), p. 255 (www.epa.gov/climatechange/emissions/down loads06/04CR.pdf); S. C. Davis and S. W. Diegel, *Transportation Energy Data Book*, 25th ed., ORNL-6974 (Washington: U.S. Department of Energy, Office of Transportation Technologies, September 2006), p. 280 (http://cta.ornl.gov/cta/ Publications/ Reports/TEDB_Edition25_ORNL_6974.pdf).

2. See Electric Power Research Institute (EPRI), *Comparing the Benefits and Impacts of Hybrid Electric Vehicle Options for Compact Sedan and Sport Utility Vehicles*, Technical Report 1006892 (Palo Alto, Calif.: EPRI, 2002); EPRI, *Comparing the Benefits and Impacts of Hybrid Electric Vehicle Options*, Technical Report 1000349 (Palo Alto, Calif.: EPRI, 2001).

3. L. B. Lave and H. L. MacLean, "An Environmental-Economic Evaluation of Hybrid Electric Vehicles: Toyota's Prius vs. Its Conventional Internal Combustion Engine Corolla," *Transportation Research, Part D—Transport and Environment* 7, no. 2 (2002): 155–62.

4. See R. R. Heffner, K. S. Kurani, and T. S. Turrentine, "Symbolism in California's Early Market for Hybrid Electric Vehicles," *Transportation Research, Part D—Transport and Environment* 12, no. 6 (2007): 396–413.

5. See H. L. MacLean and L. B. Lave, "Life Cycle Assessment of Automobile/Fuel Options," *Environmental Science and Technology* 37, no. 2 (2003): 5445–452; M. Z. Jacobson, W. G. Colella, and D. M. Golden, "Cleaning the Air and Improving Health with Hydrogen Fuel-Cell Vehicles," *Science* 308, no. 5730 (2005): 1901–905.

6. K. Funk and A. Rabl, "Electric versus Conventional Vehicles: Social Costs and Benefits in France," *Transportation Research, Part D—Transport and Environment* 4, no. 6 (1999): 397–411.

7. For cost-effectiveness analysis of HEVs, see Lave and MacLean (2002); for PHEVs, see D. M. Lemoine, D. M. Kammen, and A. E. Farrell, "An Innovation and Policy Agenda for Commercially Competitive Plug-In Hybrid Vehicles," *Environmental Research Letters* 3, no. 1 (2008): 1–10.

8. D. M. Lemoine, "Valuing Plug-In Hybrid Electric Vehicles' Battery Capacity Using a Real Options Framework" (under review).

9. Lemoine, Kammen, and Farrell (2008).

10. Jon Creyts and others, *Reducing U.S. Greenhouse Gas Emissions: How Much at What Cost?* (New York: McKinsey & Company and The Conference Board, December 2007), p. xiii (www.mckinsey.com/clientservice/ccsi/pdf/US_ghg_final_ report.pdf).

11. EPRI (2002); EPRI (2001).

12. See U.S. Energy Information Administration, *Annual Energy Review 2006*, DOE/EIA-0384 (2006) (Washington: U.S. Department of Energy, 2007).

13. Concerning the 16 percent discount rate, see D. L. Greene and J. DeCicco, "Engineering-Economic Analyses of Automotive Fuel Economy Potential in the United States," *Annual Review of Energy and the Environment* 25 (2000): 477–535.

14. EPRI (2001).

15. Concerning the USABC target of $150/kWh, see R. A. Sutula, "Progress Report for Electric Vehicle Battery Research and Development Program" (Washington: U.S. Department of Energy, 2001) (www1.eere.energy.gov/vehiclesandfuels/pdfs/ program/ 2001_pr_elec_vehicle_batt.pdf). Concerning the upper bound of $1,300/kWh, we calculated our estimate from data available on the website of Hymotion, a company that performs conversions of HEVs into PHEVs (http://www.hymotion.com). On their website (accessed Spring 2007), they listed the price of performing such a conversion for a Toyota Prius, as well as the size (in kWh) of the new battery that they install. By dividing one by the other, we obtained the estimate for $/kWh. Concerning the estimate of $500/kWh, we received this estimate from Project Better Place via a personal communication.

16. Lemoine, Kammen, and Farrell (2008); Lave and MacLean (2002).

17. See M. Wang, "Development and Use of GREET 1.6—Fuel-Cycle Model for Transportation Fuels and Vehicle Technologies," ANL/ESD/TM-163 (Argonne, Ill.: Argonne National Laboratory, Center for Transportation Research, August 2001) (www.transportation.anl.gov/pdfs/TA/153.pdf.)

18. See C. Samaras and K. Meisterling, "Life Cycle Assessment of Greenhouse Gas Emissions from Plug-In Hybrid Vehicles: Implications for Policy," *Environmental Science & Technology* 42, no. 9 (2008): 3170–76.

19. For more details, see S. Pacca and A. Horvath, "Greenhouse Gas Emissions from Building and Operating Electric Power Plants in the Upper Colorado River Basin," *Environmental Science & Technology* 36, no. 14 (2006): 3194–200; M. G. Morgan, J. Apt, and L. B. Lave, "The U.S. Electric Power Sector and Climate Change Mitigation" (Arlington, Va.: Pew Center on Global Climate Change, June 2005) (www.pewclimate.org/docUploads/Electricity_Final.pdf).

20. See Lemoine, Kammen, and Farrell (2008).

21. For more details on displacement of renewable electricity generators, see J. F. DeCarolis and D. W. Keith, "The Costs of Wind's Variability: Is There a Threshold? *Electricity Journal* (January–February 2005): 69–77.

22. See, by way of comparison, L. Sanna, "Driving the Solution: The Plug-In Hybrid Vehicle," *EPRI Journal* (Fall 2005): 8–17.

23. Concerning discount rates, see D. L. Greene and J. DeCicco, "Engineering-Economic Analyses of Automotive Fuel Economy Potential in the United States," *Annual Review of Energy and the Environment* 25 (2000): 477–535.

24. See Creyts and others (2007).

25. For more details on battery research, see R. A. Sutula, "Progress Report for Electric Vehicle Battery Research and Development Program" (Washington: U.S. Department of Energy, Energy Efficiency and Renewable Energy, 2001) (www1.eere. energy.gov/vehiclesandfuels/pdfs/program/2001_pr_elec_vehicle_batt.pdf).

26. For more details on this standard in California, see A. Schwarzenegger, Executive Order S-01-07, "Low Carbon Fuel Standard (LCFS)" (Sacramento, Calif., January 18, 2007); A. R. Brandt and others, *A Low-Carbon Fuel Standard for California Part 2: Policy Analysis* (Sacramento, Calif.: Office of the Governor, Air Resources Board, 2007); S. M. Arons and others, *A Low-Carbon Fuel Standard for California Part 1: Technical Analysis* (Sacramento, Calif.: Office of the Governor, Air Resources Board, 2007).

27. Lemoine, Kammen, and Farrell (2008).

28. Although the fleet average today is roughly 23 mpg, we use a 30 mpg comparison as a target figure, assuming increases in Corporate Average Fuel Economy (CAFE) standards and because the "first adopters" may be purchasers of hybrid vehicles, who are already selecting from a higher mpg subset of available vehicles.

29. We suggest a value close to the total ethanol purchase, hence $6,000 out of a total fuel cost of $7,000, but higher and lower costs could be reasonably proposed and justified.

30. See Creyts and others (2007).

CHAPTER TEN

Federal Policy Options to Support Early Electric Vehicle Deployment by Reducing Financial and Technological Risks

BRACKEN HENDRICKS and BENJAMIN GOLDSTEIN

Plug-in electric vehicles (PEVs) represent one of the most promising near-term technologies to reduce U.S. dependence on oil and cut the carbon footprint of our transportation sector. Yet despite their enormous potential, progress toward mass commercialization has been slowed by a variety of roadblocks, primarily related to technology, risk, and cost.

This chapter identifies a number of obstacles to commercialization of PEVs, with a specific focus on how automakers' concerns over battery safety, durability, longevity, and cost have slowed adoption of this technology and delayed deployment across the U.S. fleet. The chapter then discusses in detail three complementary federal policy options to reduce financial and technology risk for early adopters; diminish automakers' concerns over moving toward mass production; alleviate consumer anxiety about battery safety, durability, and longevity over the life of the vehicle warranty; and provide a controlled testing environment in which to monitor battery performance. These options are as follows:

—adopt a federal fleet purchasing agreement to ensure a stable market and controlled testing environment for the first massive deployment of PEVs

—create the "Federal Battery Guarantee Corporation," which would underwrite insurance on battery life for the duration of the vehicle warranty

—guarantee a secondary market for used battery assemblies, which have reduced efficacy in vehicles but generally retain 80 percent of their energy storage capacity.

In the near term, these policies are intended to reduce risk and address industry and consumer fears about battery obsolescence enough to get the first wave of PEVs on the road. Ultimately, the goal is to help the PEV industry mature to the point that government support is no longer necessary, achieve economies of scale required to make PEVs affordable for the average consumer, and move rapidly to mass commercialization of this promising technology.

Why PEVs Now?

The U.S. auto industry is in a tumultuous period and faces an uncertain future. News of plant closings, layoffs, and persistent unprofitability appears almost daily, as the Big Three automakers recoil from a business model that invested heavily in larger vehicles (SUVs, crossovers, and pickups) with low fuel economy. With oil exceeding $140 a barrel in 2008, gasoline surpassing $4 a gallon, and the reality of global warming driving new policies to limit greenhouse gas emissions, the U.S. auto industry faces a completely new landscape that demands fresh thinking about its product lines.

The vehicle market is responding to those price signals. U.S. new-vehicle sales dropped sharply in 2008, with declines in almost all major models except for fuel-efficient compact vehicles.[1] On the other hand, sales of hybrid vehicles in April 2008 had climbed nearly 50 percent since April 2007, pushing the new-vehicle market share for hybrids past the 3 percent mark for the first time.[2] Because consumers have experienced record-high gasoline prices, consumer confidence in fuel-efficient hybrids is a trend that is here to stay: in a recent poll, nearly 50 percent of Americans estimated that in ten years, roughly half of all new cars sold would be hybrid vehicles.[3]

PEVs, with the benefit of their extended electric range, enjoy enormous popular support. According to an August 2007 survey for the Automotive X Prize Team, Americans see PEVs that get 100 miles per gallon (mpg) as the single most powerful way, of six ways tested, to combat global warming. Nearly two-thirds of respondents were "extremely" or "very" interested in

buying a 100-mpg car. And Americans see the development of such cars as
an important national objective—an important detail for the politics of promoting PEVs. Seventy-seven percent say that it would be "extremely" or
"very" important to have a project that would lead to such cars being manufactured and sold in the United States in the next five years.[4] Moreover,
consumers are showing sincere interest: as of June 2008, there were 11,512
"soft" orders on the Plug-In-Partners website, which tallies pledges to purchase PEVs once they are commercially available.

PEVs are unmistakably a game-changing technology in the auto sector.
Their potential to reduce oil consumption, curb greenhouse gas emissions, and save consumers money makes them an urgent national security,
public health, environmental, and economic priority. Moreover, if the
U.S. auto industry is to reverse its downturn and succeed in the twenty-
first-century vehicle market, it needs to move fast. Asian companies like
Toyota and Hyundai are rapidly developing their own PEV lines, and U.S.
automakers do not want to be caught in another game of catch-up, as
they were with hybrids. Moreover, the auto industry is capital intensive,
and the plant conversions and retooling necessary to support electric drivetrains will take time. The moment to act is now.

Obstacles to Commercialization

What, then, is inhibiting quicker adoption of PEVs by the auto industry?
Other chapters in this volume discuss some of the challenges with respect
to battery chemistry and concerns about the readiness of grid infrastructure. Yet neither issue is serious enough to prohibit getting the first generation of vehicles on the road.[5]

PEV technology has been approached cautiously by automakers primarily because of concerns over battery durability, longevity, and cost.
Large-format battery assemblies—currently estimated to cost at least
$10,000 for a forty-mile range—will constitute a hefty portion of a vehi-
cle's value, and the relatively new technology is viewed as a liability by
an industry accustomed to ten-year, 100,000-mile power train warranties. Thus, finding policy mechanisms to help reduce the cost and
technology risk thresholds for early adopters is crucial to getting the first
generation of the vehicles to market—thus priming consumers, spurring
investment and innovation in the private sector, and scaling up to reduce
costs.

However, generous policy support from Washington cannot go unmatched by the auto industry, which historically has been resistant to higher fuel efficiency standards and sluggish in exploring alternative drivetrains. Automakers have been especially cautious about vehicle electrification, in part because it represents such a large departure from the internal combustion engine. Accustomed to controlling the entire production process and selling the auto body, drivetrain, and accessories as a complete package, automakers are concerned that problems with battery assemblies will affect the integrity of their brands.

Yet now is the time for some constructive new thinking. If concerns over battery cost, risk, and performance underlie the auto industry's reluctance to act, then let the industry take a page from its own history and approach batteries as a serviceable, replaceable, and separately warranted component of the vehicle, just like tires. Cars must be designed so that the battery assemblies can be easily serviced or replaced as they age. And automakers must be receptive to innovative business models, like that promoted by Better Place, as new synergies are created among battery manufacturers, utility companies, automakers, and consumers.

This is a period of "creative destruction" for the auto industry, especially for the U.S. Big Three. They can seize the opportunity to develop and commercialize a new generation of low- and zero-emissions vehicles, or they can continue to hemorrhage jobs, close plants, and cede their market share to more nimble, innovative companies. Washington will have an important role in facilitating the transition to low-emissions vehicles, but it is up to the auto industry to do its part as well.

Three Policy Options

As mentioned, Washington can help speed up the adoption of PEVs by implementing three policy options: adopting a federal fleet purchasing agreement; creating the "Federal Battery Guarantee Corporation"; and guaranteeing a secondary market for used battery assemblies.

Federal Fleet Purchasing Agreement

A federal fleet purchasing agreement would commit the government to purchasing a specific number of PEVs each year. Currently, the federal government acquires approximately 63,000 new vehicles annually and maintains a fleet of roughly 631,000.[6] By 2012, that number of new vehicles is likely to be closer to 65,000. Legislation mandating that 30 percent of all new vehicles purchased by the U.S. government be PEVs beginning in 2012 would equate to approximately 20,000 units a year.[7] That percentage should be ramped up over time, as production increases, costs drop, and more PEV models are introduced.

By 2012, vehicle manufacturers may not be ready with PEV versions of the full range of vehicle classes (especially SUVs, vans, and pickups). The Chevy Volt and Toyota Prius PEVs are not scheduled to be ready until at least 2010, an ambitious timeframe. With that constraint in mind, the fleet purchasing agreement would have to be responsive to the realities of the technology and vehicle availability, without sacrificing its purpose: to persuade automakers to develop PEVs and reach scale quickly by providing a guaranteed market.

The federal government should also take concrete measures to support other forms of PEV market aggregation by cities, corporate fleets, and individual consumers. Adequate tax incentives to bring down the cost of PEVs for early adopters are discussed elsewhere in this volume.

A federal fleet purchasing agreement would be an effective policy instrument to address a variety of obstacles hindering PEV commercialization. First, lack of a dependable market has inhibited automakers from pushing a large first batch of PEVs off the assembly line. Second, automakers argue that battery assemblies are still relatively untested over the long term under diverse driving and environmental conditions. Third, mainstream consumers are still relatively uniformed or skeptical about the "100-mpg" car, which sounds almost too good to be true.

The proposed agreement would address these obstacles. First, it would create a guaranteed market for PEV vehicles, giving automakers the confidence to get PEV models off the drawing boards and on the assembly lines, quickly and at scale.

Second, it could play a crucial role in helping to test PEV performance over the long term, under diverse driving and environmental conditions. Having such a large number of units deployed under one jurisdiction allows for easy performance tracking. In return for a guaranteed market, automakers, battery manufacturers, and utilities should commit resources and collaborate with the General Services Administration on a performance monitoring pilot that covers vehicle energy use and long-term battery performance. Over time, the pilot should incorporate V2H (vehicle-to-home—or building) and V2G (vehicle-to-grid) technology. Moreover, the sheer size of the federal vehicle fleet allows the flexibility to experiment with emerging technologies and incorporate them in volume without much financial burden or risk—if some of these vehicles fail to perform, the results will not be catastrophic.

Third and last, a large deployment of PEVs in the federal fleet would send a message to consumers that this technology is very much a practical reality, not a side project of vehicle hobbyists and environmentalists. Dispelling the misperception that PEVs are inaccessible and futuristic will do much to prime the consumer market for large-scale adoption.

The cost of the proposed policy is difficult to estimate, given the uncertainties in future prices for large-format battery assemblies. Yet the U.S. government, as consumer of the most prodigious quantities of oil on the planet, has a strategic interest in obtaining cost-effective and reliable PEVs, even if they are expensive at the outset. And even using current cost structures, the financial burden is minimal. Assuming a $10,000 premium for a forty-mile battery assembly, 20,000 PEV vehicles would cost $200 million a year more than comparable internal combustion engine counterparts. Yet much of that cost would be offset by government savings on gasoline consumption over the lifetime of the vehicles. And the costs for PEVs would begin to drop significantly as the scale of production increased and technology improved.

"Federal Battery Guarantee Corporation"

The idea for the proposed Federal Battery Guarantee Corporation (FBGC) was briefly introduced by David Sandalow in his book *Freedom from Oil*. The FBGC would underwrite insurance on battery life and performance for the normal automotive drivetrain warranty period of ten years, thus removing risk for both the consumer and the vendor. The FBGC would cover only pure economic loss from functional obsolescence or product malfunction. If batteries fail to perform as promised for the full ten years, the government would pay out of an established insurance pool to have the battery serviced or replaced or to refund consumers for the value remaining on their warranty.

Automakers are accustomed to providing their customers with ten-year, 100,000-mile drivetrain warranties. Understandably, they are hesitant to extend that guarantee to PEVs running on batteries that have yet to be completely proven to perform to those specifications. Moreover, when releasing a new product, automakers must normally set funds aside to ensure that their risk is covered in the event of a defect or malfunction. Estimating the amount of risk coverage is exceedingly difficult for new, large-format battery assemblies with uncertain long-term performance, and coming up with the necessary funds is nearly impossible in the current environment, when credit is tight and automakers are running in the red.

The FBGC would resolve that impasse by partially removing the risk burden. Battery assembly manufacturers would still be responsible for guaranteeing solid workmanship and for covering their existing warranties, probably for the first two or three years, after which time the FBGC would come in, much as the third parties do that currently offer extended warranty packages for most consumer electronics. Therefore, for the FBGC to work, automakers must get comfortable with the notion of two separate warranties: one for the vehicle (which they continue to cover), and one for the battery assembly, covered initially by the battery manufacturer and later by the FBGC.

In the event of battery malfunction or underperformance, the FBGC would pay out to have the battery serviced or replaced or to refund consumers for the value remaining on their warranty—whichever is the cheapest option. The FBGC would not own the battery; it would only cover necessary repairs or replacements, just as tire companies do now and IBM used to do for its electric typewriters. Also, the FBGC would not perform the actual services, which would require developing a nationwide infrastructure for repairs. Rather, it would reimburse automakers, mechanics, or new battery repair companies for their parts and labor within a pre-established rate structure.

The FBGC is loosely inspired by the Pension Benefit Guarantee Corporation (PBGC), which was created by the Employee Retirement Income Security Act of 1974 "to encourage the continuation and maintenance of private-sector defined benefit pension plans, provide timely and uninterrupted payment of pension benefits, and keep pension insurance premiums at a minimum."[8] The PBGC is a backstop for private pension plans that have ended; the FBGC would fill a similar role in underwriting and providing extended warranties for battery assemblies.

However, unlike the PBGC (which receives no funds from general tax revenues), the cost of the FBGC would be determined by the Congressional Budget Office on the basis of the probability of battery obsolescence or malfunction and the cost of repair, replacement, or refund. That, understandably, would be difficult to predict for a new technology with an uncertain market share and untested performance record.

A few flexible financing options for the FBGC include

—creating an insurance pool up front with a cash influx from the Treasury Department (as was done for the nuclear industry under the Price-Anderson Act, to the tune of $500 million)

—using government-issued securities to back the guarantee

—having automakers and battery manufacturers contribute a nominal amount (in the form of an insurance premium) at first, which would be held in escrow by the FBGC and supplemented by government funds. The private sector would then gradually increase its share of the insurance premium as sales and profits take off, the technology matures, and risk decreases.

Covering battery warranties through a lump insurance policy underwritten by the federal government also lowers per-unit costs by spreading the risks over a large number of vehicles and battery assemblies from different manufacturers.

One precondition for the success of the FBGC is that automakers recognize the battery assembly as a serviceable component and engineer their PEVs to facilitate access to the battery for service or replacement. An easily replaceable battery assembly is also important because the FBGC can make use of degraded PEV batteries for stationary power storage at government installations or for refurbishment and resale.

The policy principles embodied in the proposed Federal Battery Guarantee Corporation have ample historical precedent, the most relevant being U.S. government indemnification of the nuclear industry. First passed in 1957, the Price-Anderson Act helped a strategic industry get on its feet by underwriting the liability for claims arising from nuclear incidents. That federal guarantee was essential to reducing private sector risk, especially in the early years when the technology was still immature.

Regardless of one's opinions on the current merits of nuclear power, incubating the nascent nuclear power industry was a strategic national imperative in the late 1950s. Primarily for national security reasons (to counter the Russian nuclear threat) but also to meet the burgeoning energy needs of an explosive postwar economy, the federal government recognized from the outset that the nuclear industry needed a supportive policy framework to expedite its development. The same is true for PEVs today—and for the same national security, economic, and energy-related reasons.

PEV technology is, obviously, must less risky than nuclear technology. It also is immune from the ethical and safety dilemmas associated with nuclear energy, such as radioactive waste storage and reprocessing. Moreover, the economics of PEVs are much better at the outset: already, the technology can almost achieve lifecycle cost parity with hybrids and compact vehicles, and in an era of skyrocketing oil prices, PEVs will not require the kind of prolonged subsidization (through loan guarantees, security measures, waste disposal, and so forth) demanded by the nuclear industry to stay competitive.

One additional benefit of the proposed corporation would be to help the private insurance industry develop a system by which battery manufacturers could eventually protect themselves against financial losses. Private insurance markets have trouble quantifying the risk of any new technology; accordingly, they are reluctant to issue coverage at all or they charge premiums that battery companies cannot afford. Federal underwriting in the early stages of the PEV industry would allow private insurers time to monitor the risks involved and create adequate and affordable insurance policies.

Guaranteed Secondary Market for Used Battery Assemblies

Large-format battery assemblies generally retain 80 percent of their energy storage capacity even after they have lost their efficacy in powering vehicles. Identifying plausible secondary applications for used battery assemblies and establishing a resale market therefore could give PEV owners an opportunity to reclaim a portion of the purchase price of the battery, effectively reducing its initial cost.

Through a federal battery buyback guarantee, the government would commit to purchasing used PEV battery assemblies at a preferential rate, thus establishing a guaranteed market. That would not be a case of charity: the government has a legitimate need for dependable backup energy storage at federal buildings, electronic data storage centers, military bases, hospitals, and so forth. Once adequate performance and dependability are established, used battery assemblies charged by the grid or by distributed solar power could seamlessly replace existing diesel generators as the preferred backup energy supply in many government installations.

Complementing the federal buyback policy would be a suite of tax incentives to encourage private industry to buy used batteries. In a March 2003 report, Sandia National Laboratories identified four potential economically viable applications for used battery assemblies: electricity transmission support, light commercial load following, residential load following, and backup power for distributed node telecommunications.[9] The report found no insurmountable technical barriers to using refurbished used battery assemblies in stationary applications. Moreover, in the five years since the report was written, battery technology has improved substantially. And with the economies of scale that would accompany mass production of the vehicle fleet, battery assembly costs would be poised to drop significantly, thus strengthening the economic case for use in stationary power storage applications.

The private sector already is showing interest, and that interest will only grow as applications develop for smart grid and distributed solar energy. Pacific Gas and Electric has spoken optimistically about the possibility of using battery assemblies for storing renewable energy generated on site and releasing it to shave peak loads. And in the not-so-distant future, one could envision used battery "farms" providing the storage capacity needed to level out utility-scale wind or solar energy generated during off-peak hours. Establishing a system of tax incentives to support private sector pursuit of these promising stationary applications would help lower the cost of new battery assemblies for vehicles by creating a vibrant resale market.

Easy, Costless Regulatory Action

In addition to the three policy options, there is one easy, costless regulatory action that the Executive Branch could take immediately to help drive PEVs to market: the Environmental Protection Agency (EPA) should grant California its request to regulate tailpipe greenhouse gas emissions under the Clean Air Act.

In December 2007, the EPA denied California its request, a decision nearly unprecedented since California was first granted special status in the Federal Air Quality Act of 1967, which allows California to apply for a "waiver" in order to implement more stringent standards. Over the last forty years, the EPA has granted California fifty full waivers and forty waiver amendments; on only five occasions has it denied a waiver request outright (the last was in 1975).[10] Moreover, the April 2007 Supreme Court ruling in *Massachusetts* v. *EPA* unequivocally affirmed that greenhouse gas emissions from automobiles fall under the jurisdiction of the Clean Air Act.

The California tailpipe standards would translate into vehicle fuel efficiency gains greater than those required by the increase in corporate average fuel economy (CAFE) standards called for in the Energy Independence and Security Act of 2007. The California Air Resources Board reports: "Since the California rules are significantly more effective at reducing GHGs than the federal CAFE program, they also result in better fuel efficiency—roughly 43 miles per gallon (mpg) in 2020 for the California vehicle fleet as compared to the new CAFE standard of 35 mpg."[11] While automakers are free to deploy the low-emissions technologies of their choice, PEVs would certainly be competitive in meeting the more stringent California emissions standards.

Granting the California waiver request would drive new innovations in the auto industry, and it would affect markets beyond California. Indeed, since California first passed its emissions standards in 2004, sixteen other states—representing approximately 45 percent of the U.S. auto market—have either passed equivalent legislation or pledged to do so once the EPA grants the waiver to California. Granting the waiver therefore would help build nationwide demand for PEVs on a commercial scale.

Addressing the Moral Hazard and Related Concerns

Before leveraging significant government support for getting PEVs on the road, it is important to address the moral hazard issue and related concerns: Does too much of a safety net inadvertently reduce manufacturers' diligence in their performance engineering? Is there a risk in pushing through a technology that may not be fully ready for deployment? Are we circumventing the normal private sector product development process?

The answer to those concerns comes in four parts. First, the environment for battery assemblies is quite competitive, with both domestic and foreign manufacturers contending for a cost and performance advantage in what promises to be a large and lucrative market. Battery companies have ample incentives to produce a top-quality product, and federal battery guarantees or fleet purchasing agreements will not undermine the fundamentals of private sector competition in this vibrant emerging market.

Second, the United States already has a safety testing system in place, administered by the Department of Transportation (DOT). The DOT subjects battery assemblies to rigorous trials and ensures their relative safety and dependability before clearing them for use in vehicle drivetrains. Ramped-up funding and employee training would ensure that DOT is capable of expediting the safety approval process for this vital new technology.

Third, compared with fossil fuel vehicle technologies, low- and zero-emissions technologies historically have been disadvantaged under federal policy, for two reasons:

—Drivers of conventional vehicles have never paid the full price for gasoline and diesel, whose externalities (greenhouse gas pollution, oil spills, respiratory ailments, geopolitical costs, and so forth) have been pushed onto the general public and future generations.

—Federal support (from R&D funding, subsidies, and so forth) has been heavily skewed toward the oil industry, giving gasoline and diesel a historical advantage over low-emissions energy carriers like batteries. Resolute federal policy support for PEVs (and other clean technologies) is justified to correct for years of inequality that put them at a disadvantage with respect to their fossil fuel competitors.

Last, the urgency of the situation demands prompt deployment of PEVs. We simply do not have time to wait until the technology completely matures or the price signals materialize to make PEVs competitive with the internal combustion engine. The federal government has a mandate—on national security, environmental, public health, and economic grounds—to expedite the commercialization of this critical technology.

A New Reuther Plan

With buy-in from the auto industry and increases in R&D funding, tax incentives, regulatory changes, and other policies discussed in this volume, the four policy mechanisms described above should provide the framework needed to get PEVs on the road. However, a more ambitious program may be warranted to achieve the rapid transformation of the auto sector necessary to save Detroit, break the stranglehold that oil has on our economy, and combat global warming. During World War II, the nation adopted a progressive industrial policy to retool automobile plants to produce airplanes for the war effort. It may again need such a policy—for a new era in which the stakes are just as high.

In 1940 Walter Reuther, later president of the UAW, presented the Reuther Plan to Phillip Murray (then head of the CIO) in the form of a report entitled "500 Planes a Day—A Program for the Utilization of the Automobile Industry for the Mass Production of Defense Planes." Murray delivered the plan to President Roosevelt, who saw it as emblematic of his goal to make the United States the "arsenal of democracy" for nations under attack by Nazi Germany. Roosevelt responded with robust interest, mobilizing the necessary federal resources, and the program achieved impressive results: in 1939, the United States produced fewer than 6,000 planes; in 1944, it produced 96,000.[12]

If the transformation of our vehicle sector is truly a national priority, the United States could emulate the original Reuther Plan in today's context: producing safe, lightweight vehicles driven by electricity or sustainable, advanced biofuels (or both) with the same sense of purpose and leadership that the country exhibited during World War II. Battery technology would certainly be part of this new industrial effort, but so would lightweight chassis development, aerodynamics, cellulosic ethanol production, and more. And the effort would involve prominent roles for labor, automakers, manufacturers, farmers, universities, federal research labs, and the American people.

The major difference between the modern plan and the original is that we would not be lend-leasing planes to our allies, as we did in World War II. Instead, we would build a robust domestic market and export the next wave of automotive technology to an eager, oil-weary world. If the federal government put its full resources behind the transformation of the U.S. vehicle sector with the same determination as it did during World War II, many of the policies described in this volume and chapter would have a role. However, that would also require making the case to the American people that this transformation could not occur without a significant government presence in the market, at least at the outset.

Re-creating the basic Reuther model with modern-day adjustments would be fairly simple. As it did during World War II, credit could flow to the private sector through loans and loan guarantees administered by an umbrella government finance corporation comprising subsidiaries that would coordinate the industrial mobilization effort by targeting specific solutions to the oil crisis. The "Auto Plant Retooling Corporation," "Vehicle Electrification Services Corporation," "Mass Transit Investment Corporation," "Advanced Biofuels Development Corporation," "Smart Grid

Deployment Corporation," and so forth would coordinate and direct capital flows to industries, producing a financial and technological shockwave that would revitalize manufacturing and unleash a surge of private investment. On the boards of those subsidiaries would sit relevant stakeholders (government, labor, industry, academia, consumers, and so forth), driven by a mandate to free our country—and the world—from its deadly dependence on oil.

Galvanizing the popular will for the country to invest in this endeavor will require real leadership. And the American people may just be ready: skyrocketing oil prices, intolerable congestion, the rise of petroauthoritarianism, and the battle against climate change have primed the country for action.

Financing the front end of this industrial effort also will require leadership, along with some creative thinking and smart politics. The current deficit is an obstacle, but it is not insurmountable. While our credit is still decent, the country can continue to borrow money internationally—but use it to invest in industrial conversion instead of buying and burning imported oil. There is the possibility of an "investment dividend" as we strategically redeploy U.S. troops from Iraq. Auction revenues from a nationwide cap-and-trade system could be a dependable source of reinvestment funds, but they would not begin to flow until complex enabling legislation was hammered out.[13]

Americans may even be ready to be called to the service of their country by purchasing "American Energy Bonds," modeled after the War Bonds that helped finance the conversion of American industry during WWII. The country is hungry to buy into something positive, and a future without $4-a-gallon gasoline and runaway global warming provides a hopeful cause around which to rally. "American Energy Bonds" would appeal to a country eager to transcend the geopolitics of oil and actually invest once again in the manufacturing and transportation infrastructure of the country to promote a low-carbon future. Given the chance to change the course of the nation and confront a national security, climate, and economic emergency, many Americans would be content with modest interest on those bonds, especially in the current volatile investment climate. The opportunity to restore national pride and technological leadership could combine with the kind of creative fascination aroused by the Apollo Project to rally the country to take action and put a down payment on a better world.

Conclusion

Federal support to expedite PEV deployment is necessary because the private sector is reluctant to shoulder the entire risk burden, especially because individual investors do not capture the full net social benefits provided by reducing our dependence on oil and combating global warming. There is a public purpose in rapid deployment, so the public can share the initial risk. That is good policy.

The federal government provides grants, loan guarantees, federal underwriting, tax credits, and preferential purchase agreements to reduce risk and the cost of capital for a host of beneficial purposes, because private markets do not value their full public benefits. Low-income mortgages and housing tax credits, subsidized college loans, tax credits for hybrid vehicles, and grants to companies developing less polluting power plants are all examples. Federal support for PEVs is a natural extension of that logic.

The policies outlined in this chapter and in the book overall rest on solid—and diverse—historical precedents. Federal interventions to jumpstart strategic industries in the United States have an impressive track record, especially in the transportation sector. The Pacific Railroad Act of 1862 deeded land to private railroad companies to reduce the risks of laying track, thus facilitating westward expansion; the National Interstate and Defense Highways Act of 1956 began our interstate highway system under the rubric of national security, creating the most extensive and efficient road commerce system in the world at its time; and the Apollo Project catapulted the United States to dominance in the aeronautics and space-related industries.

These examples have many things in common: they were strategic national imperatives vital to the country's security, technological leadership, and economic growth. Vehicle electrification to end our dependence on oil and shift to a cleaner and more reliable domestic fuel certainly fits that description well. And with its ability to revitalize an important manufacturing sector—the American auto industry—and leverage rapid and deep cuts in global warming emissions, PEV technology merits immediate and significant federal support.

Notes

1. J. D. Power and Associates, "U.S. New Light-Vehicle Sales in 2008 Forecasted to Reach Lowest Point in More Than a Decade," March 18, 2008 (www.jdpower.com/corporate/news/releases/pressrelease.aspx?ID=2008031 [September 24, 2008]).

2. Green Car Congress, "Reported U.S. Sales of Hybrids in April Pass 3% Market Share of New Vehicles Sold," May 5, 2008 (www.greencarcongress.com/2008/05/reported-us-sal.html [September 24, 2008]).

3. Rasmussen Reports, "Toplines—Gas Prices—March 28–29, 2008" (http://rasmussenreports.com/public_content/lifestyle/general_lifestyle/general_lifestyle_toplines/toplines_gas_prices_march_28_29_2008 [September 24, 2008]).

4. Jeremy Rosner and Kristi Fuksa, "Americans See 100-mpg Cars as Biggest Fix for Global Warming, Have High Interest in Purchasing, but Also Sensitivity about Costs," Greenberg Quinlin Rosner Research, August 1, 2007 (www.progressiveauto xprize.org/files/downloads/auto/axp_polling_08012007.pdf [September 24, 2008]).

5. In the 1990s, a few highly regarded fully electric models were available in California.

6. General Services Administration, Office of Governmentwide Policy, "Federal Fleet Report, Fiscal Year 2006" (www.gsa.gov/gsa/cm_attachments/GSA_DOCUMENT/FFR2006_030707_R2K-g6_0Z5RDZ-i34K-pR.pdf [September 24, 2008]).

7. Exemptions can be made for military light-duty vehicles if the technology does not perform as required.

8. Pension Benefit Guaranty Corporation, "Who We Are" (www.pbgc.gov/about/about.html#1 [September 24, 2008]).

9. Erin Cready and others, "Technical and Economic Feasibility of Applying Used EV Batteries in Stationary Applications: A Study for the DOE Energy Storage Systems Program," Sandia National Laboratories, March 2003 (www.prod.sandia.gov/cgi-bin/techlib/access-control.pl/2002/024084.pdf [September 24, 2008]).

10. California Environmental Protection Agency, Air Resources Board, "Frequently Asked Questions: Climate Change Emissions Standards for Vehicles, Actions to Reduce Greenhouse Gases from Cars and Trucks," May 30, 2007 (www.arb.ca.gov/cc/factsheets/ccfaq.pdf [September 24, 2008]).

11. California Environmental Protection Agency, Air Resources Board, "Comparison of Greenhouse Gas Reductions for the United States and Canada under U.S. CAFE Standards and California Air Resources Board Greenhouse Gas Regulations," February 25, 2008 (www.arb.ca.gov/cc/ccms/reports/pavleycafe_reportfeb25_08.pdf [September 24, 2008]).

12. Alan L. Gropman, "U.S. Production in World War II (Mobilizing U.S. Industry in World War II: Myth and Reality)," August 1, 1996 (www.accessmylibrary.com/coms2/summary_0286-218124_ITM [September 24, 2008]).

13. Cap and trade is an oft-discussed policy option for reducing greenhouse gas emissions by allowing firms to trade a limited number of "emissions permits," which would be reduced gradually to comply with the tightening emissions cap. These permits should be auctioned, both to ensure economic efficiency and to raise revenue to protect consumers and reinvest in the transition to a low-carbon economy.

CHAPTER ELEVEN

Electric Vehicles:
How Do We Get Millions on the Road?

TOM Z. COLLINA and RON ZUCKER

"This is not the time for niche vehicles," says Bob Lutz, the outspoken vice chairman of General Motors. How right he is. The United States and the rest of the world will enjoy the significant oil security and climate benefits of plug-in electric vehicles *only if* industry produces them and consumers buy them *in vast numbers*. For that to happen, we must find a way to reduce or eliminate the upfront costs of the battery and the charging infrastructure—the two main barriers to developing a strong electric vehicle (EV) market. To get there, we need new business models that spread the battery and infrastructure costs over time, and we need new federal incentives.

First and foremost, we need to think differently about the electric car. In the future, with the rising price of gasoline, fuel type will be a choice, not a given. Gasoline, natural gas, ethanol, diesel, electricity, and hydrogen will all be options. In fact, fuel type may soon be the dominant consumer attraction, much as body design has been in the past. This shift will be nothing less than revolutionary for the auto industry—and few are ready for it.

Consider the telephone. Remember when you used to buy a new phone—land line, that is—and then sign up for service with the phone company, in two separate transactions? The phone maker didn't care who provided the connection service, and the phone company didn't care who sold you your phone. (If you're under thirty years of age, you probably don't remember this because you never did it.) Today, you buy a mobile phone *contract*, phone and service agreement all in one. The phone may even be free, because the service provider makes its money from selling minutes, not the phone itself.

The automobile industry may soon undergo a similar transformation. Within a decade, you may be able to buy an electric vehicle as part of a service contract. The price of the car would be discounted because you are agreeing to buy not minutes, but *miles* to drive your car. The service contract would be for some number of years, say five or ten, and the cost of the car could be spread out over that time. Furthermore, the service provider would install charging infrastructure, including charge spots at your home, your office, the mall, Starbuck's, and so forth, plus battery exchange stations along the highways (think cell towers) for your use. The car battery, also owned by the service provider, could be charged at one of the ubiquitous charge spots or traded at the exchange stations in the same time that it takes to fill your car up with gas. With enough battery exchange stations, the electric car—just like the internal combustion car—would have unlimited range.

There are many potential benefits to this approach. Owning a car could be significantly cheaper than it is today. Now, when you buy a car, you really have no idea how much fuel will cost you over the next five years. Under a set plan, you would know exactly how much you would pay and you might even be able to choose the source of your fuel—for example, you might be able to choose a plan under which 100 percent or 50 percent of your power comes from renewable sources. You might want to charge only at night, when rates are low, or to pay a premium to charge anytime.

In addition, if you used your car primarily for commuting, you could opt to charge only at home or at the office parking lot. For longer trips, you could extend your range by using recharging stations to swap the "empty" battery for a "full" one. And, as you would not own the battery, you would not get stuck with yesterday's technology.

Moreover, by buying a long-term contract, you would empower the service provider to purchase long-term contracts for renewable energy. That would enable the financing of truly zero-petroleum and zero-carbon vehicles—the "holy grail" for cutting our oil addiction and climate pollution.

The potential market for this approach is massive. Many developing countries, which skipped over telephone land lines and went right to mobile phones, could similarly avoid building a gasoline infrastructure and go right to electricity. The benefits in terms of oil and carbon dioxide reductions in China and India, for example, would be tremendous.

Better Place

This revolutionary idea is not ours, of course; it is being promoted and implemented by Better Place (BP), an innovative company founded by Shai Agassi in October 2007. He has already raised $200 million (from investors such as VantagePoint Venture Partners, Israel Corporation, Morgan Stanley, and others) and signed up Israel and Denmark to adopt his plan nationwide. He reportedly is talking with the state of Hawaii and the city of San Francisco to be his first U.S. beachhead.

Here's the idea: BP would act as the service provider (think Verizon), building the charge spots and battery exchange stations (the infrastructure), providing the batteries and electricity, and selling the cars through service plans. Renault-Nissan would build the electric vehicles (think Nokia), with Automotive Energy Supply Corporation (AESC) producing the batteries. Agassi estimated in May 2008 that Renault-Nissan would invest $500 million to $1 billion to develop the electric vehicles with a swappable battery pack. Israel Corporation chairman Idan Ofer, who has invested $130 million, said, "I consider this to be a revolutionary project, and I believe that most of the [Israeli] public will drive an electric car within a decade."[1]

"With $100-a-barrel oil, we've crossed a historic threshold where electricity and batteries provide a cheaper alternative for consumers," Agassi said. "You buy a car to go an infinite distance, and we need to create the same feeling for an electric car—that you can fill it up when you stop or sleep and go an infinite distance."[2]

BP would provide consumers with lithium-ion batteries—capable of going about 125 miles per charge—and build the infrastructure to charge them. On-board GPS would help drivers find a charging station when needed—no more driving around looking for an open gas station.

In Israel, the government will offer tax breaks to electric car buyers until 2019 that effectively make them cheaper to buy than gas vehicles. "You'll be able to get a nice, high-end car at a price roughly half that of the gasoline model today," Agassi said. He also expects the operating expenses of electrics to be half those of gas cars if users take advantage of cheaper nighttime charging. "Israel can't become a major industrial country, but it can become a daring world laboratory and a pilot plant for new ideas, like the electric car," said Israel's president, Shimon Peres. He said he also supports a larger investment in solar power, noting that "the Saudis don't control the sun."[3]

In Denmark, BP is working with DONG Energy to put electric vehicles on the road and to take advantage of Denmark's wind power resources. "With this project, we hope to contribute substantially to reducing CO_2 emissions from Danish cars. At the same time, we will achieve a new way of storing the unstable electricity output from wind turbines, as EVs are typically charged during the night, when the exploitation of power generation is low. This provides optimum exploitation of our resources for the benefit of the environment," says Anders Eldrup, CEO of DONG Energy.[4]

Indeed, the spread of electric vehicles will enable broader use of renewable energy than is otherwise possible. The car batteries act as distributed energy storage systems that allow excess power (such as wind at night) to be stored until it is needed. And the long-term contracts envisioned by BP will encourage development of more sources of renewable energy. That synergy will be a powerful boost to renewable energy.

The BP Business Model

The success of BP's plan depends primarily on its ability to deliver cost-competitive electric vehicles that people want to buy. To check the viability of the business plan, Deutsche Bank reviewed BP's numbers and concluded in a March 2008 report that "we see a potential for a paradigm shift in the way vehicles are owned and fueled. . . . Looking at [Better Place's] model, we conclude that a pure EV should not be more expensive than a gasoline/diesel vehicle."[5]

According to Deutsche Bank, a typical BP contract would cost $550 per month and provide 18,000 miles per year. That seems steep until you consider that it's only about $50 more than the average monthly loan payment for a new gasoline-powered car—and the BP price includes the cost of the car *and* the fuel.

With gas at $4 and 20 miles per gallon, Americans would pay about 20 cents per mile for gas. At that rate, the cost of gasoline for 18,000 miles a year over ten years would be $36,000 (assuming stable gas prices). You would pay at least $66,000 over ten years (more if you take out a car loan) for a $30,000 car.[6] With BP at $550 per month, you also would pay $66,000 over ten years (or 33 cents per mile, car included). So at mid-2008 prices you could have a zero-gas, zero-carbon electric car for about the same price as a conventional car. Over time, we should see an increasing price advantage for electric vehicles, as oil prices continue to rise and the cost of batteries and renewable energy declines. And because electric cars have fewer moving parts, they also are cheaper to maintain.

Deutsche Bank also notes that "entities in 5-10 countries are in the pipeline to announce deals with [Better Place] over the course of this year" in addition to deals already signed in Denmark and Israel. The bank expects other automakers, besides Renault-Nissan, to work with the company. "Frankly, we are not aware of any reason why they would not sign up for this, as the automakers do not need to commit capital for infrastructure for batteries under [the Better Place] business model," Deutsche Bank wrote. "We think companies such as [Better Place] have the potential to drive significant change in the global auto industry."[7]

BP's business model is not public, so we have to take Deutsche Bank's word for it. But there are some clear challenges to getting this right. Building hundreds (in Israel) or thousands (in the United States) of battery exchange stations and hundreds of thousands of charge spots would be extremely expensive. Battery costs also must be brought down to earth. A back-end data system to manage the battery exchange process would be complicated, although Agassi's background with SAP should serve him well there. Finally, all carmakers who wanted to partner with BP would have to build cars to accommodate BP's swappable batteries. If BP gets out front and sets a standard that others follow, then fine. But if BP sets a standard that others ignore (remember Betamax?), then we may be limited to car choices from Renault-Nissan. None of that, however, seems insurmountable. Says Agassi, "There will be a very loud splat when I hit the ground," he says, "or there's going to be a revolution."[8]

Other Business Models

That, of course, is not the only way to sell electric vehicles. Tesla Motors and other small startup companies like Fisker are building EVs in small numbers and at high prices. Once Tesla gets established in the sports car sector (in 2008 it's building 600 Roadsters, at $100,000 per car), it plans to build a luxury sedan ($60,000) and then a car for the rest of us ($30,000). The key unknown is how long it will take to get to the mass-market model and if a startup company can reach the production levels needed.

Another startup, Think, plans to enter the EV market at the low end. Think plans to start U.S. sales in 2009 with the Think City, a two-seater priced in the $20,000 to $30,000 range, car only. Battery and electricity packages will be sold separately, and Think envisions monthly pricing plans. Sometime thereafter, the five-seater Think Ox will be introduced. This business model has the benefit of starting out with a lower-priced car, but it leaves open the question of how fast a small company can ramp up production.

At the other end of the spectrum is the plug-in hybrid Chevy Volt. No one can doubt GM's ability to mass produce vehicles. Says GM's Lutz: "We can't afford to hit singles and bunts. We need triples and home runs." GM plans to start producing the Volt in late 2010 and to produce 10,000 vehicles in 2011, the first year of full production. After that, says Lutz, "We're in uncharted territory. If global demand is there, my personal guess is that vehicles like the Volt could be 500,000 a year in a few years' time."[9] Working against those high volume numbers is the projected cost of the first Volt—$35,000, creeping up from the original goal of $30,000.[10] Fuel will be sold separately.

There is room for all of these approaches and more, with some that target niche markets and some that aim for the masses, some that offer pure electric vehicles and some that offer plug-in hybrids. Deutsche Bank likes BP because "this is the only model that we know of in which the consumer can immediately benefit from lower fuel costs, without incremental upfront cost in the vehicle"—and thus has mass-market appeal.[11] Yet other mass-production vehicles like the Chevy Volt can be sold the old-fashioned way and also be cost competitive, with a little help from Uncle Sam.

Federal Incentives

Government incentives to promote increased electrification of the transportation sector are justified on many grounds, including reducing carbon pollution, cutting U.S. dependence on foreign oil, and investing in domestic energy infrastructure. The question is how best to do it.

Even the best new business models, like Better Place, would benefit from federal assistance. Startup costs to build the vehicles and charging infrastructure would be large. Congress and the executive branch need to do their part. Surprisingly, given that EV technology is so closely associated with energy independence, Congress has only recently begun to treat EVs as part of the answer to America's environmental and security challenges. In fact, the 1992 Energy Policy Act (EPAct) did not even consider EVs to be alternative fuel vehicles for the purpose of fleet purchase credits.[12] EVs were seen as peripheral to America's transportation infrastructure.

That approach has changed rapidly. With the 2005 update to the EPAct, followed closely by President Bush's declaration in the 2006 State of the Union Address that the United States is "addicted to oil," EVs have taken center stage. With that transformation has come a variety of legislation to encourage their production and purchase. These changes have focused on batteries for the cars and on the nature of the electric grid.

The 2005 EPAct update included some mention of EVs, but it was fairly minimal. The legislation included a $40 million initiative for commercialization of flexible-fuel hybrid and plug-in hybrid vehicles. It also included a section that explicitly authorized the Department of Energy to accelerate improvements in battery efficiency and provided for loan guarantees for investments in technology innovations. While those were important changes and represented an initial investment, they pale beside the $1 billion that General Motors claims to be the cost of developing the all-electric EV-1.[13]

Finally, in 2007, legislators began to truly tackle the requirements of EVs. The 2007 Clean Energy Act included $90 million a year for five years for funding for competitive grants to state, local, and municipal governments, businesses, and others to develop programs to encourage the use of plug-in electric drive vehicles and other emerging electric vehicle technologies.[14] There also was funding to support non-road electric vehicles[15] and to encourage education programs, especially in higher education engineering, to support electric drive and component design.[16]

Recognizing that battery technology is one of the most important and strategic elements in EV innovation, the bill also included loan guarantees for the construction of facilities to manufacture advanced vehicle batteries and battery systems developed in the United States.[17]

In addition, the Clean Energy Act included a large section recognizing that transportation was inseparable from the wider issue of the electric grid. When we examine the federal role in cleaner transportation, we need to consider the federal role in electricity generation and distribution. Analyses suggest that pure electric cars release up to 60 percent less greenhouse gases and consume 99 percent less oil than conventional cars using the current mix of fuels to generate electricity.[18] But it also puts new demands on the electric grid. That is why we cannot discuss electric cars without also discussing new solutions for electric power generation and storage.

One of the problems is that it is difficult, expensive, and relatively inefficient to store electricity, especially compared with other forms of energy. If you don't need your car, you simply turn it off, "saving" the gasoline for when you do need it. But you cannot "park" electric current. Some power generators, such as hydropower facilities or nuclear reactors, cannot really be shut down—even when demand is low. Others, such as wind turbines and solar panels, produce electricity intermittently.

The key is being able to store electric power and get it when you need it. The use of centralized batteries for that purpose, however, is difficult and expensive. Large batteries, capable of storing significant power, traditionally have been of the lead-acid type; although reliable, each battery typically fills a warehouse and lasts five years. Newer designs, while smaller and more efficient, typically cost about 10 percent more per kilowatt-hour than simply firing a coal power plant.[19]

However, energy technology planners see the potential for EVs to change that outlook. Cars can be charged at night, at low cost, when there is surplus electric power; the stored energy is then used during the day to power the car. Overnight charging is especially well suited for wind energy. Thus, instead of building a few, large stationary batteries to store excess energy, EVs could serve as a distributed storage system.

Once sufficient numbers of EVs are connected to a modernized grid, they could conceivably sell back electricity during the day, when the grid needs more power and prices are high. Vehicle-to-grid (V2G) technology is a powerful potential advantage for EVs. However, it requires an updated electric distribution system. Our current electrical grid has not changed much since the early twentieth century.

For V2G to reach its potential, which creates some of the ancillary economic benefits of EVs, the grid needs to be updated into a "smart grid." A smart grid would allow two-way transmission of power, so that cars could power the grid during periods of peak demand and receive power from the grid at times of low demand. Moreover, advanced metering would allow different pricing based on the cost of producing more power. Consumers could pay less for power when there is an abundance of spare capacity, typically late at night, and pay more—or conceivably even sell it back to the utility at a higher price—when power is scarce, typically at midday.

However, the nation's electric infrastructure is massive. A smart grid is a huge national undertaking. That's why the Energy Independence and Security Act of 2007 devotes almost $300 million to energy storage research and development. It also creates a new Energy Storage Advisory Council to maintain U.S. competitiveness in energy storage for electric drive vehicles, stationary applications, and electricity transmission and distribution.

In Boulder, Colorado, Xcel Energy is installing one of the first smart grids in the country. The system seeks to replace both the utility components of the system (monitors, switches, fuses, and so forth) and the consumer components (meters, monitors, device/appliance controls) with components capable of two-way communication and to enhance the new devices with integration logic to bring the system together. Although two-way communication has fairly widespread application, it is crucial for V2G. Current meters in the United States use a one-way communication system. You turn on a light, and the system registers a request for power. The power is sent to your home, and the meter notices how much power you use. For a V2G system to operate, you must also be able to tell the system that you now have a surplus of power available for the grid. Only a smart grid can provide two-way communication.

Although the idea is radical in the transportation sector, it is not new. For years, many utilities have offered "net metering," whereby homeowners who installed renewable energy generating systems, frequently solar or wind power, could effectively sell the power back to the utility if the system generated more than they needed for their homes. The homeowner could literally watch her electric meter run backward, sending electricity to the grid instead of grabbing it down. While V2G requires a more advanced version of this idea, allowing users to monitor when their cars are charged and when they are discharged, it is not beyond modern technology.

However, the costs involved are significant. Xcel Energy's pilot program is slated to cost a total of $100 million for 50,000 residences and businesses comprising approximately 100,000 people.[20] While costs are likely to come down after the lessons of the pilot project are learned, a project at that scale for every person in the United States could total a whopping $300 billion. Moreover, Boulder was selected as a pilot project in part for its high population density, which makes it easier to work in.

Last, there is not one electrical system in the United States. The nation has a patchwork of different energy systems, each with different levels of technology and information infrastructures. If an EV driver is going to be able to go from California to New York while plugging in to recharge, the vehicle will need to be able to "speak" to the local system operator. That requires standardization, which is not currently the norm.

Given this historical context, the highest priorities for federal action are consumer incentives, a low-carbon fuel standard, federal purchasing requirements, charging infrastructure, and the smart grid.

Consumer incentives. For Better Place, the key contribution of Israel and Denmark to making the plan work was offering tax incentives to consumers to make electric vehicles cheaper than conventional cars on a lifetime basis. That will be especially important in the United States, where gasoline prices are lower than in Europe or Israel and the upfront cost premium of an EV therefore will take longer to pay off.

In October 2008, the U.S. Congress passed the first tax incentives for plug-in electric vehicles—up to $7,500 in tax credits for the first 250,000 cars sold. That is a good start, but we can do better. The tax credit for full EVs should go higher—up to $10,000—and should be extended to the first 2 million vehicles. The higher credit would more effectively offset the $10,000 to $12,000 cost of the battery for a full electric vehicle. The credit could be calculated on a sliding scale, decreasing as the carbon pollution from the vehicle goes up. For example, full EVs with no tailpipe emissions would get the maximum credit. The plug-in hybrid Chevy Volt—which has a gasoline generator to extend its range—would receive the $7,500 credit. Less capable plug-in hybrids would get less than that, and so on. The credit would be reduced as needed for the next 2 million plug-ins sold.

Low-carbon fuel standard. Of course, an EV with zero tailpipe emissions may not be a carbon-neutral vehicle; it all depends on where the electricity comes from. Therefore, we need to create tough national standards for reducing the carbon emissions from electricity production and to require utilities to meet those standards. One approach is through establishing a low-carbon fuel standard (LCFS). An LCFS is a greenhouse gas standard on the mix of transportation fuels—including electricity—sold in the United States. It requires fuel providers to reduce the amount of lifecycle greenhouse gases per unit of energy that they sell. They can meet the standard through a mix of technologies. Rather than pick a winning technology, an LCFS simply sets the performance level and allows providers to innovate to meet the standard.

For EVs, that requires a change in how we think about driving. We are all used to thinking about fuel efficiency in terms of miles per gallon. For each gallon of gas that I add to my car, I will travel so many miles. We need to be able to convert that into greenhouse gases emitted. That means figuring out not just the conversion of the input fuel to electricity—whether it is energy from coal, nuclear power, wind, or any other energy source—but the total carbon content of each bit of power that we use to refuel.

That is a tricky standard to meet. The California Air Resources Board (CARB) is charged with evaluating all fuels to determine their total "wells to wheels" carbon footprint. If fuel for electricity generation is required, where does it come from? How hard and expensive is it to transport? What does each actual mile traveled mean in terms of carbon output?

Moreover, those numbers vary by region. In California, where a great deal of energy comes from geothermal and hydroelectric sources, generation of electricity is relatively low carbon. However, if the addition of electric cars requires the state to "import" electricity generated in other, less environmentally friendly regions of the country, how do we account for that electricity under an LCFS? These are all questions that CARB is trying to answer, and we will need similar answers for the whole country if an LCFS is to succeed at setting a standard that will actually reduce greenhouse gas emissions.

Despite the challenges, setting a low-carbon fuel standard is what the movement to EVs is all about. EVs allow consumers to lower their greenhouse gas emissions in a simple, cost-effective way. Moreover, since it is easier to clean up a power plant than each individual car on the road, producers can meet their targets more quickly. And since the electric grid is run largely on domestic power, an LCFS contributes to America's energy independence and to national security without encouraging high-carbon solutions like converting coal and oil shale to liquid fuel.

Currently there is no national LCFS in the United States. The state of California has joined other influential fuel markets, including the European Union and two Canadian provinces, in initiating an LCFS. Other states in the United States are beginning to consider following suit, including Illinois, Iowa, Kansas, Michigan, Wisconsin, and Massachusetts. However, global warming and oil dependence are not issues that affect only a few states. We need a national LCFS.

Federal purchasing requirements. The federal government buys tens of thousands of vehicles each year, and it should use that buying power to energize the automobile industry. Congress should require 50 percent of all federal noncombat vehicles bought by 2015 to be plug-ins, and it should go out and find producers who can fill that order. That would be a great inducement to any car company that is considering a shift to EVs.[21]

Charging infrastructure In addition to subsidizing the car, we also must create incentives for building a national charging infrastructure. It would be tragic if the first million plug-ins were sold to consumers who then could not find convenient places to recharge. (That scenario would be familiar to the owners of flex-fuel vehicles who still cannot find ethanol.) Infrastructure will be an expensive part of the equation and can be deployed much faster with federal assistance.

For example, homeowners, developers, builders, and businesses would get tax credits for installing charging spots in driveways and parking lots. Service providers would get tax credits for building battery exchange stations, much like current incentives for domestic ethanol production. One of the best forms of advertising for plug-ins would be the public perception that the charging infrastructure already was in place; conversely, the perception that charge spots could not be found would be devastating for the EV market.

Smart grid. Developing a smart grid would be a major undertaking, although some infrastructure improvements are within current capabilities. European experience shows that a step as simple as creating a unified power-trading market in which generation and transmission are auctioned jointly on a day-ahead market can help avoid outages.[22] Small-scale technical innovations, such as composite conductors to increase thermal ratings of lines and phase-shifting transformers to relieve bottleneck constraints, can have immediate effects on grid reliability.[23] The technology for improvements is well known and proven.

However, the constraint on our electric infrastructure is not just technological. We have a patchwork quilt of seven independent system operators and four regional transmission operators negotiating for power with independent generators. This balkanization of power distribution forces ratepayers in one area of the country to pay for upgrades to the grid that will largely benefit another area of the country. Meanwhile, power companies are forced by political pressure to keep utility rates low.

That is why true change will require federal action and massive investment. Specifically, these are the minimum requirements to upgrade the infrastructure to support EVs:

—An "extra high voltage" backbone: Our national grid was largely built in the 1960s, using even older technology. Much of it is reaching the end of its useful life. Meanwhile, thanks to the deregulation of electricity that began in the late 1970s under President Carter, more of our electricity comes from farther away on the open market. It frequently is cheaper to increase capacity far from the urban centers. To enable that, we need a newer grid made up of newer, more capable transmission centers.

—A smart distribution grid, with transformers and meters capable of two-way digital communication. This would be a nationwide extension of Xcel Energy's Boulder experiment.

—A real-time monitoring system to quickly adapt to surges in capacity or demand.

The Department of Energy has investigated these ideas and proposed a three-stage upgrade.[24] While the price tag through 2030 has been estimated at as high as $900 billion for a full upgrade,[25] it must be noted that the electric utility sector is projected to spend up to $10 billion a year for piecemeal upgrades.[26] Moreover, current power interruptions cost the United States more than $79 billion *per year*.[27] We cannot afford to ignore these needs any longer. We, as a nation, need to make the investment in our clean energy future.

Finally, in addition to providing for the electricity needed for EVs and providing incentives for consumers to buy electric vehicles, the government could also seek to buy up older cars and get them off the road. Given how the resale value of gas-guzzling SUVs has plummeted, the government could become the "buyer of last resort" to help consumers switch to EVs. The government could also create a floor price for oil to give added confidence to investors in the electric car field. Although the long-term trend is clear, we will still experience short-term drops in oil prices that will spook risk-averse investors.

By joining innovative thinking on electric vehicles with smart federal policy, we can reach our goal of getting millions of these vehicles on the road in the United States and across the globe. The challenges posed by oil dependence and global warming are vast, and our solutions must match the challenges. This is no time for niche-market thinking. "If what I'm saying is right, this would be the largest economic dislocation in the history of capitalism," says Agassi.[28]

Let's hope Agassi is right, and let's help to *make* him right.

Notes

1. "Project Better Place Presents Prototype; Renault Seen Investing up to $1 Billion in R&D," Cleantech Investing in Israel, May 11, 2008 (http://cleantech-israel.blog spot.com/2008/05/project-better-place-presents-prototype.html).

2. Steven Erlanger, "Israel Is Set to Promote the Use of Electric Cars," *New York Times*, January 21, 2008 (www.nytimes.com/2008/01/21/world/middleeast/21israel. html?_r=1&ref=world&oref=slogin).

3. Ibid.

4. "DONG Energy and California-Based Project Better Place to Introduce Environmentally Friendly Electric Vehicles in Denmark," Reuters, March 27, 2008 (www. reuters.com/article/pressRelease/idUS120477+27-Mar-2008+BW20080327).

5. Rod Lache, Dan Galves, and Patrick Nolan, "Paradigm Shift for the Global Auto Industry," Deutsche Bank, March 16, 2008.

6. In 2007 the average cost of a new car was $28,797. Information courtesy of the National Automobile Dealers Association, *AutoExec Magazine*, May 2008, p. 45.

7. Lache, Galves, and Nolan, "Paradigm Shift."

8. Steve Hamm, "The Electric Car Acid Test," *Business Week*, January 24, 2008 (www.businessweek.com/magazine/content/08_05/b4069042006924.htm).

9. "Bob Lutz: No Chevy Beat but Maybe 500,000 Chevy Volts," July 15, 2008 (http://gm-volt.com/2008/07/15/bob-lutz-no-chevy-beat-but-maybe-500000-chevy-volts/).

10. Chuck Squatriglia, "Wipers, Stereo Raise Price of Chevrolet Volt to $35,000," Wired, February 12, 2008 (http://blog.wired.com/cars/2008/02/wipers-stereo-p.html).

11. Rod Lache and others, "Electric Cars: Plugged In," Deutsche Bank, June 9, 2008, p. 12.

12. See Energy Policy Act of 1992 (HR776), section 508, and the Energy Independence and Security Act of 2007 (HR6), section 133.

13. Among others, see quotes from Keith Cole, director of legislative and regulatory affairs, General Motors, at 2020 Vision's National Summit on Energy Security, National Press Club, Washington, July 12, 2007.

14. CLEAN Energy Act of 2007, section 131(b).

15. Ibid., section 131(c).

16. Ibid., section 131(d).

17. Ibid., section 135.

18. Sherry Boschert, "The Cleanest Cars: Well-To-Wheels Emissions Comparisons," updated May 2008, p. 6 (www.sherryboschert.com): "The [Argonne National Laboratory] GHG chart suggests that an ICE produces approximately 500 g/mile, compared with nearly 300 g/mile from HEVs, 220 g/mile from EVs on the U.S. grid, 200 g/mile from HFCEVs using hydrogen from natural gas reforming stations, 500 g/mile from HFCEVs using hydrogen from electrolysis, and nearly 1,000 g/mile from hydrogen ICEs (not FCEVs) using hydrogen from electrolysis."

19. Paul Davidson, "New Battery Packs Powerful Punch," *USA Today*, July 5, 2007.

20. Ron Zucker's interview with Craig Eicher, Xcel Energy, July 1, 2008.

21. For more on federal purchases, see David Sandalow, *Freedom from Oil* (New York: McGraw-Hill, 2007), p. 70.

22 See, for example, European Federation of Energy Traders, "Intra-Day Power Markets within and across European National Frontiers: A Practical Approach to Facilitate Wholesale Liquidity," December 2006.

23. U.S. Climate Change Technology Program, "Technology Options for the Near and Long Term," November 2003, pp. 1.3–4.

24. U.S. Department of Energy, Office of Electric Transmission and Distribution, "'Grid 2030': A National Vision for Electricity's Second 100 Years," July 2003.

25. Kurt Yeager, testimony before the House Energy and Commerce Committee, *Facilitating the Transition to a Smart Electric Grid*, 110 Cong., 1 sess., May 3, 2007, p. 10.

26. James Kelly, "Intelligent CIS: The Missing Link for MDM Success," *Electric Energy T&D*, September-October 2008, p. 24.

27. Kristina Hamachi LaCommare and Joseph H. Eto, "Cost of Power Interruptions to Electricity Consumers in the United States," Ernest Orlando Lawrence Berkeley National Laboratory, February 2006.

28. Hamm, "The Electric Car Acid Test."

CHAPTER TWELVE

Electric Utility Issues in Replacing Oil with Electricity in Transportation

STEVE MARSHALL

Imagine a business that made a fuel that could replace petroleum in cars and trucks for less than the cost of gasoline at a dollar a gallon—a fuel that would emit far less CO_2 than gasoline, virtually end urban pollution from cars, cut the U.S. trade deficit by a billion dollars a day, and significantly improve national security. Such a business would be expected to go all out to work with automakers to produce cars that used the fuel, relentlessly lobby Congress to remove roadblocks and create incentives to facilitate a fast transition to its use, and widely advertise it to the public as the ideal fuel to replace petroleum.

That business would be expected to make the same aggressive effort that producers of corn-based ethanol made to get Congress to enact a $0.51-per-gallon tax credit for producers and to set aggressive ethanol production goals—or to make the effort that hydrogen fuel cell proponents have made to obtain billions of federal research dollars.

The business that makes this fuel is real, not imaginary. It is the electric power industry. And the energy source that can supplement and then supplant oil as the preferred fuel for cars and trucks is, as this book details elsewhere, electricity.

A sea change in public policy away from the use of oil and remarkable advances in battery technology mean that plug-in electric vehicles—vehicles that connect to the power grid—will increasingly power surface transportation. And that means that electric utilities will, in effect, be the gas stations of the future—and could become a major counterbalance to the oil and gas industry.

The critical role that utilities must play in the transition from oil to electricity was recognized by General Motors in a July 2008 announcement. GM said that it was teaming with dozens of utilities to "smooth a path" for its plug-in cars, including the Chevy Volt that it will start selling in 2010.[1] Vice chairman Bob Lutz has said that GM's future depends on the success of the Volt.[2]

The announcement was encouraging to those who have asked why utilities, with some notable and laudable exceptions, have for the most part been bystanders in expediting the transition from oil to electricity in transportation. Questions remain about what can be done to broadly encourage electric utilities to take a more active role to help meet the challenges that the United States faces in overcoming its dependence on oil.

What institutional and regulatory constraints limit utility electric transportation initiatives? What reforms are needed to remove those constraints and create the necessary incentives to accelerate the transition from mostly foreign oil to domestic electric power? What can we learn from those exceptional utilities that took an early lead in the effort to replace oil with electricity in transportation? This chapter addresses those questions.

The Early History of Electric Utilities and Transportation

Thomas Edison patented the idea of an electric distribution system in 1880 and later that year created the first electric power utility, the Edison Electric Illuminating Company. On September 4, 1882, Edison himself switched on the Pearl Street generating station, which powered a distribution system that extended lines to twenty-nine customers in lower Manhattan. From that small start, the electric utility industry has grown into one of the foundations of the modern global economy. Today, virtually everything in the United States runs on electricity—except most cars and trucks. But it wasn't always that way.

Soon after Edison opened the Pearl Street station, electricity was being generated by ever-larger power projects from Niagara Falls to Snoqualmie Falls near Seattle. With extra power to sell, electric utilities sought uses for power besides lighting. The idea was to expand and diversify electricity's uses in order to better utilize the costly system of generating plants and wires. If there were multiple uses for power throughout the day, electric utilities would become more efficient and the cost of power for each customer would go down.

Transportation was one of the first uses of electric power other than lighting. Before the mass production of gasoline engine cars, some electric utilities formed electric traction companies. In one early example, the predecessor of the Puget Sound Power, Light, and Traction Company created an interurban electric trolley line in the Seattle area.[3] The interurban made efficient use of the available power capacity of the Snoqualmie Falls hydroelectric power plant that otherwise would have been wasted.

Early on a pattern was set for the operation of electric utilities. In order to become more efficient and to make power more affordable, they needed to become bigger and they needed more diversified uses for their power. The key was to keep demand for power as constant as possible over all twenty-four hours of the day because power moved at the speed of light and could not be stored for later use the way food, clothes, and most other manufactured goods can be.[4]

Electric utilities also became the nation's most capital-intensive business. To make electricity, with its high fixed costs, more affordable, it was necessary to find predictable and efficient uses for power by filling in gaps in demand and reducing demand spikes. Electric transportation systems were one early effort to even out demand for power and make the best use of the power system. But the interurban electric trolley line in Seattle did not last long. Henry Ford's innovative assembly lines started turning out millions of affordable gas engine cars. Cars meant freedom to come and go without being tied to a schedule and to go where there were no train or trolley tracks. The freedom and convenience of affordable individual mobility was an irresistible and transforming force.

Some of the first cars were powered by electricity, but the batteries of that era were no match for the stored energy that gasoline provided. Even though electricity costs dropped fast in the first decades of the twentieth century, gas prices dropped even faster, with a seemingly endless series of domestic oil field discoveries and John D. Rockefeller's consolidation of a system (and then monopoly) for pumping, refining, and distributing gas to fuel internal combustion engines. While metropolitan subways and some commuter train lines continue to use electricity for energy, 96 percent of transportation in the United States is now based on oil.[5]

Electric Utility Regulation and Its Intended and Unintended Effects

The electric power industry and the oil industry went through parallel periods of consolidation that gave rise to trusts and holding companies and then monopolies. But the resulting government response and the remedies for the two industries were fundamentally different, with far-reaching consequences.

Teddy Roosevelt made Rockefeller's Standard Oil a trust-busting target and broke it into several independent companies, but the oil industry has remained mostly free of government price regulation. A different outcome, however, was in store for electric power holding companies. Sam Insull was an Edison protégé who saw the need to consolidate electric utilities and set up a system of regulated local utilities that could use exclusive service areas as a way to finance long-term investments in expensive power generation and distribution facilities. His system, like Rockefeller's, helped to dramatically reduce the cost of energy. But behind the scenes, Insull also created holding companies that leveraged his control beyond the view and reach of regulators. His leveraged system eventually crashed, Insull was ruined, and the system of state government regulation of the price of electric power emerged stronger and more pervasive.

Today, there are dozens of regulated investor-owned electric power utilities and a number of public electric power utilities run by cities, public utility districts, and rural cooperatives. The regulatory and institutional controls on pricing and policies that have emerged have had intended and unintended consequences.

Regulated Costs and Limited Return on Utility Investments

State regulation of utility companies centers on setting the rates that utilities can charge their customers. In not much of an overstatement, the book *Megatrends* said that the real business of regulated utilities was winning rate cases.[6] In a state rate case, regulators review utility costs and set a rate of return for shareholder investments. In general, the idea is that the prudent costs of running a utility will be passed on to customers through rates and that investments by shareholders will be allowed a regulated rate of return.

This system worked well when costs were broadly declining as utility consolidation and larger and more efficient means of power generation worked to decrease the cost of making power. But the system hit a wall in the 1980s. Until then, "the risk of large [utility] losses attributable to regulatory action was more theoretical than real."[7] There was significant regulatory discretion to disallow recovery of utility investments before then, but because costs had been declining, there was little reason or pressure to do so.

The regulatory climate changed in the late 1980s as state regulators disallowed recovery of tens of billions of dollars in electric utility investments, mostly by imposing huge regulatory losses on investments in nuclear power plants. Utilities that requested large rate increases to cover large investment costs met a hostile regulatory environment as angry consumers pressured state regulators to hold down the level of rate increases, and the term "rate shock" emerged to describe consumers' reaction. The favored tool for disallowance was to find that the investment was "imprudent."

In one example, Louisiana regulators disallowed as imprudent $1.4 billion of the $3 billion invested by Gulf States Utilities in its River Bend nuclear power plant. The plant had been started and then suspended when demand for power dropped. But then Congress passed the 1978 Fuel Use Act, which prohibited a utility from burning natural gas under boilers to generate electricity after 1989. In order to replace 3,400 megawatts of its natural gas generation before the deadline set by Congress, Gulf States revived the River Bend project and completed it on time and on budget. But the costs required a significant rate increase, and state regulators found a way to disallow recovery of nearly half of those costs.[8]

What makes this case remarkable and instructive today is that the state regulators concluded that a *lignite coal plant* might have been a lower-cost option and thus the utility was imprudent in restarting River Bend. In 1991 the Supreme Court of Louisiana upheld the regulator's determination that a lignite coal generating plant would have been a better choice. It is hard to imagine that result today—not just because the law has changed (again allowing the use of natural gas), but because burning lignite coal to make electricity produces more carbon dioxide than almost any other option and would have been strongly opposed if proposed today.

That decision and dozens like it fundamentally changed utility industry behavior, making utility executives aware that their business costs could be disallowed based on a regulator's broad view of what is imprudent. Utilities became even more conservative, cautious, and unwilling to take risks. One term that emerged to describe the situation was "asymmetric regulation." If a utility took a risk and it paid off, the upside for utility shareholders was limited by the rate of return allowed by regulators. But if a utility took a risk that did not pay off, the costs would be disallowed and shareholders would take the loss. That was a formula that discouraged innovation and risk taking.

Regulation of Electric Power Demand and its Effects

In addition to asymmetric regulation and prudence reviews, many state regulators and legislators became active in encouraging and then ordering utilities to adopt aggressive measures to reduce demand for electricity. Energy efficiency—sometimes called the fifth fuel (or negawatts)—became a benchmark that many regulators used to judge utilities in rate cases. If a utility asked for a rate increase to pay for added generation capacity, it was met with calls to ensure that the utility was first was doing all that it could to encourage customers to conserve power. That was a fundamental shift in policy.

Utilities had promoted the use of more of their product since Edison's first utility system opened in Manhattan. To encourage more use and thus reduce unit costs, utilities charged less per unit the more electricity that a customer used (declining block rates), promoted new uses, created special rates for all-electric homes, and generally encouraged consumption, just like any other seller of a product.

But utility programs promoting more use of electricity hit another regulatory wall with the end of inexpensive generation of new capacity. Utilities were encouraged and then required to promote less use of their product; to end all-electric home rates; to charge more per kilowatt, not less, as total use went up (tiered rates); to encourage customers to switch from electricity to natural gas for home heating and water heaters; and to promote and provide conservation measures, such as insulation and new compact fluorescent light bulbs. Under regulatory prodding, utilities established educational campaigns to encourage customers to use less electricity.

Some regulators recognized that with high fixed costs, if a utility cut demand and sold fewer units of electricity, the cost per unit would have to go up; otherwise utilities would not be able to make enough on the sale of the remaining units to cover their costs. In response, some regulators have experimented with "decoupling," whereby a utility would be rewarded for selling less power and penalized for selling more power.

For example, California first decoupled sales and profits for electricity in 1982, and in 2007 the state adopted what is called "decoupling plus," designed to make investments in energy efficiency more profitable for a utility than building a new generating facility.[9] California regulators now allow a fee to be added to each utility bill to pay for the demand reduction targets that they set. If a utility hits 85 percent to 100 percent of its target, it is allowed to keep 9 percent of the savings; if it saves more than the target amount, it keeps 12 percent. But if it falls short of the target, it gets no return at all, and if it falls far short (less than 65 percent of the target), the utility has to pay a fine. California now spends a billion dollars a year on energy efficiency programs, and utility regulators hope to meet "half of all projected demand growth through increased energy efficiency."[10]

The Advent of Deregulation, Enron, and Continued Confusion

In the 1990s, as the cost of electricity continued to rise, a public policy debate emerged about whether to "deregulate" the generation of electricity in order to allow independent power producers to compete for customers. California was one of the first states to deregulate electric utilities following an all-out lobbying effort by Enron and other companies. A few years later, in 2000–01, California and the entire West Coast experienced an energy meltdown, due to tight supplies and Enron's manipulation of markets. Enron went bankrupt, California governor Gray Davis was recalled, and the future direction of U.S. energy regulation, or deregulation, continues in a state of uncertainty.

Increasing Regulation of New Generation Sources

Although the deregulation debate is unresolved, there is an increasing trend for regulators and legislators to specify the type of energy sources to be used in new electric generation facilities. With concerns over climate change, it is becoming less and less likely that a significant number of new coal power plants will be built without a means to capture and sequester the resulting carbon dioxide. Many states have enacted renewable portfolio standards that require a percentage of new or even existing generation facilities to use renewable sources such as wind and solar power, and in 2008 Congress came close to passing a national renewable portfolio standard. Prices for natural gas continue to be volatile, thus making it difficult to predict future costs and creating regulatory risks for new gas-fired generation facilities. And the high cost of alternative power that would result from portfolio standards that essentially required use of wind and solar energy would create rate shock worries and concern over full cost recovery through consumer rates.

Utilities' Response to Replacing Oil with Electricity in Transportation

Since the 1980s, the broad trend toward regulation has created conditions that are not compatible with supporting the broad and strong leadership in utility companies needed to help transportation move away from oil to electricity. In some states regulations now reward utilities for selling less, not more, power in the name of energy efficiency. New generation is more expensive and options are more limited, creating new and higher levels of regulatory risk. It is not surprising that most U.S. utilities have taken a wait-and-see attitude about promoting cars that connect to the grid.

Although many utilities are generally positive in their public statements about plug-in electric vehicles, they are anxious to see what regulators and legislators will do. They worry about whether they will be penalized by existing measures designed to cut demand for electricity if they give strong support to electric vehicles. And they are concerned that the costs that they incur in preparing for or promoting the transition from oil will not be allowed in rate cases. Such concerns have led many, if not most, utility executives to take the position that it is not their job to tackle this issue head on. Some executives add that their utilities do not have sufficient power to meet the potential demand from cars; others look for assurance that they will not alienate regulators before they will take action. Some notable utilities, however, have taken an exceptional leadership role, including Southern California Edison, Austin Energy, and Pacific Gas and Electric, along with electric utility trade groups such as the Edison Electric Institute and the American Public Power Association as well as the Electric Power Research Institute. Two Oregon-based utilities, Portland General Electric and Pacific Power, have recently announced plug-in vehicle initiatives with encouragement from Oregon's governor, Ted Kulongoski.[11]

The question is what public policy changes need to be made and new directions taken to fully realize the potential of electric utilities in meeting the challenge of replacing oil with alternative fuels for transportation.

The Need for National Legislative Direction and State Regulatory Change

Because the rates and practices of utility companies—and thus their business direction—are inextricably bound by government regulations, it is essential to ensure that legislation governing utilities clearly supports the national goal of radically reducing oil use in transportation. As this chapter shows, utilities already are subject to laws and regulations that govern the most basic aspects of their business—rate design, renewable portfolio standards, decoupling of rates, prudence reviews, deregulation, and conservation mandates. New legislation and modified regulations will be necessary to ensure that utilities, which have come to expect pervasive regulation, are provided with a clear set of new directions. Otherwise there will be a wasteful period of delay, confusion, and lost opportunities while the United States confronts an energy crisis in fueling national transportation.

That will require, among other changes, a new perspective on energy efficiency that recognizes that the broader goal needs to be to make total U.S. energy use more efficient and more secure. Utilities need a broader focus that includes more than just simply reducing the use of electricity. If the United States substitutes electricity for oil in transportation, total energy use will be substantially conserved, because the use of electricity in cars is much more efficient than the use of gas and diesel in internal combustion engines. Energy use should be measured by a more universal standard and utilities given direction, incentives, and credit for assisting with overall energy reduction—specifically for reducing the country's damaging dependence on petroleum in transportation—even if it means increasing use of electricity in some regions at some times of the day.

Reform is needed in four broad areas for the necessary change of direction to take place. First, Congress and state legislatures need to pass clear cost recovery legislation for utilities that invest in electrifying transportation.

Utilities need to know that the money that they spend to expedite the transformation of transportation will be defined and allowed in rates as "necessary and prudent" costs.

Second, Congress needs to enact legislation that provides incentives for utility companies to participate in the electrification effort, such as enhanced rates of return on capital invested in projects designed to electrify transportation, including credits for carbon dioxide reduction.

Third, current national and state utility regulations need to be revised so that they mesh with and support a new national policy to electrify transportation and eliminate unintended barriers. State pricing and decoupling regulations need to be revised to accommodate the fueling of cars with electricity. Renewable portfolio standards should provide incentives to utilities to electrify transportation and to better integrate intermittent wind and solar power with vehicle battery storage capability. Integrated resource planning (IRP) regulations need to be modified.

Fourth, we need a new system that will enable cars to communicate with the power grid in ways that make the grid more efficient by shifting recharging to off-peak times, enable intermittent renewable power to be more easily integrated into the power grid, provide incentives for drivers who use electricity, and ultimately provide for vehicle-to-grid power flows to help meet peak demand for power and to provide other services, including voltage support and spinning reserves. Although we could wait for standards to evolve state by state, Congress should establish and expedite implementation of standards through national legislation, in coordination with Canada, because electric-powered cars will move from one utility area to another across North America. The way that electricity is provided, priced, metered, and billed will have to be redesigned for cars and trucks at the national level. Because our vast power grid is so interconnected with that of Canada (recall the 2003 blackout that affected Canada as much as the United States, where the outage started), we need a coordinated North American system.

Done correctly, such a system will substantially accelerate the production and integration of the new plug-in vehicles needed to end the near-monopoly that oil has on the U.S. transportation sector. It will reduce total U.S. energy use, enable utilities to integrate intermittent renewable energy sources such as wind and solar power, and more efficiently utilize existing utility investments by tapping unused capacity at night and during other off-peak times—and thereby ultimately reduce peak demand.

Recovery of Costs

The first reform needed is clear direction from Congress to allow utilities to recover the costs that they incur in supporting the transition from oil to electricity in vehicles. One initial hurdle will be to respond to those who say that regulations regarding cost recovery are a state prerogative. Fundamentally, the transition away from oil in transportation is an issue of national economic and environmental policy. (As a preface to a set of legislative reforms, Congress should summarize and quantify the benefits to the environment and national economic security.) It also is a growing national security issue, given the extraordinary transfer of wealth from the United States, directly and indirectly, to unstable and potentially hostile oil-exporting countries.

Will allowing cost recovery make a difference? In the case of Southern California Edison (SCE), the reasonable assurance of cost recovery and a mechanism to provide funding for those costs have helped make SCE a national leader in the move toward electrifying transportation. Starting with the mandates in the 1990s for zero-emissions cars, California also created a system of charges that could be used to fund the infrastructure needed to provide electricity to those cars. SCE set up an electric transportation department to focus on what was needed, and the costs of its efforts were recovered under state-mandated policy. Although the mandates and experiment in the 1990s with electric cars faded (the documentary *Who Killed the Electric Car* relates the history of that effort), SCE continued its effort and remains one of the few utilities to have an electric transportation department.[12] All utilities should have that electric transportation capability in order to accelerate production and integration of vehicles that plug into the grid. Other California investor-owned utilities have now joined SCE in taking major steps to move to electrify transportation, including Pacific Gas and Electric, San Diego Gas and Electric, and California public utilities such as the Sacramento Municipal Utility District and the Los Angeles Department of Water and Power.

Cost recovery cannot be a blank check, but there must be clear congressional mandates on what categories of costs utilities will be allowed to recover through rates. For costs outside of specified areas, there should be a requirement that state regulators provide prior approval of programs so that costs cannot be disallowed under prudence reviews long after the fact. Rate reviews based on prudent cost grounds should be carefully and narrowly circumscribed.

Finally, Congress needs to mandate the recovery through current rates of what is sometimes called the cost of work in progress. It sometimes takes investment of capital over a period of several years to build new generation and transmission facilities or, in the case of electric vehicles, an integrated system of recharging, billing, metering, and pricing systems. During the period that the systems are being built but yet not completed (work in progress), there is a regulatory gap in which cost recovery is delayed—and then sometimes denied. Congress should address that issue in the context of electrifying transportation.

Enhanced Rates of Return and Carbon Dioxide Credits

Congress should enact legislation to provide for enhanced rates of return on invested capital in projects designed to electrify transportation, including credits for carbon dioxide reduction. When the Federal Energy Regulatory Commission (FERC) recognized the need for more high-voltage transmission lines, it turned to one of the basic regulatory tools available to encourage utility investment—enhanced rates of return for capital devoted to new transmission lines. In order to encourage rapid utility support for the national goal of oil reduction, Congress should enact legislation to provide incentives in the form of enhanced rates of return on equity invested in oil reduction and direct FERC to provide specific guidelines for an incentive program.

Utility projects that reduce total U.S. carbon dioxide emissions also should receive credits to offset other costs. That would send a signal and help reduce the regulatory uncertainty created by proposed cap-and-trade and other mandates that will affect utility investments.

Total U.S. energy use can be converted into British thermal units (BTUs), and mandated energy efficiency and conservation programs should be measured by overall savings in BTUs, not just reductions in the use of electricity measured in kilowatt-hours. Measuring overall carbon dioxide reduction also would favor electricity over petroleum, and utilities should be given credit for contributing to the reduction of CO_2 even if it means more use of electricity.

Offset credits for reducing carbon dioxide by substituting electricity for petroleum need to be clearly defined and ensured during the transition from oil to electricity in transportation. Just as production tax credits are provided to wind power equipment manufacturers and ethanol producers, carbon offset credits in addition to traditional rate incentives are needed for utilities.

It is interesting to note that the current ethanol production tax credit of $0.51 a gallon is equal in some parts of the country to the entire cost of producing the electric equivalent of a gallon of gas.[13] In the Pacific Northwest and in other areas, utilities could produce power for less than the current ethanol production tax credit subsidy. Overall across the country, the estimated cost for the electric equivalent of a gallon of gas is less than one dollar. In other words, if the equivalent of the ethanol credit were applied to utilities, the cost of electricity for cars could be reduced to somewhere between the equivalent of zero to 50 cents a gallon.

Tax credits, however, do not work for utilities, so another mechanism must be used. Because the rates of investor-owned utilities are regulated, a tax increase or decrease has no effect on their bottom line. Municipal utilities and other consumer-owned utilities pay no corporate income tax and thus have no need for tax incentives either. One potential incentive that would work and is needed is carbon dioxide offset credits.

As Congress considers and refines proposed cap-and-trade legislation and national renewable portfolio standards, it needs to incorporate incentives tailored to the realities of utility decisionmaking, including enhanced rates of return on certain transportation investments as well as carbon credits for utility initiatives that reduce U.S. oil use and dependence.

Reforming Current Utility Regulations

Existing national and state utility regulations create unintended barriers and should be revised to support a new national policy to electrify transportation. State policies on pricing and decoupling regulations need to be revised to accommodate the fueling of cars with electricity. Renewable portfolio standards should provide incentives to utilities to electrify transportation and to better integrate wind and solar power with vehicle battery storage capability. Integrated resource planning regulations need to be modified.

Some states require utilities to charge more for electricity the more a home or a business uses it in order to encourage electric conservation. But if cars are to be recharged without that penalty, they will have to be separately metered or otherwise identified so that the use of electricity in transportation does not have the unintended consequence of discouraging the transition from oil to electricity. Smart meter systems in homes can provide part of the solution. But a better solution is to have the car also serve as the meter since it is mobile and will connect to the grid at places other than the home. The technology to make that possible already exists (one example is being used in a pilot project in the Seattle area funded by the U.S. Department of Energy through the Idaho National Laboratory).

Vehicle-to-Grid Communication and Coordination

We can enable cars to communicate with the power grid in ways that will make the grid more efficient by shifting recharging to off-peak times, enable intermittent renewable power to be more easily integrated into the power grid, provide incentives for drivers who use electricity, and ultimately provide for vehicles to supplement grid supplies to help meet peak demand for power and other services.

If use of electric vehicles is metered and priced separately from other uses of electricity, incentives can be tailored to encourage use in cars while continuing to provide price signals to conserve in other areas. There is another, perhaps more fundamental, reason to provide for communication directly from utilities to vehicles. Because the electric cost of an equivalent gallon of gas is so much lower than the cost of gas, many if not most electric vehicle owners would choose to recharge whenever they could, including at peak times when they arrive home from work.[14] Adding new demands on utility generation at peak times will be expensive and will undermine other efforts to reduce carbon dioxide emissions. Instead, there needs to be a system of interruptible rates controlled by utilities under legislative guidelines that can eliminate or mitigate peak-time charging and shift it to off-peak times, making the power grid more efficient. A system that ties vehicles to the grid so that they act as backup power sources is within current technological capability, but it needs to be refined through national demonstration projects.[15]

If utilities could control the timing of recharging, it would permit the integration of wind, solar, and other intermittent renewable sources of energy. Batteries in vehicles do not care whether they are continuously charged or intermittently charged overnight or during the day. When wind power is available at night, batteries in vehicles can store that power and use it during the day. Solar power in the middle of the day, when demand is less than in the morning or afternoon peaks, also is a good source for recharging vehicles.

One of the most powerful benefits of separate metering for vehicles comes with the ability to encourage more conservation. Decoupling of rates from electric use is intended to prompt utilities to invest more in conservation even though the fixed cost of power does not change. But when we switch from oil to electricity in vehicles, utilities will see demand for power increase, which will cover their fixed costs even as they reduce demand for other uses in homes and businesses. Potentially, the current system of decoupling rates may no longer be needed if a new system is devised for recharging vehicles that maintains utility investments and covers fixed costs.

The advent of plug-in electric vehicles provides a new set of options in making the power grid more efficient, which will further serve to make total U.S. energy use more efficient and less carbon intensive. Electric vehicles can be powered by an increasingly carbon-free grid with electricity supplied by the sun, wind, water, waves, atoms, and conservation.

Conclusion

Thomas Edison is best known for inventing the electric light bulb, but his most important invention may have been the integrated system that he created to generate, distribute, and finance affordable electricity. We need a system like Edison's to tie together the opportunities presented by the coming transition from oil to electricity in transportation. By rethinking and reforming current legislative and regulatory constraints on utilities and providing needed incentives, Congress can advance a new era of more rational, integrated, economical, and secure energy.

We need a national program to jump-start a clean, secure energy future. And we need an enduring system of utility regulation that provides the right incentives to turn utilities into what can be thought of as the gas stations of the future.

Notes

1. General Motors announced "that it will collaborate with 34 electrical utilities in the United States and Canada to study how plug-ins will affect the electrical grid, hoping to iron out any problems before the first wave of mass-market plug-ins arrives. The Electric Power Research Institute of Palo Alto will also participate in GM's study group. 'Utilities are about to become the gas stations for these vehicles, and they have to get it right.'" *San Francisco Chronicle*, July 23, 2008 (www.sfchroniclemarket

place.com/cgi-bin/article.cgi?f=/c/a/2008/07/23/BU6711TF9S.DTL [October 8, 2008]).

2. Bob Lutz, Remarks to Seattle Chamber of Commerce, June 18, 2008. See also David Welch, "GM: Live Green or Die," *BusinessWeek*, May 26, 2008 (www.business week.com/magazine/content/08_21/b4085036665789.htm?chan=magazine+channel_top+stories [October 8, 2008]); Ángel González, "GM Recharges on Future of Electric Car," *Seattle Times*, June 30, 2008: GM "is betting big bucks—most of its current research-and-development budget—that the internal-combustion engine's time is running out" (http://seattletimes.nwsource.com/html/businesstechnology/2008003356_electriccar18.html [October 8, 2008]); Bob Lutz, "The Road Ahead," *Newsweek*, February 25, 2008: "The electrification of the automobile is inevitable"(www.newsweek.com/id/112736 [October 8, 2008]).

3. Robert C. Wing and others, *A Century of Service: The Puget Power Story* (Puget Sound Power and Light Company, 1987), pp. 17–38.

4. There is significant unused capacity in today's electric power grid. Using conservative estimates, a study for the Department of Energy reported that unused off-peak electricity generation and transmission capacity could fuel 73 percent of the U.S. light-duty vehicle fleet, if they were plug-in hybrid electrics: "If all the cars and light trucks in the nation switched from oil to electrons, idle capacity in the existing electric power system could generate most of the electricity consumed by plug-in hybrid electric vehicles." Michael Kintner-Meyer and others, *"Impacts Assessment of Plug-in Hybrid Vehicles on Electric Utilities and Regional U.S. Power Grids"* (Pacific Northwest National Laboratory, 2007).

5. See "U.S. Primary Energy Consumption by Source and Sector," Energy Information Administration, 2007 (www.eia.doe.gov/emeu/aer/pecss_diagram.html [December 31, 2008]); David Sandalow, *Freedom from Oil* (New York: McGraw Hill, 2008), p. 14.

6. John Naisbitt, *Megatrends: Ten New Directions Transforming Our Lives* (New York: Warner Books, 1982).

7. C. Studness, "A Test of the Reinterpretation of Utility Imprudence," *Public Utilities Fortnightly,* July 1, 1991, pp. 39–42.

8. Ibid.

9. For a brief summary, see "The Elusive Negawatt," *The Economist*, May 10, 2008, pp 78–80.

10. Ibid., p. 80 (quoting Dian Grueneich, California Public Utilities Commissioner).

11. Amy Hsuan, "Kulongoski Lobbies to Bring China's New Hybrid Car to Oregon," *Oregonian*, November 21, 2008 (www.oregonlive.com/business/index.ssf/2008/11/kulongoski_lobbies_to_bring_ch.html [December 31, 2008]).

12. "Who Killed the Electric Car?" released in theaters in June 2006, was written and directed by Chris Paine, produced by Jessie Deeter, and executive produced by Tavin Marin Titus and Richard D. Titus of Plinyminor and Dean Devlin, Kearie Peak, Mark Roskin, and Rachel Olshan of Electric Entertainment. Sony Pictures Home Entertainment released a DVD of the movie in November 2006.

13. See, for example, Steve Marshall and Bill Gaines, "Washington Should Be Leader In Push For All-Electric Cars," *Tacoma News Tribune*, February 24, 2008.

14. See, for example, Loren Baker and Steve Marshall, "Are Utilities the Gas Stations of the Future?" *Northwest Public Power Association Bulletin*, June 2007.

15. For a discussion of smart charging of electric vehicles, see the presentations of David Kaplan and Shai Agassi at "Beyond Oil: Transforming Transportation," Fifth Annual TransTech Conference, September 4–5, 2008, online at www.Cascadiaproject. org. See also "Driven: Shai Agassi's Audacious Plan to Put Electric Cars on the Road," *Wired*, August 18, 2008.

CHAPTER THIRTEEN

Promoting Use of Plug-In Electric Vehicles through Utility Industry Acquisition and Leasing of Batteries

PETER FOX-PENNER, DEAN MURPHY, MARIKO GERONIMO, and MATTHEW MCCAFFREE

Petroleum is the predominant transport fuel in the United States. It is supported by a vast and ubiquitous infrastructure, it is easy to transport, and until recently it was relatively inexpensive. But as prices continue to rise, there is greater recognition of the destabilizing geopolitical effect of the country's overdependence on petroleum. Looming federal greenhouse gas (GHG) regulation will add to the price of petroleum-based fuels in the years to come, and it provides greater motivation to address transportation GHG emissions today. While multiple alternatives are being sought, one of the most promising near-term solutions—one that will leverage existing infrastructure, reduce GHG emissions, and allow drivers the same freedom and mobility as they enjoy with today's vehicles—is the plug-in electric vehicle (PEV), or "plug-in."[1]

While plug-in electric vehicle technology exists today and holds the greatest promise to reduce demand for oil, PEVs currently carry a price premium, in large part due to the extra cost of the high-capacity battery that they require. In order to bring these cars to market more rapidly, it is in the interest of consumers, manufacturers, the federal and some state governments, and utilities to work to remove this initial first-cost barrier. Since PEVs would rely on electricity from the grid, either wholly or partially, electric utilities could be on the brink of becoming a major part of the transportation sector and could benefit considerably from the widespread deployment of PEVs. They are uniquely positioned to collaborate with the federal and state governments and car manufacturers to bring the vehicles to market quickly and to use creative approaches to do so.

The Role of Plug-In Hybrids in U.S. Energy Strategy

Most Americans drive less than thirty miles a day, which means that PEVs would give them the option to fuel their cars at home on domestic fuel with fewer emissions. The potential for PEVs to contribute to a comprehensive energy strategy has led to broad agreement across the U.S. political spectrum that this technology is one key to achieving U.S. energy security and reducing greenhouse gases. The Bush administration, both candidates in the 2008 presidential election, leading environmental groups, and congressional leaders from both sides of the aisle are on the record supporting PEV development to reach those goals.

Aggressive research, development, and demonstration (RD&D) is under way for plug-ins, financed by both public and private funding. The Energy Independence and Security Act of 2007 provides for grants and RD&D programs to develop PEVs, and proposals to spur sales through tax credits (much like those introduced for hybrid vehicles) have enjoyed bipartisan support. A123Systems is now selling its Hymotion conversion kits to turn internal combustion hybrids into plug-ins. GM, Toyota, and Nissan are all in a race to develop the first successful mass-market PEV, with expected release dates from 2010 to 2011. The momentum is shifting from producing boutique, aftermarket solutions such as conversion kits to producing cars with mass-market appeal. However, in order to achieve high-volume sales of plug-ins, the cars not only must have easy-to-use, reliable technology but also must sell at a price that most customers can afford.

Recent advances in battery technology have allowed for the development cycle of PEVs to be shorter than that of new car models. For example, new lithium-ion batteries are much lighter than they used to be. For an equivalent charge, today's batteries are about one-quarter as heavy as they were ten years ago. But the unique specifications for electric vehicle batteries require extensive research and testing to ensure that they are stable and perform consistently before they are mass produced. The pace of current battery technology development suggests that they will be ready for the market in the near term, and as long as PEVs are produced on a large scale with readily available materials, their cost is certain to decline. Meanwhile, manufacturers are understandably cautious about selling cars with batteries that add several thousand dollars to the sales price and whose performance is uncertain.

An Opportunity for Electric Utilities

While car companies fret over the cost of batteries, electric utilities are uniquely poised to benefit from a U.S. vehicle fleet with a greater number of PEVs. By fueling a significant portion of national transport, electric utilities could become, in the words of GM spokesman Robert Peterson, "more important than the oil companies."[2] PEVs not only would provide the utilities with a large new source of energy sales, they also would serve as a potential resource for helping to manage the grid. If PEVs incorporate emerging vehicle-to-grid (V2G) technology for grid and load management, they will help reduce the chance that electric utilities will have to invest in increasingly expensive generation assets. There is even discussion of having utilities use old PEV batteries after they are retired from vehicles for some stationary grid applications.

The efforts currently under way are helping to create a market for PEVs, but to further accelerate their widespread introduction in a way that benefits utilities, car manufacturers, and customers, it may be useful to create a program to directly offset the added costs and risks of the batteries used in the cars. Performance issues can be addressed through warranties, but the question remains of how these new vehicles can achieve price parity with hybrids and even internal-combustion cars.

A rate-base approach by electric utilities could be the answer. The basic idea is that the utilities would own the PEV batteries sold in their area and treat them as their own assets, much as they do with generation, transmission, and distribution infrastructure. They would lease the battery to the car owner, thus offsetting the incremental battery cost at the time of the purchase of the vehicle, and utilities would recover the added cost through utility rates.

Here's how it could work. When a PEV with an integral, manufacturer-installed battery is purchased, the battery is seamlessly, automatically, and simultaneously sold to the local electric distribution utility. The vehicle's sticker price would not include cost of the battery—or perhaps more accurately, it would already reflect the battery lease payments. The battery lease would be integrated into the sales price of the car; the only difference to the customer would be the reduction in the sticker price due to the electric utility's ownership of the battery. The battery would be the utility's property, and the customer would automatically become the battery lessee until the car was sold or destroyed. The utility would amortize the battery investment through a small surcharge on distribution rates. If the car is resold, the battery lease would transfer to the new owner. The battery of a car that is retired would be removed for load-balancing by the utility, or the manufacturer would remove and retire or recycle the battery, just as today.

The program would be needed only for the first five to ten years of PEV sales, its duration perhaps linked explicitly to the number of vehicles sold (say, the first million or two million PEVs). After that, production volume and manufacturing cost savings should reduce costs to the point that much less support would be needed. A similarly structured program is being used for current hybrids: tax incentives are offered for the first 60,000 hybrids sold by a particular manufacturer and then slowly phased out. The incentives, not including the phase-out period, cover roughly 300,000 hybrids. More ambitious incentives for PEVs with more ambitious sales targets would likely increase initial demand.

During the initial market introduction phase, the cost of the batteries would be recovered by utilities through electricity rates. The program would be in effect while PEV sales were in their infancy and discontinued once sales reached full commercial scale. Conservatively assuming that each battery cost $3,600 and had an average vehicular service life of five years, the annual carrying cost for the utility would be about $902 per battery.[3] If, starting in 2010, PEV sales were to follow a trajectory similar to that of hybrid electric vehicle sales, then there could be a 0.2 percent fleet penetration of about 500,000 vehicles (or just over 0.4 percent of households with PEVs) within five years of the start of commercial sales (see table 13-1).

Spreading the cost of the batteries across all electric customers, at a half-million vehicles in cumulative sales, battery cost recovery would increase the average residential customer bill by just 7 cents a month, or 84 cents a year. By the time there were 2 million PEVs in cumulative sales (just under 1 percent of the light-duty vehicle fleet), the goal of accelerating PEV battery technology to commercial production levels would be

Table 13-1. Estimated PEV Sales and Program Costs, 2015 and 2020

Item	2015	2020
Additional cost of battery (assumed)	$3,600 per vehicle	
$902 per vehicle-year (five years)	$3,600 per vehicle	
Total number of subsidized PEVs		
(cumulative since 2010)	0.5 million	2.4 million
LDV fleet penetration (total)	0.2 percent	0.9 percent
Total cost for battery program	$0.29 billion	$1.41 billion
Annual cost per residential electric customer	$0.84	$3.92
Percentage increase to average residential		
electric utility bill	0.1 percent	0.3 percent

achieved. The first-cost barrier to introducing PEVs to consumers would be reduced immensely, and PEVs could compete on a level playing field with traditional internal-combustion vehicles as well as vehicles using alternative technologies. At that level, where the subsidies are largest, the impact on the average residential electricity bill would be about 33 cents a month, or $3.92 a year.

The lease arrangement with the local electric utility would leave the choice of battery, warranty, and other terms undisturbed. Car and battery manufacturers would come to their own commercial terms regarding performance guarantees, warranties, and service agreements. Car owners would be entitled to the same protection that they would have if they owned the battery, and utilities would be in the business of providing electricity, not guaranteeing car parts. In order to make the process as seamless as possible, every segment of the electric power industry should be able to participate in the program, from investor-owned utilities to cooperatives to municipal utilities. Furthermore, commercial or utility fleets should be able to opt out of the program.

Of course, a large portion of the initial cost would be due to ongoing development of batteries that can carry a sufficient charge for the vehicles, particularly if they rely wholly on electric power. The program would require that the leasing arrangements be made regardless of battery technology. Thus the program allows for continued innovation because the relationship between the car and battery manufacturers would be independent of the leasing program. Car manufacturers would still have the same incentive to incorporate the most innovative, cost-effective technology in their cars.

Cooperation between State and Federal Government Agencies and Electric Utilities

Admittedly, the proposal does not present what is a traditional business model for the electricity sector. Utilities are used to having fixed assets that have well-known operational lives, amortization schedules, and project finance strategies. When similar ideas have been raised in the past, there has been resistance on the part of utilities to having assets that move around between areas and states for fear that their assets may not even be used by their own customers and grids. But electric utilities are on the brink of entering the transportation sector, and they will benefit in the long run by taking an active role at the outset. If managed correctly and with sufficient collaboration between regulators and utilities, transfers from one service area to another could be imperceptible to both utility and car owner.

There are several advantages to having electric utilities own the batteries. Utilities have a low cost of capital and the ability to amortize the incremental first costs over a large sales base. In addition, it is the electric utilities whose sales will benefit from PEV growth, and they will have the best resources available to measure PEVs' impact on electricity infrastructure. It is highly likely that the batteries are going to be a part of the nation's electric power grid, either through residual battery use for load management or through more advanced V2G technology. Utilities not only are poised to profit from electric drive vehicles by providing the fuel, they also are the best entities to promote off-peak battery charging, to ensure user safety, and to institute pilot projects for V2G and residual use programs.

Ideally, the proposed program should be implemented nationally and with the participation of state and federal government and regulatory agencies, giving the utilities regulatory support for tracking changes in ownership. After a PEV was sold, the battery would be linked to the location where the car was garaged (that is, the owner's location) for insurance purposes. If the car changed ownership within the service area of the same distribution utility, that utility would not have to make any changes. If the car was moved to a location outside the original service area, the asset should shift to the new local distribution utility's rate base.

Initially, owning and managing batteries may be seen as being beyond the core capabilities of most utilities, requiring them to take on a new set of administrative responsibilities. There are a variety of ways in which the industry could pool and greatly reduce its administrative burdens, thereby allaying fears that each individual utility would be responsible for tracking batteries in its service area. One alternative is to create a dedicated public-private acquisition and leasing corporation that acquires the batteries and administers the program for all utilities, allowing utilities to invest in the corporation rather than the batteries themselves. The newly established national corporation, designed with the input of electric utilities and subject to federal oversight, would be able to administer battery tracking through a single central database. Each utility would contribute capital to the corporation, and its investment would be put into the rate base for all utilities, allowing them to recoup their investments through rates (with a reasonable return on investment, as for other capital assets). In turn, program administration would be centralized, allowing for tracking of battery sales and vehicle life.

The federal government also could administer a PEV battery ownership program simply by creating a fund to subsidize the cost of the battery to the PEV buyer or by giving grants or tax credits directly to buyers or automakers. However, such a program would typically require significant taxpayer funding; without it, the first-cost barrier would remain large.

Regardless of whether the battery ownership or public-private corporation approach is adopted, the role of the federal government would be to ensure national participation in the program. All utilities would have to participate in order to allow customers to take advantage of it anywhere in the United States. If utility participation was not universal, the automatic battery buy-down/lease could be offered only to cars in certain areas. If federal policymakers wanted to make the program universal, it would be easy to legislate a federal surcharge on power distribution rates and fund the public-private leasing corporation that way. Under that approach, there would be no rate-basing of the batteries and local utilities would be just collection agents.

Federal measures would have to be in place to help standardize the financial structure of the program. Utilities would definitely want—and should receive—legislative assurances that they could amortize the costs. Such assurances have been provided to utilities for other purposes in the past.

All of these approaches would be reasonable if they were implemented wisely. However, many citizens frown on direct federal subsidies to retail purchases, and the federal government would be in the difficult position of justifying a battery ownership program to the wider public. Utilities have the means to raise capital for battery purchases, and they have a well-tested framework for recouping their investments. If the federal government cannot afford to remove the first-cost barrier, then utilities are the next logical choice.

Nearly every president, all former secretaries of energy, and many congressional leaders have pledged at one time or another to reduce or end U.S. dependence on foreign oil. These approaches—utility battery ownership or a federally administered public-private corporation—can deliver on that perennial promise. At the same time, either approach would prepare utilities to be a vital part of the national transportation infrastructure.

Plug-ins are a crucial part of the solution to rising emissions and overdependence on oil. Battery costs are the main barrier to broad-scale deployment of PEVs. Every possible acceleration strategy should be put to work, but utilities alone have the customers, synergies, and balance sheets needed to help get the cars on the road as soon as possible.

Notes

1. In this chapter, the term *plug-in electric vehicle* (PEV) encompasses both fully electric and plug-in hybrid electric vehicles (PHEVs).

2. Rebecca Smith, "Utilities, Plug-In Cars: Near Collision? Electric Firms Say Daytime Charges May Raise Costs," *Wall Street Journal*, May 2, 2008, p. B1.

3. The estimate for vehicular service life takes into account predicted battery calendar life and deterioration due to regular charging and discharging. A uniform cost per battery of $3,600 is assumed for both all-electric and hybrid-electric vehicles, although the former would likely house larger batteries.

Contributors

Samuel M. Arons
Google

Tom Z. Collina
2020 Vision

Peter Fox-Penner
The Brattle Group

Mariko Geronimo
The Brattle Group

Benjamin Goldstein
Center for American Progress

Benjamin H. Harris
*Brookings Institution and the
Urban–Brookings Tax Policy Center*

Bracken Hendricks
Center for American Progress

Holmes Hummel
University of California, Berkeley

Daniel M. Kammen
University of California, Berkeley

Derek M. Lemoine
University of California, Berkeley

Deron Lovaas
Natural Resources Defense Council

Alan L. Madian
LECG

Steve Marshall
*Cascadia Center for Regional
Development*

Matthew McCaffree
Institute for Electric Efficiency

Irving Mintzer
Potomac Energy Fund

Dean Murphy
The Brattle Group

Dan Reicher
Google

Chelsea Sexton
Lightning Rod Foundation

Saurin D. Shah
Neuberger Berman

Kim D. Simpkins
LECG

Dean Taylor
Southern California Edison

Luke Tonachel
Natural Resources Defense Council

Lisa A. Walsh
LECG

Jon Wellinghoff
Federal Energy Regulatory Commission

R. James Woolsey
Booz Allen Hamilton

Ron Zucker
2020 Vision

Index